WRITING-ENI
MODELS OF ꜰACULTY-DRIVEN AND DEPARTMENTAL TRANSFORMATION

PERSPECTIVES ON WRITING

Series Editors: Rich Rice, Heather MacNeill Falconer, and J. Michael Rifenburg
Consulting Editor: Susan H. McLeod

The Perspectives on Writing series addresses writing studies in a broad sense. Consistent with the wide ranging approaches characteristic of teaching and scholarship in writing across the curriculum, the series presents works that take divergent perspectives on working as a writer, teaching writing, administering writing programs, and studying writing in its various forms.

The WAC Clearinghouse, Colorado State University Open Press, and University Press of Colorado are collaborating so that these books will be widely available through free digital distribution and low-cost print editions. The publishers and the Series editors are committed to the principle that knowledge should freely circulate. We see the opportunities that new technologies have for further democratizing knowledge. And we see that to share the power of writing is to share the means for all to articulate their needs, interest, and learning into the great experiment of literacy.

Recent Books in the Series

Alexandria L. Lockett, Iris D. Ruiz, James Chase Sanchez, and Christopher Carter (Eds.), *Race, Rhetoric, and Research Methods* (2021)

Kristopher M. Lotier, *Postprocess Postmortem* (2021)

Ryan J. Dippre and Talinn Phillips (Eds.), *Approaches to Lifespan Writing Research: Generating an Actionable Coherence* (2020)

Lesley Erin Bartlett, Sandra L. Tarabochia, Andrea R. Olinger, and Margaret J. Marshall (Eds.), *Diverse Approaches to Teaching, Learning, and Writing Across the Curriculum: IWAC at 25* (2020)

Hannah J. Rule, *Situating Writing Processes* (2019)

Asao B. Inoue, *Labor-Based Grading Contracts: Building Equity and Inclusion in the Compassionate Writing Classroom* (2019)

Mark Sutton and Sally Chandler (Eds.), *The Writing Studio Sampler: Stories About Change* (2018)

Kristine L. Blair and Lee Nickoson (Eds.), *Composing Feminist Interventions: Activism, Engagement, Praxis* (2018)

Mya Poe, Asao B. Inoue, and Norbert Elliot (Eds.), *Writing Assessment, Social Justice, and the Advancement of Opportunity* (2018)

Patricia Portanova, J. Michael Rifenburg, and Duane Roen (Eds.), *Contemporary Perspectives on Cognition and Writing* (2017)

WRITING-ENRICHED CURRICULA: MODELS OF FACULTY-DRIVEN AND DEPARTMENTAL TRANSFORMATION

Edited by Chris M. Anson and Pamela Flash

The WAC Clearinghouse
wac.colostate.edu
Fort Collins, Colorado

University Press of Colorado
upcolorado.com
Louisville, Colorado

The WAC Clearinghouse, Fort Collins, Colorado 80523

University Press of Colorado, Louisville, Colorado 80027

© 2021 by Chris M. Anson and Pamela Flash. This work is licensed under a Creative Commons Attribution-NonCommercial-NoDerivatives 4.0 International.

ISBN 978-1-64215-129-9 (PDF) | 978-1-64215-130-5 (ePub) | 978-1-64642-243-2 (pbk.)

DOI: 10.37514/PER-B.2021.1299

Printed in the United States of America

Library of Congress Cataloging-in-Publication Data

Names: Anson, Chris M., 1954– editor. | Flash, Pamela, 1958– editor.
Title: Writing-enriched curricula : models of faculty-driven and departmental transformation / edited by Chris M. Anson and Pamela Flash.
Description: Fort Collins, Colorado : The WAC Clearinghouse ; Louisville, Colorado : University Press of Colorado, 2021. | Series: Perspectives on writing | Includes bibliographical references.
Identifiers: LCCN 2021036580 (print) | LCCN 2021036581 (ebook) | ISBN 9781646422432 (paperback) | ISBN 9781642151299 (pdf) | ISBN 9781642151305 (epub)
Subjects: LCSH: Composition (Language arts)—Study and teaching (Higher)—United States. | Language arts (Higher)—Correlation with content subjects—United States. | Interdisciplinary approach in education—United States.
Classification: LCC PE1405.U6 W744 2021 (print) | LCC PE1405.U6 (ebook) | DDC 808/.0420711—dc23
LC record available at https://lccn.loc.gov/2021036580
LC ebook record available at https://lccn.loc.gov/2021036581

Copyeditor: Don Donahue
Designer: Mike Palmquist
Cover Photo: Matthew Luskey, from the 2018 International WEC Institute. Used with permsission.
Series Editors: Rich Rice, Heather MacNeill Falconer, and J. Michael Rifenburg
Consulting Editor: Susan H. McLeod

The WAC Clearinghouse supports teachers of writing across the disciplines. Hosted by Colorado State University, and supported by the Colorado State University Open Press, it brings together scholarly journals and book series as well as resources for teachers who use writing in their courses. This book is available in digital formats for free download at wac.colostate.edu.

Founded in 1965, the University Press of Colorado is a nonprofit cooperative publishing enterprise supported, in part, by Adams State University, Colorado State University, Fort Lewis College, Metropolitan State University of Denver, University of Alaska Fairbanks, University of Colorado, University of Denver, University of Northern Colorado, Univesity of Wyoming, Utah State University, and Western Colorado University. For more information, visit upcolorado.com. The Press partners with the Clearinghouse to make its books available in print.

CONTENTS

FOREWORD

Michael Carter
North Carolina State University

The writing-enriched curriculum (WEC) has had a significant impact on writing in university settings, a model that has been adapted at multiple schools in the US and abroad. So I may be pardoned if I tried to claim that WEC had its origin in 1997 at my own university, NC State. At least that's what I wrote when I originally began this foreword. But I quickly realized that this claim was both an overstatement and an understatement, an overstatement in that it gave the impression that there was from the beginning an intentional goal in mind and an understatement in that others soon brought their own ideas and experiences with writing that converged in the underlying principles that drive approaches to the writing-enriched curriculum.

My own experience began with one of the most mundane actions of the academy, empaneling a task force. Our Council on Undergraduate Education (CUE) had a problem. A few years earlier, it had established General Education Requirements that included the stipulation that in addition to the two semesters of first-year writing and an additional advanced writing or speaking course, undergraduates were to be assigned writing in their majors, at least two papers. Not surprisingly, this requirement was difficult to define and certainly to enforce; thus, there being no agreement as to what counted as a *paper*, pretty much anything went, if it went at all. The charge of a new task force, the Writing Work Group, was to clarify the ambiguities of the two-paper requirement and to propose a way to evaluate its effectiveness across the campus.

Skipping over the two years of deliberations, in spring 1997 the task force submitted its report to CUE. Instead of continuing to wrangle with the issue of two papers in the majors, we proposed that the university commit to a program in writing across the curriculum (WAC). This proposal reflected the mainstream of composition at that time: a centralized university program emphasizing designated writing-intensive courses in each major and training of faculty teaching those courses. It mainly followed the WAC program at the University of Missouri, which was considered a model at the time.

Upon approval of the proposal by CUE, we began to consider the next steps of implementation. But that effort soon came to an abrupt halt—the rejection of our proposal by the university's deans' council, comprised of the provost and deans of the colleges. We were stunned, especially those of us, like me, who were

DOI: https://doi.org/10.37514/PER-B.2021.1299.1.2

too lowly in the university hierarchy at that time to be aware there even was a deans' council. And what, we asked each other, did they know about teaching writing?

In place of our proposal, the deans' council stipulated that any new program must meet three demands. First, it should include speaking in addition to writing. Yes, we could incorporate speaking, but we had no expertise on campus in the field of speaking across the curriculum. Second, instead of a centralized oversight and guidance by experts in the field, responsibility for writing and speaking in the majors was given to deans and department heads to enforce. This decentralization eliminated the possibility of the WAC program we had proposed. And third, to assure that deans and department heads would indeed take responsibility for writing and speaking in their curricula, the efficacy of these programs was to be evaluated through outcomes-based assessment.

Outcomes-based assessment? This was a completely new term for us. Obviously, the focus was on outcomes, but outcomes from what? And what exactly were we expected to assess? There was no direction at all from the university administration. Today, of course, outcomes assessment permeates the academy, largely because it is required of our regional accrediting agencies. But at that time, at least for us, we did not know what to make of it.

Somehow, and I really don't remember how, it fell to me to undertake the task of implementing this unwanted program. I had the summer of 1997 to figure it out. And though I didn't yet know exactly what an outcome was or how it could be produced, I realized that what I would be asking of faculty was revolutionary, and they were unlikely to be happy about it. First, the primary unit of measure for the assessment process must be the program: computer science, history, psychology, chemical engineering, business, etc. If assessment were to be meaningful in terms of improvement, then it was the program that was to be improved. This contrasted sharply with the primary measures at the time, the individual faculty member and his or her courses. The sources of data for those evaluations were mainly end-of-term student course evaluations and peer reviews of faculty teaching, typically applied to third-year reviews, promotion, and tenure. I knew that the tectonic shift to evaluating programs would be a serious challenge.

Second, if the program were to be the primary unit of measure, what was to be measured? The answer, of course, was the outcome, what came out of a process, in this case student learning. But this also required a dramatic adjustment on the part of faculty very much comfortable with curricula that relied on inputs, not outcomes. By inputs, I mean prescribing a set of required and elective courses and perhaps certain other learning experiences and simply assuming a result, viable knowledge and skills. Under the new system, however, faculty would be required to measure the extent to which their programs enabled students to meet designated learning outcomes.

As I faced the approaching fall semester, I was confronted with the reality that outcomes assessment would demand a mammoth effort on the part of faculty. I couldn't simply expect them to create program outcomes and measures of outcomes on their own, especially since at that point I didn't even know what outcomes would look like or how they would be generated. So I decided to make a five-year plan in which I would work with faculty department by department in all nine colleges with undergraduate students. Because there was no hiding from faculty the fact that this was a top-down requirement from university administrators, I needed the backing of college and departmental administrators. Thus, before I would meet with faculty groups from each college, I planned to meet first with the dean and then department heads to explain what I was doing and why, trying to establish what good will I could. Then for each department I would arrange to work with members of the Curriculum and Instruction Committees, responsible for undergraduate education.

Inescapably, the day came for me to meet with my first group of faculty. I didn't have a plan because I had no idea what to expect. And I was concerned with how faculty from my largely science and technical university would respond to me, a young associate professor, completely unknown to them, and from the English department no less. After introductions, I opened with the only justification I had for my presence there: the provost required them to do outcomes assessment. For the scheduled 90 minutes, the first hour was given over to their sturdy and implacable resistance. The provost has no right to make us do this. He was only going to use these outcomes as an excuse to cut our budgets. What if we don't want to do outcomes assessment? Who's going to make us? What evidence was there that our program needs improvement? What if we just made up information about our program? How would anybody know? Who says this is going to work at all? Can you give us examples of how this has worked at other universities? And on and on.

I am faculty, too, and had attended enough of my own department meetings not to be terribly surprised at their reaction. Finally, after an hour of this, I said, "OK. We have a half-hour left. Just humor me for the rest of our time and tell me about your program." The tenor of the meeting suddenly changed. For them, I became this tabula rasa in their department eager to learn about a program they were clearly quite proud of. I scribbled notes as fast as I could hoping for some insight later. Afterward, I discovered that there was enough information there for what amounted to proto-outcomes. When we met again, I read them what I had found, and that set off a productive discussion shaping and then generating more outcomes. And, critically, I came to understand that learning outcomes were what students should be able to do that demonstrated their learning but also at the same time as a way of learning itself.

As I worked with more departments, I found a pattern emerging. Nearly all the initial meetings were dominated by resistance. I learned that faculty needed to establish their opposition; they wanted to be heard, to feel that they had been understood. And I would give them sufficient space for that. Once that point had been reached, I would ask about their programs and, based on a list of open-ended questions, started taking notes. Then I applied experience I had in coding interviews, generating what I called objectives, the broad learning goals students were expected to achieve, and then operational definitions of outcomes for each category. This meant that the next time I met with a faculty group I could show them learning outcomes that reflected an understanding of their programs and revise as necessary (Carter, 2002).

In my deep dive into the wide reach of departments across my university, I learned that the writing of faculty and students was intimately disciplinary. The writing in my own discipline, rhetoric and writing, became visible to me only in contrast to the other ways of writing I encountered. I was particularly struck by the faculty of the Departments of History and Mathematics. They each readily acknowledged that it was highly unlikely that their students would become professional historians or mathematicians. The goals of the faculty, then, were to shape students' ways of thinking as modes of problem solving appropriate to history or to mathematics, described in their program outcomes (Carter, 2007).

Once we realized that outcomes assessment was becoming established on our campus, it was time for some administrative structure. We convinced the provost to fund a Campus Writing and Speaking Program (CWSP). And we constituted a Campus Writing and Speaking Board comprised mostly of faculty. Over the following year, Chris Anson, who had been offered the position of Director of the CWSP but had to delay his move from the University of Minnesota for a year, travelled frequently to NC State to work with faculty as I continued as interim director. During that year, he was able to participate in an *ex officio* capacity in the search for an assistant director who would bring expertise in oral communication across the curriculum. That search attracted Deanna Dannels, a new Ph.D. who had focused her dissertation research on speaking in the engineering and other curricula at the University of Utah. Chris and Deanna arrived in the summer of 1999 and began to establish a well-respected program extending our outcomes work by assisting departments with implementation and assessment and shaping an institutional culture of writing, while I continued to evangelize outcomes assessment on campus.

I completed my five years of working with faculty in the colleges in the 2002–2003 academic year. By that time, I had become involved with a broad university committee implementing outcomes assessment across the university, grounded in the understanding that what students produce through their writing and speaking is how we can judge learning. In 2004 I began working with our graduate school in outcomes assessment of graduate programs. And NC State sponsored its first Undergraduate Assessment Symposium in 2007, attracting faculty from around the US and beyond. I presented a workshop entitled Program Assessment 101: A Beginner's Guide, which became a staple in the annual symposia, later sponsored by Meredith College of Raleigh. Outcomes assessment had caught on, accrediting agencies requiring it, so lots of faculty came to get the basics that they could take back to their colleges and universities. In 2007, after Pamela Flash at the University of Minnesota had received funding to develop and model what she called a writing-enriched curriculum, she invited Chris Anson and me to visit and talk to members of the WEC Advisory Committee about our work. So it turns out that the provost and deans who had blocked our original plan must have known what they were talking about after all.

In retrospect, though we certainly were not aware of it at the time, we were part of a much longer history in the United States of gathering data to test advanced learning and accountability, dating back to World War I (Shavelson, 2007, 2010). Within this broad scope of time, the key innovation at the root of WEC is the focus on writing outcomes in disciplinary programs generated, managed, and tested by faculty in those programs. WEC is now surely one of, if not the, most robust models for integrating writing in the disciplines. In the following pages, scholars offer a wide range of exciting perspectives on this model, opening and broadening its potential for teaching and learning.

REFERENCES

Carter, M. (2002). A process for establishing outcomes-based assessment plans for writing and speaking in the disciplines. *Language and Learning Across the Disciplines, 6,* 4–29. https://doi.org/10.37514/LLD-J.2003.6.1.02.

Carter, M. (2007). Ways of knowing, doing, and writing in the disciplines. *College Composition and Communication, 58*(3), 385–418.

Shavelson, R. J. (2007). *A brief history of student learning assessment: How we got where we are and a proposal for where to go next.* Association of American Universities.

Shavelson, R. J. (2010). *Measuring college learning responsibly: Accountability in a new era.* Stanford University Press.

WRITING-ENRICHED CURRICULA: MODELS OF FACULTY-DRIVEN AND DEPARTMENTAL TRANSFORMATION

INTRODUCTION.

WEC AND THE STRENGTH OF THE COMMONS

Chris M. Anson

North Carolina State University

In 1978, the farmers in Xiaogang, a small rural village in China, signed a secret pact that risked getting them all executed by the government. At that time, the government took all the food grown by the farmers and redistributed it nationally, but the farmers' share in return was so small that many of their families were near starvation. Worse, the government did not have enough local knowledge to allow the farmers to be productive, and mandated disastrous crop experiments (Dikötter, 2010) which, together with persistent droughts, had brought the village to near collapse. As farmer Yan Hongchan recalls, even the cows were too weak to plow (Dandan, 2018, para. 15).

Driven to desperation, Yan Hongchan called a special meeting in which the villagers decided to defy the government's system by signing a secret agreement that they would illegally farm their own small plots of land in addition to contributing to the Chinese collective farming program. This extra food would be distributed equally within the village without the knowledge of the government. If each family grew enough food for both the government and the needs of the new village collective, there was an additional benefit: they could also keep any surplus for themselves. The secret pact, which one of them hid inside a piece of bamboo on the ceiling of his mud house, had a provision that if any of the farmers were jailed or executed because of the plan, the rest would take care of their children.

Because the farmers were newly incentivized to do well for their own community, they redoubled their efforts, and the harvest—66,500 kg of rice—was greater than it had been for the five previous years combined (Xinhua News Agency, 2018). Local overseers soon noticed, and the news eventually reached the highest level of the Communist Party leadership. Mao-Zedong had recently died, or the farmers would likely have been severely punished or sentenced to death under his rule. But newly empowered Deng Xiaoping was interested in economic reform. When his government realized what was happening, instead of punishing the villagers, they studied their practices with interest and used their analysis to reform China's entire economic system. The result was over 500 million people being elevated out of

DOI: https://doi.org/10.37514/PER-B.2021.1299.1.3

poverty—"the greatest economic advance the world has ever seen, and the greatest improvement in history in the living standards and life chances for ordinary people" (Pirie, 2018). The secret pact is now in a museum, and all Chinese schoolchildren learn the story of the farmers of Xiaogang (see also Eckholm, 1998).

For some economists, this case demonstrates one version of Garrett Hardin's (1968) "Tragedy of the Commons," more recently taken up by the late Nobel laureate Elinor Ostrom, which theorizes the tensions that arise between self-interest, the collective good, and who manages local decisions for a community. Ostrom critiques farming and herding analogies made by earlier scholars, some of whom argue that centralization—a "leviathan," or controlling agency—is required to avoid individuals' self-interest from interfering with collective goals (Ophuls, 1977), and to counteract the tendency for people to become "free riders," that is, enjoying the efforts of others without contributing. For example, Dandan (2018) explains that under the Chinese collective farming program, everyone was guaranteed the same wage, so that when some farmers put in less effort, the result was a "vicious cycle [sic]: Farmers worked at half-pace, crop yields fell, the state handed back less grain for food, and so farmers worked even slower" (para. 9). According to Jingchang, a signer of the document, "there was no incentive to work hard—to go out to the fields early, to put in extra effort" (Kestenbaum & Goldstein, 2012, para. 5).

In contrast, Ostrom argues that "tragedy" is likely to happen to the commons when some authority or power has a controlling interest in what local communities do or produce, but without understanding their context. "Missing from the set of accepted, well-developed theories of human organization," she writes, "is an adequately specified theory of collective action whereby a group of principals can organize themselves voluntarily to retain the residuals of their own efforts" (1990, p. 24). Without such a theory of self-governance and self-organization, "major policy decisions will continue to be undertaken with a presumption that individuals cannot organize themselves and always need to be organized by external authorities" (Ostrom, 1990, p. 25). For the farmers of Xiaogang, the imposition of a collective good (from above, and afar) was ignoring their local knowledge, subverting their incentive, and leading to a kind of passive resistance. But in contrast to a purely capitalistic and self-aggrandizing orientation in defiance of the communist farming program, the secret pact also meant providing for more than just one person or family's needs—it meant sharing the resources collectively within a particular community.

～～～

The writing-across-the-curriculum (WAC) movement has become one of the most enduring educational reforms in history, influencing curriculum and pedagogy across content areas and at every level from primary school to graduate programs (Russell, 2006). Survey research has shown that formal programs for WAC have grown dramatically across the U.S. and around the world (http://mappingproject.ucdavis.edu/). Long predicted to end up on the ash heap of bygone educational fads, WAC continues to develop in new directions and promote extensive research, theory, and instructional practices.

The WAC movement had its genesis close to the earth, in initiatives on small liberal-arts campuses like Central College in Pella, Iowa, where Barbara Walvoord reputedly held the first WAC workshop in 1970 (Walvoord, 2006), or at Carleton College in Minnesota, or at Beaver College (now Arcadia College) in Pennsylvania (McLeod & Soven, 1992). Wherever its true genesis, it is often characterized as a grass-roots movement, "a story of serendipity and community" (Bean, 2006, p. 115), something that sprang up from the fertile ground of small, student-oriented institutions and was nourished by those committed to teaching and learning—and then slowly spread.

Descriptions of these early programs are remarkably consistent. Typically, a group of energetic faculty began sharing ideas, usually through a coordinator with some charisma and a background in writing and pedagogy. As Russell (2002) explains, the impetus for these collaborations varied from small grant programs to a focus on admissions standards to an interest in assessing students' competencies. At the heart of the efforts, however, was a "bottom-up" orientation that inspired faculty to enhance their uses of writing in their own discipline-based courses. The contagion of their enthusiasm then led other faculty to join the often socially dynamic enterprise.

This model has effectively served the needs of many campuses, especially because there is something compelling about colleagues who share their inspiration and excitement about teaching with writing. But such programs sustain themselves only because someone is loudly trumpeting their causes: there is nothing particularly "institutional" about the activity. When the grant program dries up or the leader moves on to other pursuits or retires, or the sometimes modest funding for their course release(s) disappears, the effort often shrivels up or goes with them, leaving behind only the fond memories of a once vibrant collective dedicated to curricular and pedagogical change. Or the group never expands beyond a self-chosen few who work on writing in small interstitial curricular spaces, in the form of socially dynamic meetings that are open to all, but already solidifying into a kind of microculture with certain terms of membership. Students lucky enough to take courses with these enlightened faculty often come away with an intellectually rich experience and improved abilities. But many others miss out, and the scattershot nature of the entire endeavor fails to contribute to the broader, campus-wide enhancement of writing and other communication practices. Instead, little verdant spaces for disciplinary writing are surrounded by a more barren curricular landscape.

The history of WAC eventually shows the establishment of the earliest organized programs, first in the form of institutional support for grass-roots efforts and then, inevitably, as systematic, campus-wide initiatives written into general-education or other curricular plans by or with administrators—who sometimes are beneficent stewards and sometimes behave like the park police. Broader concerns about intellectual development and engagement can be replaced by a preoccupation with the skills of writing and vocational preparation. Accompanying this normalizing is increasing concern for regularity and distribution of the effort imposed, like the Chinese collective farming program, by a central body. The popularity of writing-intensive programs partly reflects a desire to create and control a universal *requirement,* representing a shift away from the development of teachers and toward a focus on students' accumulation of credit hours. All eyes turn to the generic requirements for the design of courses as the context for implementation; the syllabus, not the instructor, earns certification from an overseer—a committee or administrative body charged with monitoring the program, which may do little to transform the way faculty integrate and support writing in their courses or learn strategies for accommodating a broad range of student needs and populations. Siloed in specific, required courses, writing may even disappear from non-WI courses. Faculty members' unchallenged, tacit assumptions about writing and writing instruction can block their ability or willingness to sustain instructional change around writing, and beyond the WI courses there may be no change at all. As they are assigned to different (sometimes untenured) faculty who often see them as an additional burden, or shuffled off on adjuncts, the courses can eventually lose their original writing intensity, as I learned from a newly-hired assistant professor at one institution who was required to teach all three different WI courses in her department, leaving no room in her schedule for courses in her area of expertise. As a result, course-based integration may fail to create systemic or sustainable change and perpetuates a binary between writing and content (where writing is "added on" to disciplinary coverage).

Of course, some excellent campus-wide WI programs have remained successful for decades. When such programs are supported over time, and when different faculty cycle through the teaching of WI courses (and are appropriately prepared to do so), they can create lasting change. But as Holdstein (2001) explains in "Writing Across the Curriculum and the Paradoxes of Institutional Initiatives," by the 1990s, leaders of the movement were attempting to address "the problems inherent in a double-edged trend: WAC's becoming a top-down phenomenon" (p. 43). Holdstein points to McLeod and Soven's (1991) concern about the increased mandating of WAC and their anecdote about a writing program administrator who was told by her dean to deal with reluctant faculty by "ramming WAC down their throats" (p. 25). And as White lamented in a brief but oft-quoted article, "The Damage of Innovations Set Adrift," many unsupported WAC programs end up desiccated, leaving behind the dried up detritus of the program's once living initiative (White, 1990; see also Cox et al., 2018 on the sustainability of WAC programs).

When WAC is organized by structures outside individual departments and programs, whoever is responsible for implementation carries the burden—and it can be a heavy one—of "selling" the increased and enhanced use of writing down to the level of individual teachers. In that role, the leader may encounter faculty who resist WAC for a range of reasons, including feelings of inadequacy or unpreparedness to "teach" writing, fear that the focus will intrude on their coverage of material, worries about workload, or beliefs that the job of preparing writers should fall to writing teachers and that a "one-shot inoculation" should be adequate.

Over time, these problems have contributed to the demise of WAC on some campuses: over half of the WAC programs identified in 1987 had disappeared by 2007 (Thaiss & Porter, 2010). Many short-term, grant-funded, QEP-sanctioned, and personality-driven programs don't reach the level of sustainability to which they aspire (Cox et al., 2018). The reasons for the downfall of specific programs are many and complex: loss of leadership, loss of funding, faculty resistance to the effort, turnover of personnel, malaise, and lack of continued faculty development, to name a few. But the approach itself can also be to blame.

A few years after White expressed his dismay about the too-frequent disintegration of WAC programs, it became clear that the movement needed to evolve structurally, partly in response to these limitations and concerns about sustainability. McLeod et al. asked in *WAC for the New Millennium* (2011) how the movement would survive: "How will it grow and change—what new forms will WAC programs take [and] what new WAC theories and research will help lay the groundwork for future WAC programs?" (2001, p. 4). Their collection explored the future of WAC from political, curricular, and pedagogical perspectives, focusing especially on inter-unit collaborations, diverse student populations, emerging technologies, and various institutional initiatives such as service-learning.

Spurred on by these questions and the limitations of existing approaches, WAC leaders started to recognize that programs must be intentionally shaped to best match the cultures, missions, populations, disciplinary emphases, and faculty interests of specific institutions. Experiments have yielded portfolio models, vertical curricular models (see Yancey, Chapter 3 of this volume), individual consultation models, writing fellows programs (see Bastian, Chapter 10 of this volume, and Hall & Hughes, 2011), tripartite models such as the program at the

University of St. Thomas, which involves extensive development of faculty who then choose to teach general-education WI courses, writing-to-learn courses, and/or writing-in-the-disciplines courses—see https://www.stthomas.edu/wac/), and many other initiatives reflected in the wide range of activities documented in the WAC/WID Mapping Project (Thaiss & Porter, 2010). In addition, increasingly WAC began focusing more specifically on the needs, contexts, and genres of individual disciplines, resulting in an offshoot of WAC, writing in the disciplines (WID). But these efforts to explore the communities and genres of specific disciplines remained scattered and idiosyncratic, often motivated by department chairs or curriculum committees worried about students' unrefined writing abilities but unsure of what to do about the problem.

Unanticipated in *WAC for the New Millennium*, an ambitious and rapidly growing model[1] for college-level WAC programs sees the disciplinary unit of the *department* or *program* as the locus of activity. In this approach, a WAC leader or an institution decides to adopt the model and sets to work, often initially recruiting one or two departments that are the most eager to participate. Faculty within departments work together to define goals and outcomes, compare beliefs about writing, map their curriculum, plan for change, and decide how and when to collect data (the process is described in detail in many chapters in this volume). WAC experts serve as guides, listeners, and distillers of information—a role in stark contrast to those who police syllabi for adherence to WAC criteria or ensure that faculty are complying with some institutional requirements. Theoretically, this approach encourages ownership and responsibility; it recognizes disciplinary interests and the importance of complex, evolving genres of communication and varying departmental cultures; it understands differences in curricula, courses, and student populations; and it endorses the view that writing is learned within situated practice (Lave & Wenger, 1991; New London Group, 1996; Russell, 1995). As departments join the effort, they can then influence and help other departments. Eventually, many departments are engaged, all of them working through their own processes of curricular revision, faculty development, and writing assessment.

Across higher education, there are many examples of individual departments that have decided to focus on writing (see Blank, Chapter 5 of this volume), and most WAC leaders can point to specific units on their campuses that have moved well beyond whatever institutional structure and support may already exist. In some cases, for example, writing-intensive programs have inspired a department

---

1   Throughout this collection, authors use the terms "model," "approach," "program," "effort," "system," and "method" interchangeably to refer to various aspects or developments of the writing-enriched curriculum. Although each term carries some semantic distinctions, they all refer to the underlying principles of WEC.

to go beyond the basic university requirement of one or two demand-based courses and have expanded their focus on writing internally. But *systematically* organized programs—that is, long-term endeavors in which eventually every department on a campus collectively focuses on the role of writing in its curriculum—are still rare. The chapter on "New Programmatic Directions" in the *Reference Guide to Writing Across the Curriculum* (Bazerman et al., 2005) describes the role of writing-intensive programs, writing centers, peer tutors and writing fellows, ESL programs, interdisciplinary learning communities, service learning, and e-CAC, but the departmentally localized model is not mentioned.

Although activity within specific departments focusing on writing has been a part of WAC from long before the start of the movement, the earliest known systematic, university-wide, departmentally-localized model was implemented on my own campus. In the late 1990s, North Carolina State University was experimenting with an approach to curricular implementation and assessment of learning that focused on and empowered individual departments and programs to engage in continuous improvement (Carter, 2002; see Gary Blank's full history in Chapter 5 of this volume, and Michael Carter's Foreword). As part of this broad interest in teaching and learning, NC State's Campus Writing and Speaking Program was established in 1997. In 1999, Deanna Dannels (as Assistant Director and expert in oral communication across the curriculum) and I (as Director) were hired to lead the program. The CWSP was created to help each department across the university to focus specifically on written and oral communication through the implementation of curricular plans, faculty development, and outcomes assessment (Anson, 2006; Anson et al., 2003). The departmental model became transformative because, with the help of our program, all decisions about expectations for student writing, plans to realize those expectations, and methods to assess the results of those plans were "uniquely shaped by the department, molded to best fit its faculty, students, and curriculum" (Anson & Dannels, 2018, p. 5).

The model involved extensive consultation with members of individual departments, first to help them articulate their expectations for student writing and oral communication, eventually framed as learning outcomes embedded in the acquisition of disciplinary knowledge. The next step in the process was to consider methods to reach the outcomes. Because the outcomes were aspirational, no department believed they were already accomplishing them, so the focus shifted to the creation of implementation strategies that might include faculty-development activities, extensive curricular mapping, surveys of how faculty contributed to the effort, and consultations with individual faculty about their courses. The final stage involved figuring out ways to determine the effectiveness of the innovations.

As the success of this model became apparent, other campuses began to take notice and adapt it to their campus cultures. In 2006, inspired by the work at North Carolina State, the University of Minnesota began to pilot a structured model that they named the writing-enriched curriculum (WEC). With WEC, the University of Minnesota's WAC program, directed by Pamela Flash, created a faculty-directed set of procedures for the development, implementation, and ongoing assessment of undergraduate writing plans, collectively-authored documents that guide the curricular integration and assessment of relevant writing abilities (Anson, Dannels, et al., 2014; Flash 2016). This model, which Flash further describes in Chapter 1 of this volume, has established a portable, customizable, and sustained method for supporting curriculum-wide approaches to writing's integration, as other contributors to this collection describe.

The acronym "WEC," first branding the Minnesota program, is becoming the more generic term that characterizes the departmental model of WAC. This model is characterized by, at the least, the core features shown in Table 1 (collaboratively drafted with Pamela Flash), which are further elaborated and exemplified in this collection.

Table 1. Core features of the WEC model

Locus	Locates within academic departments and empowers and gives ownership to the faculty (and students) to name and describe relevant writing aims, and to determine their *curricular* integration and terms of assessment.
Orientation	Conceptually-oriented: recognizes the power of writing-related assumptions to drive or block the integration of writing instruction across the disciplines and is designed to draw out often tacit knowledge about writing that defines ways of knowing and doing in the discipline.
Data use	Collects local data (including writing assignments, student writing, survey data, direct assessment of student writing) and involves faculty in recurring episodes of data interpretation and analysis.
Mediation	Involves an intermediator (a writing expert) who facilitates the work of articulating writing knowledge, planning interventions, assessing results, and engaging in an ongoing partnership with departmental stakeholders.
Support	Is bolstered by the ongoing partnership of writing and teaching support offices, and by administrative, financial, and other support for individual units, but is not entirely dependent on these.
Sustainability	Promotes long-term practices, scales gradually, is sensitive to internal change and inertia, and periodically or regularly revisits and revises the original efforts.

Although developed in response to localized needs, the models at North Carolina State University and the University of Minnesota are being successfully implemented on university and college campuses across the US and in Europe. For example, along with the institutions represented in this collection, Hobart and William Smith Colleges, Eastern Oregon University, McDaniel College, Bielefeld University, Stephen F. Austin State University, Elon University, the University of Mississippi, and others have been implementing programs, in most cases directly through the help of the co-editors. The approach has gained such interest that symposia organized at the University of Minnesota have attracted attendees from dozens of institutions who want to strategize efforts on their own campuses, and my orientation toward the approach has met with strong interest at the newly established WAC Institute sponsored by the Association for Writing Across the Curriculum (https://www.wacassociation.org/).

This collection is the first volume to bring together theory, research, and campus-specific examples of the writing-enriched curriculum—the faculty-driven and departmentally focused model of WAC/WID implementation. The purpose of the collection is to inform writing program administrators, teachers, scholars, and university officials about the potential of the model to transform the way writing is used and supported across all courses and curricula in higher education. The collection includes theoretically grounded accounts of departmentally focused writing- or communication-across-the-curriculum programs, including localized research that demonstrates the effectiveness of the model. The result of targeted solicitations of WAC/WID coordinators who have implemented departmentally focused efforts on their campuses yielded ten chapters alongside the co-editors'.

The essays are divided into three sections. The first section provides the historical, theoretical, and curricular principles and methods that define the WEC model, grounded in extended descriptions, analyses, and research from its implementation. In Part Two, four chapters further theorize the WEC model through explorations of the authors' own implementation efforts. Part Three then considers the WEC model in the context of other initiatives and programs.

Instead of including descriptions of each chapter here, we asked authors to provide previews that precede the body of their chapters. Readers can use these to guide their selection of chapters to read (or to reorder the sequence of chapters) based on their particular interests.

~~~

It would be unprincipled to compare the plight of the farmers in Xiaogang during the 1970s—laboring under oppressive rules and threatened with imprisonment or execution for disobedience—with the context of higher education institutions, or any academic department, no matter how marginalized it feels in the institution's hierarchy or how put upon to do things it doesn't want to do. Nor do the economic reforms precipitated by the farmers of Xiaogang absolve the Chinese government of continuing concerns about human rights. But there is also a lesson in the famous story, not only for those leading WAC programs but for those leading most curricular and pedagogical reforms: incentive has its roots in what matters locally—in ownership and personal investments in work. In turn, the resulting energy and inspiration will contribute to the collective good. At the same time, the sustainability of such localized efforts is usually guaranteed only through partnerships with a central administration. Too many organically grown programs or initiatives have failed from lack of funding or other support. WEC programs work effectively with faculty ownership recognized and supported by upper administrations and through essential partnerships with WAC experts and their programs, which can help with significant bureaucratic and infrastructural needs (communication and follow-through, web support, materials, meeting arrangements, budgeting, and the like).

When members of academic departments and programs are inspired to focus on writing and how best it should be integrated into their curricula and their goals for students' success, and are given the support needed to bring out their understandings and examine their practices, they rise to the challenge in remarkable ways. Decades of compartmentalization and the association of writing with people outside of their disciplinary contexts have denied them the rights of ownership—of deciding what their students should be able to do, on their own terms, and then figuring out how best they can achieve those goals in their own ways. In sharing the successes of those who have contributed to this volume, as well as the challenges they have overcome or are struggling to overcome, it is our hope that this collection documents a new approach to WAC that can lead other institutions and their departments toward the kinds of transformations that result in entire cultures of writing—within and across academic and co-curricular units.

REFERENCES

Anson, C. M. (2006). Assessing writing in cross-curricular programs: Determining the locus of activity. *Assessing Writing, 11*, 100–112.

Anson, C. M., Carter, M., Dannels, D. P. & Rust, J. (2003). Mutual support: CAC programs and institutional improvement in undergraduate education. *Journal of Language and Learning Across the Disciplines, 6*(3), 26–38. https://doi.org/10.37514/LLD-J.2003.6.3.06.

Anson, C. M. & Dannels, D. P. (2018). Handing over the reins: Ownership, support, and the departmentally-focused model of communication across the curriculum. In M. Cox, J. Galin & D. Melzer, *Sustainable WAC: A whole systems approach to launching and developing WAC programs* (pp. 5–7). National Council of Teachers of English.

Anson, C. M., Dannels, D. P., Flash, P. & Gaffney, A. H. (2012). Big rubrics and weird genres: The futility of using generic assessment tools across diverse instructional contexts. *Journal of Writing Assessment, 5*(1).

Bazerman, C., Little, J., Bethel, L., Chavkin, T., Fouquette, D. & Garufis, J. (2005). *Reference guide to writing across the curriculum.* Parlor Press; The WAC Clearinghouse. https://wac.colostate.edu/books/referenceguides/bazerman-wac/.

Bean, J. C. (2006). Montana, Mina Shaughnessy, and microthemes: Reflections on WAC as a community. In S. H. McCleod & M. I. Soven (Eds.), *Composing a community: A history of writing across the curriculum.* Parlor Press.

Blank, G. B. (2021). Forty years of writing embedded in forestry at North Carolina State University. In C. M. Anson & P. Flash (Eds.), *Writing-enriched curricula: Models of faculty-driven and departmental transformation.* The WAC Clearinghouse; University Press of Colorado. https://doi.org/10.27514/PER-B.2021 .1299.2.05.

Carter, M. (2002). A Process for establishing outcomes-based assessment plans for writing and speaking in the disciplines. *Language and Learning Across the Disciplines, 6,* 4–29. https://doi.org/10.37514/LLD-J.2003.6.1.02.

Carter, M. (2021). Foreword. In C. M. Anson & P. Flash (Eds.), *Writing-enriched curricula: Models of faculty-driven and departmental transformation.* The WAC Clearinghouse; University Press of Colorado. https://doi.org/10.27514/PER-B.2021.1299 .1.2.

Cox, M., Galin, J. R. & Melzer, D. (2018). *Sustainable WAC: A whole systems approach to launching and developing writing across the curriculum programs.* National Council of Teachers of English.

Dandan, N. (2018, August 21). The farmer who changed China forever. *Sixth Tone.* http://www.sixthtone.com/news/1002783/the-farmer-who-changed-china-forever.

Dikötter, F. (2010). *Mao's Great Famine: The history of China's most devastating catastrophe, 1958–62.* Walker.

Eckholm, E. (1998, September 19). Xiaogang journal; village of small farmers marks own great leap. *The New York Times,* A4. https://www.nytimes.com/1998/09/19 /world/xiaogang-journal-village-of-small-farmers-marks-own-great-leap.html.

Flash, P. (2016). From apprised to revised: Faculty in the disciplines change what they never knew they knew. In K. B. Yancey (Ed.), *A Rhetoric of reflection* (pp. 227–249). Utah State University Press.

Flash, P. (2021). Writing-enriched curriculum: A model for making and sustaining change. In C. M. Anson & P. Flash (Eds.), *Writing-enriched curricula: Models of faculty-driven and departmental transformation.* The WAC Clearinghouse; University Press of Colorado. https://doi.org/10.27514/PER-B.2021.1299.2.01.

Xinhua News Agency. (14 October 2018). *Forty years on, Xiaogang still testbed of China's economic reform.* China Daily. https://www.chinadaily.com.cn/a/201810/14 /WS5bc32642a310eff30328237b.html.

Hall, E. & Hughes, B. (2011). Preparing faculty, professionalizing fellows: Keys to success with undergraduate writing fellows in WAC. *The WAC Journal, 22,* 21–40. https://doi.org/10.37514/WAC-J.2011.22.1.03.

Hardin, J. (1968). The tragedy of the commons. *Science, 162*(3859), 1243–1248.

Holdstein, D. (2001). "Writing across the curriculum" and the paradoxes of institutional initiatives. *Pedagogy, 1*(1), 37–52.

Kestenbaum, D. & Goldstein, J. (2012). The secret document that transformed China. National Public Radio, https://www.npr.org/sections/money/2012/01/20/14536 0447/the-secret-document-that-transformed-china.

McLeod, S. & Miraglia, E. (2011). Writing across the curriculum in a time of change. In S. H. McCleod, E. Miraglia, M. Soven & C. Thaiss (Eds.), *WAC for the new millennium: Strategies for continuing writing-across-the-curriculum programs* (pp. 1–27). National Council of Teachers of English.

McLeod, S. & Soven, M. (1991). What do you need to start—and sustain—a writing-across-the-curriculum program? *WPA: Writing Program Administration, 15*, 25–34.

McLeod, S. & Soven, M. (1992). *Writing across the curriculum: A guide to developing programs.* Sage.

Nandan, N. (2018, August 21). The farmer who changed China forever. *The Sixth Tone.* http://www.sixthtone.com/news/1002783/the-farmer-who-changed-china-forever.

New London Group (1996). A pedagogy of multiliteracies: Designing social futures. *Harvard educational review, 66*(1), 60–93.

Ophuls, W. (1977). *Ecology and the politics of scarcity.* Freeman.

Ostrom, E. (1990). *Governing the commons: The evolution of institutions for collective action.* Cambridge University Press.

Pirie, M. (2018). The document that changed the world. https://www.adamsmith.org /blog/the-document-that-changed-the-world.

Russell, D. R. (1994). American origins of the writing-across-the-curriculum movement. In C. Bazerman & D. R. Russell (Eds.), *Landmark essays on writing across the curriculum* (pp. 3–22). Hermagoras Press.

Russell, D. R. (1995). Activity theory and its implications for writing instruction. In J. Petraglia (Ed.), *Reconceiving writing, rethinking writing instruction* (pp. 51–77). Erlbaum.

Russell, D. R. (2002). *Writing in the academic disciplines: A curricular history* (2nd ed.). Southern Illinois University Press.

Russell, D. R. (2006). WAC's beginnings: Developing a community of change agents. In S. H. McLeod & M. I. Soven (Eds.), *Composing a community: A history of writing across the curriculum* (pp. 3–15). Parlor Press.

Schoolland, K. (2012). The China model: Is it a golden formula? *Economic Affairs, 32*(2), 88–90.

Thaiss, C. & Porter, T. (2010). The State of WAC/WID in 2010: Methods and results of the U.S. Survey of the International WAC/WID Mapping Project. *College Composition and Communication, 61*(3), 534–570.

Walvoord, B. E. (2006). Gender and discipline in two early WAC communities: Lessons for today. In S. H. McLeod & M. I. Soven (Eds.), *Composing a community: A history of writing across the curriculum* (pp. 142–156). Parlor Press.

White, E. M. (1990). The damage of innovations set adrift. *AAHE Bulletin, 43*(3), 3–5.

PART ONE. THE WEC APPROACH

CHAPTER 1.

WRITING-ENRICHED CURRICULUM: A MODEL FOR MAKING AND SUSTAINING CHANGE

Pamela Flash

University of Minnesota

To provide a foundational framework for ensuing chapters in this collection, this chapter overviews the genesis and design of the WEC approach and details components of the WEC model developed at the University of Minnesota and adopted in other institutional settings. From its grounding principles and basis in WAC/WID and educational research, to its systems for engaging academic faculty groups in creating, implementing, and assessing locally relevant undergraduate writing plans, the WEC methodology is outlined and substantiated with departmental case studies. Finally, this chapter identifies six essential features of the WEC model and considers ways in which these features represent shifts from established WAC/WID programming.

The writing-enriched curriculum model, or WEC, enjoys a certain commonsensical appeal. As compositionist and rhetorician Kathleen Blake Yancey remarked during a consulting visit in 2009, "What I want to know is why everyone isn't *already* doing this. It just seems so obvious." Her question was logical because what we have in WEC is a tested strategy for putting control of writing instruction and assessment into the hands of the people best positioned to make informed, locally relevant decisions about instruction and assessment—namely, a department's faculty. Still, anyone who has overseen an academic initiative knows that obvious and actionable are not conjoined characteristics. Putting a comprehensive program of curriculum development into the hands of people who don't always, or even often, agree on matters related to writing, instruction, or much else might be a dicey proposition. How is it, then, that a faculty-directed model, one that locates inside a department's regularly scheduled faculty meetings, focuses on contentious beliefs about writing and instruction, and welcomes expansive candor has succeeded, endured, and spread? Fifteen years into WEC's implementation, with a majority of my research university's undergraduate departments enrolled in the program, and with an increasing number of WEC adaptations underway in colleges and universities across the country, we're in a good position to pursue that question, to probe the model's design, development, impacts, and portability. In this chapter, I lay some groundwork for our probe by tracing the model's genesis, explicating its constituent moves, and distilling its six critical features (departmental location and control, conceptual orientation, grounding in data, use of an external mediator, forms of support, and sustainability). These features, detailed at the end of this chapter, provide insight into the model's potential and clarify differences between WEC and established writing across the curriculum (WAC) and writing in the discipline (WID) initiatives.

In essence, WEC is a facilitated process designed to support the integration of relevant writing and writing instruction into departmental curricula and to increase the rate at which students' writing meets local faculty expectations. A department's faculty works toward these hinged goals by engaging in a sequential process of generating, implementing, and assessing comprehensive documents called writing plans. In its plan, the faculty articulates local writing and instructional values and plans for instructional change. Importantly, in meetings convened to generate plan content, members are urged to talk candidly and think collectively—often for the first time—about what they believe to be true about discourse-relevant writing and locally-feasible forms of instruction. They're supported in making pragmatic decisions about which, how, and where desired writing abilities are (or might be) supported within their curricula, about structural or instructional interventions and modifications they'd like to enact to better integrate writing and writing instruction and what forms of support are needed to implement those interventions and modifications. Ultimately, all these insights, decisions, and requests are compiled into the plan which then moves through an ongoing sequence of implementation and revision over the course of the next decade. Plan revisions are partially informed by regular cycles of direct writing assessment, panel ratings of capstone-level writing against faculty-identified, graduation-level writing criteria.

Contextualized intellectually, WEC emerges from a confluence of research currents and pedagogical movements. Indeed, one reason for the model's apparent obviousness is that research and practices that help us interpret its impact and potential have been in the air for decades. In ways that I'll signal in this chapter (and others in this collection will scrutinize in more thorough detail), WEC enacts elements of influential and pragmatic educational theories that include backward design and valid evidence-based assessment (Broad, 2003; Huot, 2002; Messick,

1989; O'Neill, 2003; Wiggins & McTighe, 1998) and department-based, cyclical action research (Kemmis et al., 2014). Its emphasis on iterative, local data collection and local stakeholders' interpretation of those data draws on long-established ethnographic research methods and the interplay between emic and etic perspectives (Goodenough, 1956; Harris, 1976; Pike, 1954). Aligning with more current scholarship, WEC operationalizes research into ways that student writers transfer writing insights from one curricular location to another (Nowacek, 2011; Yancey et al., 2014, 2018) and provides opportunities for the faculty to identify and address critical points of influential conceptual struggle (Adler-Kassner et al., 2015; Meyer & Land, 2006). In these ways, the WEC framework is geared to catalyze change from within departmental activity systems (Engstrom et al., 1990; Russell, 1995; Walvoord, 2000) and to increase what educational theorist Michael Fullan calls a faculty's "change capacity" (Fullan, 2016). Finally, with hindsight I can see that the model's durability and portability rely on its conscientious consideration of components and heuristics helpful to sustainable program development (Cox et al., 2018; Fullan, 2005).

As to methodological forebears, WEC has drawn philosophical and logistical inspiration from an array of institutional programs implementing faculty-centered curricular reform. The facilitative approach Michael Carter, Chris Anson, and Deanna Dannels have used to engage departmental faculty groups in identifying writing and speaking outcomes at North Carolina State University (Anson, 2006; Anson et al., 2003; Carter, 2002;) has been particularly influential. Although NCSU's approach to working with departments involves multiple comprehensive components, it was Carter, Anson, and Dannel's approach to conducting disarmingly generative faculty meetings that helped to launch the design of WEC. At Seattle University, John Bean and colleagues developed a similar assessment-based approach, and collaborated with departments to building "writing infused" curricula (Bean et al., 2005). From George Mason University, the deliberate approach Terry Zawacki and colleagues took to embedded, departmental WAC work and especially to devising multimodal programmatic assessment (Zawacki et al., 2009) inspired WEC's menu of formative local and programmatic assessments. Finally, the model's grounded methodology, its recursive practice of putting locally collected writing samples, curricular maps, and assessment data into the hands of departmental faculty members in order to prompt their formative interpretation, was inspired in large part by the dynamic criteria mapping processes Bob Broad developed for surfacing context-relevant writing values (Broad, 2003). So, while the WEC model and WEC acronym were developed at the University of Minnesota, elements of its approach have been theorized about and implemented in diverse intellectual and geographical contexts.

GUIDING PRINCIPLES

Implementing the WEC model involves daily travel into diverse departmental subcultures, curricular structures, genre norms, and teaching practices. An established grounding in principle helps balance customization with consistency. From its inception, our WEC activity has been guided by the following five interconnected principles relating to the nature of writing and writing instruction:

- that writing is an articulation of thinking and involves choosing among an array of modes or forms, only some of which involve words,
- that writing is instrumental to learning and as such is continually developed and is the shared responsibility of all academic disciplines,
- that those who infuse writing instruction into their teaching require ongoing, partnered support,
- that unchallenged, tacit-level conceptions of writing and writing instruction inform the ways writing is taught and the degree to which writing is meaningfully incorporated into diverse undergraduate curricula,
- that systemic, curricular incorporation of writing into "content instruction" can be most meaningfully achieved when those who teach are provided multiple opportunities to articulate, interrogate, and communicate their assumptions and expectations.

The first two of these principles, and particularly the second, will sound familiar to anyone working in WAC; they're entwined in our shared programmatic and theoretical DNA. The third, with its "ongoing, partnered support" clause may raise a few eyebrows, particularly among those more familiar with the episodic forms of instructional support (e.g., the workshop or instructional consultation). The final two principles in this list are particularly foundational to WEC methodology and will be evoked throughout this chapter and in the chapters contributed by others who have adapted the model.

WEC MODEL GENESIS

In *Sustainable WAC*, Cox et al. suggest that people interested in establishing durable writing initiatives will find less value in narrative accounts of individual, contextually idiosyncratic programs and observation-based analyses than in analytic frameworks and tested administrative heuristics (Cox et al., 2018). I agree, and therefore preface the following abridged account of WEC's institutional backstory by clarifying that it's my intention to highlight ways that the model developed to address *shared* (rather than institutionally idiosyncratic) circumstances.

When, in the early 1990s, 28% of respondents to the University of Minnesota's annual student exit survey reported that they'd been required to write no more than two ten-page papers in the course of their entire degree programs, a faculty taskforce was convened to address this question: "How can we ensure that students in all degree programs receive adequate writing instruction?" This committee's interest in dispersing writing and writing instruction into all disciplinary curricula and its insistence that "students should be asked to write more often, in contexts that give greater purpose to their effort" (Task Force on Liberal Education, 1991) inspired them to propose an ambitious four-course writing-intensive (WI) requirement. In the mid-nineties the University Senate agreed, and in 1999, the initiative began full implementation. The hope was that a decentralized, yet uniform, cross-curricular requirement might deliver sustained attention to writing throughout students' undergraduate experiences.

In 2001, as the newly appointed WAC director, I began to insert myself into lots of departmental faculty meetings in each undergraduate-enrolling college. My interest was in gauging the extent to which our bi-directional approach—our combination of top-down writing intensive requirement with bottom-up, elective workshops and consultations—was successfully moving us toward our goal of what Anson, Hall, and others call a "vertical incorporation" of writing (Anson, 2006, p. 110; Hall, 2006, p. 6). By vertical incorporation, Anson and Hall refer to writing's intentional and expanded relevance up the ladder from course-specific, to departmental, collegiate, and ultimately, institution-wide systems. To get a sense of how department faculty thought this was working, I began with logistical questions: "Which of your courses have been certified as writing-intensive? Why were those courses selected? Who teaches them? How well is all this working?" In response, I was given an earful of confusion and consternation. Why, departmental faculty wanted to know, was a certain course certified WI when a certain other course—a course that invariably involved a *lot* of writing—was not? Why should a course that was not designated WI include any attention to writing? Yes, of course academic writing is vitally important, some acknowledged, but was it reasonable to ask them to add writing to their already chock-full courses, particularly in the face of expanding course enrollments and diminishing TA support? Was it *un*reasonable for them to expect that students would enter their courses having developed *basic* writing proficiency somewhere else? What, after all, were students learning in their *writing* courses? Inevitably, someone would pipe up to ask about what, if any, concrete incentives the administration was prepared to offer to induce them to teach these courses.

These initial discussions with faculty groups surfaced what seemed an intractable dilemma. Regardless of department and discipline, faculty participants articulated a variant of the same three-part claim: (1) student fluency in relevant forms and styles of writing was absolutely critical to scholarly success in their fields of research and study, 2) insufficient numbers of students in their courses were demonstrating the writing abilities they, as discourse insiders, were looking for, and (3) *they* couldn't be expected to address this problem because they were not experts in writing or writing instruction. This is a wearyingly familiar impasse to anyone engaged in WAC work. It's this sort of situation, after all, that inspired David Russell to suggest that "WAC exists in a structure that fundamentally resists it" (Russell, 1991, p. 295) and Susan McLeod to characterize WAC professionals as missionaries, diplomats, and Peace Corps volunteers (McLeod, 1995).

Instead of arguing with faculty groups, I scheduled myself into even more of their meetings, electing to pursue rather than contradict this set of assumptions. I revised my line of questioning, looking for specifics. I asked, for instance, "What sorts of things do you write and publish in mechanical engineering? In apparel design? In forest resources? Can you refer me to some examples?" "What sorts of things do you ask *undergraduates* to write? Can I take a look at some samples?" "What are some of the routine writing challenges students face here?" Responses to these questions were illuminating both for what was said and for what was not. Faculty members' current writing projects rarely looked anything like the writing projects they were assigning to undergraduate students. In some departments, particularly those that prioritize technical or design-oriented modes, a few bold instructors insisted that writing played no role at all in their research or teaching. And yet complaints about the quality of student writing remained plentiful, impassioned, if still vague: it's disorganized; it's uninteresting; it's not clear. My follow-up questions, "When you say unclear, what can you tell me about what makes it unclear?" "How might you describe the sort of organizational logic you look for?" "How critical is that structure relative to other features?" weren't so readily answered. It was in these awkward silences, as these faculty colleagues sat searching for answers to these questions and they described and questioned the writing they were doing and the writing that their students were doing, that I realized we had hit upon a situation with enormous change-making potential. If the specifics of their writing-related expectations were hidden from them, was it any wonder that meeting these expectations could feel confusing to students or that the prospect of incorporating writing instruction into their teaching could confuse faculty? It was in discussions like these, I understood, rather than in unilateral WI requirements, that advances could be made toward the goal of integrating relevant writing instruction into all degree programs.

After years of WI implementation, was our bi-directional approach to WAC working? From the sounds of things, the answer was no. Although by some metrics our WI requirement was achieving success in that many hundreds of WI courses were on the books and filling, our cross-curricular writing requirement

and corresponding programs offering elective instructional support weren't cata-
lyzing sustainable systemic change. Pedagogic insights and strategies sparked by
instructional consultations and workshops with individual instructors weren't
catching on in departments. WI courses remained atomized and over-burdened.
As a faculty participant from horticultural science remarked on the last day of
my annual five-day Teaching with Writing seminar, "Oh great, now I have to
go back to my department where nobody talks about this stuff. I'm going to get
dumped with teaching *all* the WI courses!"

My meetings in departments had made it apparent that our writing integration stalemate had at least two causes: (1) the writing-intensive requirement and
instructional support offered through our WAC program focused on individual
courses rather than curricular systems and (2) unchallenged faculty assumptions
about discourse-relevant writing—about what it should look like and how it is best
learned—presented powerful roadblocks to the initiative's goal of integrated writing instruction. No matter what changes we might require of individual courses,
we would fail at activating a systemic, curricular embrace of writing instruction
if by "writing," the University intended lengthy prose-based papers, and if by
"writing instruction," the University intended didactic explications of grammatical structures or the provision of lengthy diagnostic commentary on multiple,
lengthy drafts. These problematic and inaccurate assumptions obstructed a view
of assigned writing tasks as a way of moving students toward the department's
curricular objectives, as a tool to conceptual learning, and thus worth integrating
into departmental curricula. Systemic change would require entirely different perspectives about the relevance of writing to a department's shared curricular goals.

Thus, our 2006 question revised our 1990 question. In 1990 we'd asked,
"How can we ensure that students in all degree programs *receive adequate writing instruction?*" In 2006 we asked, "How can we ensure an *intentional and sustainable infusion* of relevant writing instruction into our diverse undergraduate curricula?" Fresh from all those faculty meetings, I recognized that finding
meaningful answers to this new question would help us to shift responsibility for
designing the curricular integration of writing into the hands of departmental
faculty members, the people who are in the best position to determine what's
meant by relevant and what intentional infusion might look like in the context of their curricular structure and pedagogical norms. Because discourse and
departmental norms are dynamic, we were going to need to engage the faculty
in a process that Kemmis et al. call "a self-reflective spiral of cycles of planning,
acting and observing, reflecting and then re-planning . . . successive cycles of
improvement" (2014, p. 2). The model we piloted and subsequently institutionalized implements this spiral by participating in an ongoing cycle of creating,
implementing, and assessing undergraduate writing plans.

THE WRITING PLAN

Writing plans are documents composed of five sections (see Table 1.1). A department's faculty establishes a broad description of writing's relevance to a discipline and field before identifying a list of writing abilities they expect of undergraduate majors. From there, they work in a reverse-engineering mode to describe where, in their course offerings, explicit attention to developing named writing abilities does or might occur. These writing abilities are translated into a menu of grading criteria from which departmental faculty members can select and adapt items to specific courses and assignments. Because these criteria are also used in triennial ratings of capstone-level writing facilitated by the WEC team (more about this later in this chapter), they stand as benchmarks in assessing the impact of the plan over time. Once these steps have been accomplished, the faculty proposes activities and changes they'd like to undertake over a specified period to effect curricular integration of relevant writing and writing instruction. All these insights and plans are compiled into a document that moves through multiple editions and follows an evolutionary path from initial and exploratory to departmentally sustained.

Table 1.1. Five sections included in the undergraduate writing plan

Section	Topic
1	Characteristics of writing in the broad discipline
2	Writing abilities expected of graduating majors
3	Curricular address of expected writing abilities
4	Methods and criteria used to assess writing
5	Proposed activity and support

Although each writing plan follows a similar outline and although some of the writing expectations, when broadly construed, are shared (see Yancey, this volume), these plans highlight differences in discourse expectations, departmental culture, and pedagogical preferences. The plan developed by my university's art history department, for example, contrasts in all sorts of ways from the one developed by our mechanical engineering department. In art history, where students can take courses like "Baroque Art in 17th Century Europe," or "African American Cinema" in no pre-established order, the faculty's list of graduation-level writing abilities includes the expectation that students "develop and fully prosecute an argument throughout their work, so that the presentation of all forms of evidence (e.g., historical information, visual observation, analysis of existing literature) clearly relates to and further develops the core thesis" (Department of Art History,

2015). In its early edition writing plans, the faculty emphasized a need to support the on-time completion of high-quality senior papers. To achieve this, the faculty focused on piloting a capstone course that would provide seniors, despite their disparate research foci, with a structured and paced workshop experience. In an adjacent move, the department developed an annual senior paper prize to be awarded to papers that most effectively demonstrate proficiency with writing criteria the faculty had listed in its writing plan. To publicly recognize award winners—and to publicly reinforce attributes of successful art historical writing—the department also launched an annual research symposium and award ceremony. Over the years, this event began to attract standing-room-only crowds which inspired the department chair to characterize it as, "*the* event of the year." Based on these successes, art history used its second and third-edition writing plans to propose strategies for exposing pre-capstone students to desired writing abilities in courses throughout its lower- and upper-division curricula.

In the Department of Mechanical Engineering, on the other hand, where the undergraduate curriculum is constructed of carefully delineated course sequences and where desired abilities include, "record[ing] and analyz[ing] activity related to laboratory and design projects," and "visually represent[ing] technical concepts and designs in ways that explain their salient features" (Department of Mechanical Engineering, 2016), re-gathering students from diverging curricular pathways and ensuring on-time graduation isn't a big concern. Because engineering courses move according to predetermined paths, the faculty was able to embed writing activities of increasing sophistication into courses in all years of their major. Of more concern to mechanical engineering faculty is persuading majors of *why* they would want to attend to writing and of *how*, specifically, they can go about meeting writing requirements. Acting on these concerns, the mechanical engineering faculty attained support for a graduate student who developed a series of genre-specific writing guides which include, "The Problem Set," "The Lab Report," and "The Design Proposal." Collectively, these guides make a case for discipline-relevant acts of audience-based communication and contradict the notion that writing is an import from an alien discipline. Exploded diagrams and annotated excerpts help mechanical engineering majors see that documenting their logic as they solve computational and design problems is fundamental to the work they'll be doing in courses and in the field. The published style guides are incrementally inserted courses and referred to where students are first introduced to these different kinds of "deliverables." (An excerpt from the Problem Set Style Guide can be seen in Figure 1.1.)

In my work with the mechanical engineering faculty, I initially raised questions about whether autodidactic materials of this sort would make much impact on student writing. Might these resources end up on a dead website, unused and increasingly out of date? I was quickly overruled. According to my colleagues in mechanical engineering, shelf-life was not a problem as not much changes in these genres ("a problem set is a problem set!"). I also learned that a willingness to refer to ancillary manuals and to comply with specifications and instructions may be distasteful to me but is routine for engineers. After conducting a controlled test of the problem-set style guide, implementing it in one section of a thermodynamics course and comparing students' problem sets and grades against those derived from a section where it wasn't used, the faculty was satisfied with the results and henceforth made the guides a required part of course materials. In these two disparate examples, we see ways in which the WEC model is driven by departmental faculty (rather than by the WAC consultant) and adjusts to address departmental norms and practices.

3. Annotated Example

Below is an example problem, with its components labeled and explained.

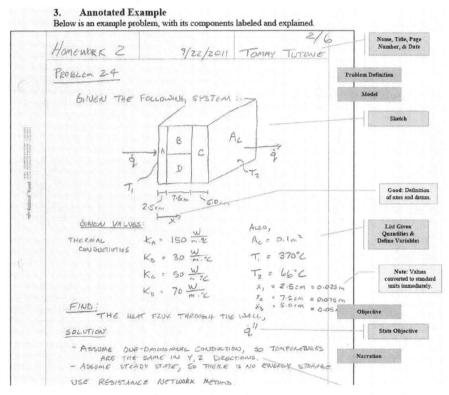

Figure 1.1. An excerpt from a mechanical engineering writing style guide in which expected components of a problem set are specified using an annotated example. Rhetorical purposes (noted in the green annotations) are interspersed with specifications (noted in the blue annotations). Evaluative comments pertaining to the sample are also provided (in yellow annotations) (Adams & Durfee, 2011).

DEVELOPING FIRST-EDITION WRITING PLANS

A first-edition writing plan is generated in a series of faculty discussions, each one focused on one or two questions related to local writing and writing instruction and each grounded by faculty review and interpretation of a form of locally collected data (see Table 1.2). Importantly, the discussions take place within a department's regularly scheduled faculty meetings. Although some department chairs may be quick to suggest that WEC discussions get assigned to a voluntary subcommittee, we're usually successful in dissuading them from this move. As Michael Carter suggests in his forward to this volume, surfacing challenges and resistance is a vitally important to the WEC process. If the resulting plan is going to succeed in overcoming internal roadblocks, those roadblocks need to become apparent. To this end, it has proven critical to involve a critical mass of departmental instructors, a group that intentionally includes people who think that talking about undergraduate writing is important *and* people who think that this topic is irrelevant and thus any discussion about it is a waste of their time. As I have evidenced elsewhere (Flash, 2016), these facilitated conversations can be transformative, triggering changes in instruction by surfacing and disrupting tacit-level assumptions about writing and writing instruction, assumptions that can cause some faculty members to resist the notion that they are the right people to support students' development as writers.

In each of these meetings, the department faculty peruses and interprets locally derived data and, in reaction to framing and clarification questions supplied by a WAC consultant, generates content, section by section, for its writing plan. These meetings are typically audio-recorded so that the discussion can be summarized and subsequently distributed back to the faculty, making this one more form of data that the WAC team collects and routes back to the department as grist for discussion. The recurring provision of local data and their collective interpretation are critical components of WEC's grounded and inductive epistemology. In the role of curious and facilitative interlocutor, a WAC consultant can help the faculty engage in the sorts of constructive discussion that they tell us would be impossible otherwise. A faculty member who participated in a 2017 focus group study affirms this impression: "The process was very helpful for getting the entire department to articulate understandings that . . . had never really been voiced or articulated. And, I think we discovered that our discipline is so closely linked to *writing*, not simply to communicating findings." (WEC Focus group transcripts, 2017). Another focus group participant, when asked what element of the WEC processes seemed most useful in effecting change, responded this way: "It was that group discussion; I don't think we would've had that just by going through faculty meetings. I think it needed to be someone asking those questions as an outside person to have us come and realize, 'Oh, we're not talking about writing the same way at all!'" (WEC Focus group transcripts 2017).

Table 1.2. The order and content of four WEC meetings in which department faculty creates a first-edition writing plan

Topic	Questions Addressed	Data Discussed	Writing Plan
Meeting #1 (M1)			
Characteristics of writing	What are the noticeable features of academic and professional writing in this department's discipline and subfields?	Samples of student writing collected from gateway-level, midway-level, and capstone-level courses	Section 1
Desired writing abilities	What writing abilities should students in this major be able to demonstrate by the time they graduate?	Stakeholder surveys (students, faculty/instructors, professional affiliates)	Section 2
Meeting #2 (M2)			
Curricular address of expected writing abilities	Given the department's desired writing outcomes, how is writing instruction best integrated into its undergraduate courses? What forms does this instruction take? With which of the desired writing abilities do students typically struggle?	Curricular maps, matrices, schemes	Section 3
Meeting #3 (M3			
Methods and criteria used to assess writing	How is student writing best assessed in this department? How might desired writing translate into valid grading criteria?	Samples of capstone-level student writing	Section 4
Meeting #4 (M4)			
Proposed activity and support	What forms of action and support are needed to optimize the integration of relevant writing instruction into this department's curriculum? What forms of support are needed to enact these plans?	List of potential plan implemental activities mentioned previous meetings	Section 5

Because WEC processes require considerable logistical and contextually savvy, departments appoint a faculty member to serve an embedded WEC coordinator. These individuals—we call them faculty liaisons—broker the fit between departmental culture and WEC activity and take a leading role in coordinating the entire endeavor. At the start of the process, they make strategic choices directing our collection of local data and ensuring that a critical mass of departmental colleagues engage in (and are thus represented by) the faculty discussions. Ultimately, liaisons draft and vet editions of writing plans and oversee iterative implementation and assessment of these plans. Thus, the importance of these faculty leaders to the success of WEC programming cannot be overstated. Serving as inside players and links to the WAC team, they successfully maintain departmental motivation and follow-through at all stages of WEC activity. If the approach is going to fulfill its faculty-driven mission, if the process is going shift responsibility for department-relevant writing instruction over to departmental faculty, WAC consultants need to be careful not to overstep. They can co-plan and co-facilitate meetings, collect and present local data, document discussions, and they can serve as important implementation partners, but they can't run the show or author the writing plan.

Faculty Meeting 1

In the first and arguably most important of four WEC meetings, a department's faculty takes up two questions that align with the first two sections of its writing plan: "What are the noticeable features of academic and professional writing in this department's discipline and subfields?" and "What writing abilities should students in this major be able to demonstrate by the time they graduate?" To prompt discussions that are more concrete than abstract and unrealistically aspirational, we distribute results from stakeholder surveys and samples of undergraduate writing.[1] As meeting participants react to these data and start generating ideas, the consultant transcribes their ideas onscreen. Refraining from altering words or adding new ideas, the consultant types away and asks clarifying questions, like, "Right here, when you say that you expect cogent analysis, what can you tell me about how that looks? What are the analytic moves that work toward cogency?" Or, "You say you want writing that is clear and precise. What typically muddies desired clarity?" Or, "You all seem to agree that you want students to demonstrate control over grammar and mechanics. What does that mean, really? At what point in the writing process might that expectation be

---

1   Elsewhere (Anson et al., 2012; Flash, 2016), I've provided detailed descriptions of survey results, recounted faculty members' interpretative reactions to these data points, and provided evidence of the impact these discussions have on the ways that meeting participants are conceptualizing writing and writing instruction within the context of their teaching.

particularly germane?" Responses to these queries are added to the onscreen document which is then shared with liaisons to use and work-up into their draft writing plan's first two sections. In this way, the faculty groups are engaging in the practice of unearthing a shared set of writing concepts or key terms, a critical component of teaching for transfer (Yancey et al., 2018).

By the end of the first meeting, faculty members will have generated two rough lists: the first uses adjectival phrases to characterize the broad territory of their disciplinary discourse as composed by academics and professionals; the second is composed of writing abilities the local faculty expects from their graduation-level majors. To achieve this result, they will have engaged in a dynamic and unusual process, a discussion about some of the hallmark epistemological moves and discourse features guiding not only their teaching, but their *own* intellectual and pedagogical work. In most cases, this discussion is illuminating and unusual, i.e., not at all what they were expecting when they elected to allow "the writing people" to invade their faculty meeting to talk about "writing."

Faculty Meeting 2

As we begin the second WEC meeting, the faculty reviews (and inevitably fiddles with) its lists of discipline-relevant writing characteristics and expected undergraduate writing abilities before moving on to consider where writing instruction occurs—or might occur—within the collection of service, core, and elective courses they offer. To prompt this analysis, they look at curricular schematics (maps and matrices) constructed from survey-generated data. In departments where poring over complex matrices may be more repellent than productive, instructors prefer to present their colleagues with oral profiles of the courses they teach and the writing they assign. In our architecture department, for example, the faculty chose to pin course materials up on modular walls and move gallery-walk style from one course to another, listening to colleagues describe how writing and design were addressed in their courses and then discussing their reactions.

Shifting faculty focus from negotiating lists of individual writing abilities to considering how and where these writing abilities might receive explicit attention in departmental offerings is a primary objective of Meeting 2. Now that the faculty has developed a group of exit-level criteria, consideration of where and how students are developing these valued writing abilities as they take lower- and upper-division courses can expose instructional gaps and opportunities. This meeting can help faculty members recognize that what they emphasize in course instruction and grading may not align with the writing abilities they collectively prize. It can also reveal the random location of writing-intensive courses, and the limited power these courses have if they are isolated within the curriculum. Finally, Meeting 2 discussions allow the faculty to locate opportunities for overt instructional reinforcement or collaboration, increasing the likelihood that students will be able to transfer what they've learn about writing between course contexts, helping them to develop the awareness they need to serve as "agents of integration" (Nowacek, 2011).

FACULTY MEETING 3

In their third WEC discussion, faculty participants shift focus again. Here, in order to generate content for the fourth section of their writing plan, they move from considering the curricular location of writing activity to considering the ways in which student writing is assessed. More specifically, they use this meeting to discuss ways in which their list of expected writing abilities translates into valid grading criteria they might adapt for use in their courses. An excerpted example from one meeting's outcome can be seen in Table 1.3. As I'll describe later in this chapter, these criteria are used in triennial WEC-sponsored rating panels, a form of direct assessment in which a faculty panel assessed students' capstone-level writing against the faculty-articulated list of criteria in order to assess the impact of WEC activity on student writing.

Table 1.3. Partial list of the biology program's expected writing abilities translated into writing criteria

Writing abilities (generated in Meeting 2)	Writing criteria (generated in Meeting 3)
By graduation, students should be able to . . .	*The text . . .*
Explain the relevance and importance of the topic under study.	Conveys the importance of an experiment by placing it into the context of a broader scientific field, highlighting known experimental precedents, and naming overall goals of the successful experiment.
Define a hypothesis in order to clarify the purpose of the work.	Presents a hypothesis as a direct statement that can be tested with experiments conducted by the student.
Explain results logically (and not necessarily chronologically) so that the results section presents a readable, efficient expression of experimental outcomes.	Demonstrates the writer's ability to select, present, and describe experimental procedures/results by providing only essential information such that the procedure can be reproduced by other scientists familiar with the field of study.
Discuss experimental results and data concisely. (Explanatory writing should effectively communicate only the essential information for reproduction of the experiment by one skilled in the art.)	Draws final conclusions from results and places them in context of the goals of the experiment. Includes key results that support or refute the hypothesis in concluding remarks.

FACULTY MEETING 4

In the fourth and final meeting in this series, the faculty develops content for the fifth section of its writing plan. In this section, members describe ways of putting ideas into action, activities that are intended to help them make some headway in addressing issues surfaced in the meetings. Proposed activity is designed around questions like, "Now that we've figured out what we're looking for, how can we incorporate our group of desired writing abilities into our courses?" "How can we do a better job of sequencing writing instruction into our flat and random-feeling curriculum?" "How can we motivate students to see the relevance of writing to their major courses of study?" In addressing these sorts of questions, some departments are keen to continue curricular research, to create a comprehensive portrait of writing instruction as it currently occurs in departmental courses and what the writing instruction looks like. Others are ready to take structural or pedagogical action by restructuring capstone courses or developing a series of customized workshops or locally relevant instructional materials.

It is at this juncture that the liaison, in possession of four comprehensive meeting summaries, sets about drafting the department's first-edition writing plan. Once drafted, the plan is circulated to departmental colleagues for comments and, ultimately, approval. On our campus, completed plans are presented for approval to our Campus Writing Board, a subcommittee of our faculty senate which evolved from the advisory board I assembled when I began to develop WEC. Other institutions implementing the WEC model assign approval responsibilities to other existing or newly established writing- or curriculum-related committees.

IMPLEMENTING WRITING PLANS

Approval of a writing plan moves a department from plan creation to plan implementation. As I've described above, implementation activities are informed by the faculty's insights and its recognition of departmental circumstances, so these activities vary significantly in both scope and design across departments. Two brief case studies illustrate divergent and contextually informed approaches departments have taken to writing plan implementation.

The first involves the Department of Ecology, Evolution, and Behavior, where, after reviewing survey results and curriculum matrices, faculty members recognized two significant points of disconnection. First, they realized that they had very little idea of where, how, or even if, students in core and elective courses were being offered any explicit writing instruction. As a result, it was difficult for individual instructors to know how, or even whether, they were positioned to introduce, to reinforce, or to simply expect key writing abilities. For students taking their courses, this murkiness made writing instruction into something of a hit-and-miss affair, and as a result, they sensed that the writing they were asked to do in their major was due more to individual instructor preferences than because writing was considered a discipline-relevant mode of thinking and communicating. Second, in reviewing stakeholder survey data, the faculty found little connection between student and faculty perceptions of high priority writing abilities. Student data revealed a majority opinion that the appropriate use of scientific terms and the ability to create precise descriptions were most important. Faculty members, on the other hand, gave top ranking to synthesizing disparate ideas, interrogating existing research and sources, and to reporting complex data using logical organization. It should also be noted that elsewhere in the survey, faculty members registered their collective and specific disappointment with students' abilities to demonstrate synthesis and interrogative reading in the writing students turned in.

Wanting to remedy their hazy understanding of what their colleagues were up to and wanting to better understand why student and faculty populations valued writing abilities so differently, the faculty contracted a graduate student to gather writing assignments and grading criteria from each of their undergraduate courses and to analyze these instructional materials for explicit mention of the writing abilities they valued. This analysis confirmed their growing suspicion that the most highly valued writing abilities were the least likely to be explicitly mentioned in writing assignments or grading criteria. Frequent and explicit mention was, however, made of accuracy and precision. Recognizing the wisdom of making their tacit-level expectations more explicit, the faculty partnered with their WAC consultant to develop a set of specific instructional approaches and materials that would provide students with low- and high-stakes writing activities that require the use of synthesis and guide students to approach texts analytically. The faculty liaison unveiled these curricular tools in two well-attended faculty/instructor workshops and posted materials on a departmental site. In this way, this department's faculty went about making durable instructional changes using just the sort of empirical methodology for which it is known: analyze some data, generate a question, develop a protocol for gathering more data, analyze results, and conclude with a substantiated answer to the question.

In youth studies, a department within our School of Social Work, writing plan implementation has looked quite different. This department's faculty is composed of a small core of tenure-track faculty and a large collection of part-time "community faculty" members. The latter are professionals in discipline-related fields who teach one course per semester or per year. To the faculty liaison's surprise, despite not being paid to attend faculty meeting of any kind, the community faculty embraced WEC meetings and the entire amalgamated group focused productively on building consensus around a set of desired writing abilities that includes the expectation that student writers be able to convey "personal and practice-oriented reflections that concretely describe a situation," and that they "evidence their experience and where necessary, draw from relevant theoretical, scholarly, and community sources" (Department of Youth Studies, 2018, p.8).

In the first year of plan implementation, as youth studies' faculty members began to intentionally incorporate these writing expectations into their teaching, concern began to arise about the actual fit between their list of writing expectations and the academic needs and abilities demonstrated by students enrolled in their courses. Youth studies attracts a high percentage of first-generation college students and students from traditionally underrepresented populations and both full-time faculty and part-time community faculty members are uniformly focused on addressing the needs and interests of these students. In its second-edition plan, therefore, the faculty proposed to address alignment concerns by developing assignments that provide students with opportunities to blend spoken and written expression into writing projects. To this end, a cohort of faculty members became trained in digital technologies and developed digital story assignments that invite students to create multimodal texts, illustrating stories from their lives and literacy traditions using videos, soundtracks, and scripted narration. To highlight the relevance of assigned writing to students' future careers, the department organized annual panel discussions in which program alumna discuss the writing they do as educators, activists, and researchers. Both implementation activities are designed to enhance the relevance of writing to departmental coursework.

A few years into the process, when discussing a batch of disappointing assessment results, members of the faculty again asked questions about the relevance of the criteria they'd named to the needs of students they enroll. This time around, in its third-edition plan, the faculty outlined a more direct approach. Enacting disciplinary expertise in designing comprehensive program evaluation protocol, the faculty designed an incremental series of activities that will involve a group of undergraduate majors in discussing and formally evaluating the department's writing plan, the faculty's current set of writing criteria, writing assignments, and approaches to writing instruction. Students' plan assessments will be shared with the entire departmental community as the faculty determines next step activity. Also, in collaboration with its WAC consultant, the department has launched an annual series of faculty discussions focused explicitly on issues of academic literacy and writing assessment in communities defined by race, gender, class, culture, and language.

WEC ASSESSMENT METHODS

Perpetual data collection and multimodal assessment processes are hardwired into every phase of the WEC model. These assessments serve two primary purposes: (1) they provide a department with information that can help its faculty develop, implement, and revise iterative writing plans and (2) they provide WAC consultants with information that will allow us continue supporting departments and also to maintain or modify components of the model itself. As illustrated in Table 1.4, these two purposes are addressed with four interrelated questions and associated indices, timing, and primary audiences.

Whether a WEC-sponsored assessment maneuver aims at gathering quantitative or qualitative information using direct or indirect instruments, the data generated by these instruments are brought to department faculty members for their interpretation and analysis. In response to the first assessment question listed in table, baseline assessment data, including de-identified writing samples, responses to stakeholder surveys, and comprehensive curricular maps and matrices, are discussed as the faculty develops its first-edition plan. Once that plan has begun implementation, additional assessments are designed to address the second assessment question. Here, the department is measuring impacts of the specific writing and instructional activities it has designed or requested. Whether the faculty has elected to organize writing-oriented programming (e.g., workshops, guest speakers, teaching consultations, or discussions), develop resources (e.g., assignment archives or student-facing support sites), implement structural changes (e.g., alter course sequencing or develop new courses), or continue to conduct curricular or instructional research (e.g., code faculty assignments and grading criteria to assess their alignment with the list of desired writing abilities), these activities are assessed in accordance with departmental goals.

Finally, to address questions about the impact WEC activity is having upon the quality of student writing (the fourth question listed in the table), departments participate in episodes of direct writing assessment every three years, beginning almost immediately after passage of their first-edition writing plan. In these assessment sessions, panels of raters measure a set of randomly selected capstone-level writing samples against lists of criteria that departments include in Section 4 of their writing plans. (On my campus, rating panels are composed of faculty members and others who have been selected by the department's liaison and, where feasible, we add "writing specialist" raters, usually a member of the WAC team.) As I've delineated elsewhere (Anson et al., 2012; Flash, 2016), these sessions begin with preliminary training and norming activity and conclude with detailed debriefing sessions. Debriefed reactions are captured and compiled along with the numeric rating scores into comprehensive reports which are subsequently brought into faculty meetings for collective interpretation and discussion.

Table 1.4. WEC's multimodal menu of assessment questions, instruments, timing, and primary audience

Assessment Question	Instruments or indices	Timing	Audience
What is the **initial status** of writing and writing instruction in a participating department?	WEC stakeholder surveys (students, instructors, professional affiliates) Meeting summaries Curricular maps and matrices	Baseline (year 1)	Department faculty
	1st edition Writing Plan		Department faculty and interdisciplinary approval board
What effect does creating, implementing, and assessing Writing Plans have upon **writing instruction and curricular design** in participating departments?	Implementation activity assessment	Variable (developed and conducted by departmental faculty)	Department faculty
	2nd and 3rd Edition Writing Plans	Year 2; Year 5	Department faculty and interdisciplinary approval board
What effect does creating, implementing, and assessing Writing Plans have upon **student writing** in participating departments?	Rating student writing against faculty-articulated criteria	Triennially	Department faculty
	Student Experience in Research Universities (SERU) survey	Biennially	Provost's Office
How successfully does the **WEC model design and process** function to support the iterative development, implementation, and assessment of departmental Writing Plans?	Writing Plan review	Year 1 (first edition); Year 2 (second edition); Year 5 (3rd edition)	Department faculty and interdisciplinary approval board
	Liaison survey	Annually (2009–2016)	WAC consultant team
	Faculty focus group	2017+	WAC consultant team

The step of bringing the results back to the faculty for its reaction is critical to ensuring the valid interpretation of results and to sustaining a department's active involvement in the program. In cases where comparative results are reported (i.e., at least two triennial rating sessions have been conducted), members of the faculty are familiar with the criteria and courses from which samples were drawn and are thus best situated to interpret and address rising or dropping scores. As co-facilitators in these discussions, WAC consultants emphasize two questions: In what ways do the assessments contained in these reports align with or diverge your own evaluations of student writing? What next-step activities do these results inspire? Answers to these questions underscore the formative intention of the rating process and steer discussions toward action and forward momentum. Ultimately, by providing departmental faculty with recurring opportunities to both interpret and *use* assessment results, we're integrating considerations of content, criteria, and consequences in order increase the value implications of ratings (Huot, 2002; Messick, 1989; O'Neill, 2003).

In a final note related to the triennial rating of student writing, I'll point out that the decision of whether or not to report on rating results in its publicly posted writing plan (or elsewhere) is left entirely to the faculty. This provision can have a powerfully disarming impact on faculty members who might suspect that the WEC Program in general (and the rating process in particular) will be somehow used by central administration to justify department changes or budget reductions. Realizing that the WEC Program invests in the process (collecting and redacting samples, paying raters, generating reports) but relinquishes control over the data helps cement faculty trust in the process, and this trusting relationship is central to the model's power to provoke and sustain local change.

Aside from triennial ratings, a tool for addressing questions about WEC's impact on student writing abilities can be found in student engagement surveys like the National Survey of Student Engagement (NSSE)[2] or the Student Experience in Research Universities survey (SERU). On our campus, students' responses to items on the biennial SERU survey have allowed us to compare the frequency with which students inside and outside departments participating in WEC engage in high-impact writing and learning practices. As members of my institution's institutional research office reported in 2015, students majoring in WEC-participating majors reported engagement critical learning habits and abilities at a higher frequency than did students whose majors had yet to engage in the program (Office of Institutional Research, 2015). These habits and abilities included concept mastery, thinking critically and/or creatively about

---

2   For more on the piloting and addition of 27 writing-related NSSE items, see Anderson, et al. (2017).

course content, and understanding the criteria instructors have used to grade their writing.

Lastly, several related data points help us assess the design of the WEC model—its sequence of meetings, data collection, and assessment and so forth. One indication of its success is the rate of elective enrollment. On my campus more than sixty departments have elected to enroll in the process and we add more each year. On other campuses where our WEC model is being adapted, willing departments queue up waiting to begin. Another indication of the method's effect is the rate at which faculty-authored writing plans are approved. On my campus, writing plans are submitted to the Campus Writing Board, a sub-committee of the faculty senate. Approval is based on a set of criteria that assess the plan's ability to address interests and concerns expressed by a critical mass of departmental stakeholders and the feasibility of proposed activity. Finally, model components can be assessed by faculty participants. On my campus, we've used annual liaison surveys, focus groups, and biannual all-liaison meeting to capture the impressions (and advice) of faculty members in participating departments. Over the past 15 years, we've relied heavily on data generated from these assessments as we've built and refined the WEC model.

SIX CORE FEATURES

In the process of collaborating on this book project, Chris Anson and I negotiated a list of WEC's core features, the practices and principles that have proven fundamental to successfully promoting and sustaining departmental implantation of writing-enriched curricula. Our negotiation required us to separate essential elements from site-specific adaptations and logistical apparatuses we've developed to organize and administer WEC programs on our sites. The resulting list is included in Anson's Introduction to this volume and I provide a briefly annotated version here.

Departmental Location and Faculty Control

Academic departments elect to participate in a WEC initiative and, to the extent possible, WEC activity takes place inside regularly scheduled departmental faculty meetings to ensure participation of most (if not all) members. In generating its writing plan, the faculty is invited to review locally derived data sets and to define writing in ways that are disciplinarily and departmentally relevant. Most importantly, the faculty achieves consensus on a list of graduation-level writing abilities its members expect of students enrolled in the department's major(s) and makes collective decisions about how and in which of their courses these writing abilities will be addressed with explicit forms of instruction. Members determine what (if any) instructional innovations they'd like to implement to ensure that the writing instruction they offer in their courses adequately supports the development of desired writing abilities, and they decide how they'll measure the success of these innovations. Finally, WEC activities are led by a member of the faculty who takes on the role of WEC Faculty Liaison. In all these ways, WEC methods are designed to leverage and enhance a department's existing structural and interpersonal connections. WEC doesn't focus on writing in a discipline per se; instead, its deliberate focus is on writing in a *department*.

CONCEPTUAL ORIENTATION

As I've described here and elsewhere (Flash, 2016), the WEC approach takes aim at inconspicuous but powerful presumptions that circle around writing and writing instruction. Because these ideas—convictions about what does (and does not) count as effective academic text, suppositions about how and where academic writing should (and should not) be taught and learned—can exert profound influence on instructors' willingness to devote instructional time to writing in their own courses, we begin with them. Each facet of the model, from its capacious definition of writing (visual marks conveying meaning) to its perpetual collection of diverse data sets and its insistence on departmental faculty control, is designed to loosen convictions that writing and writing instruction are irrelevant to specific fields, courses of study, or individual instructors.

DATA USE

As professional scholars and researchers, faculty members in virtually all academic disciplines spend significant time analyzing various forms of data and developing a healthy mistrust for unsubstantiated hunches and hearsay. Intent upon provoking grounded and pragmatic discussion of writing and writing instruction, the WEC model leverages this disposition and skillset by hardwiring data collection and interpretation into all phases of its activity. In virtually all WEC meetings, those charged with creating writing plans as well as those charged with assessing WEC-related activity, faculty members review, analyze, and interpret locally derived artifacts, instructional models, and assessment data. As I've described, these data include stakeholder survey results, curricular matrices, rating reports, and samples of student writing. These data, intended primarily as springboards to discussion, help departments address questions such as: What forms of writing are being assigned and in which courses? What strengths and weaknesses are showing up in student writing? What effect is all this WEC activity having on student writing? On our instruction? Without the grounding that data provide, these discussions would likely be composed of unreconcilable opinions which would make unified action hard to identify. Throughout the WEC process, WAC team members provide the service of collecting, preparing, presenting, and archiving local data that department members wouldn't have the time or resources to collect.

MEDIATION

At each stage of WEC activity, departmental faculty groups are joined by a WAC consultant, an outsider to the department and discipline but an insider to issues of writing and writing instruction. The model and approach are built upon the idea that a WAC consultant's ability to clarify issues and help catalyze changes that would have been unlikely otherwise resides in our ability to leverage what Susan McLeod describes as our *foreigner* status. The WAC consultant's advantage lies, says McLeod, in our "not being part of the local departmental power structure; they have no stake in disciplinary arguments . . . they can ask questions no one else can ask" (McLeod, 1995, p. 108). In WEC work, the role of foreigner is intentionally and consistently inhabited. As many contributors to this collection, Luskey, Emery, Fodrey, Hassay, and Sheriff among them, have affirmed, WAC consultants cede control, problematize expertise, hold ideas up to the light, listen carefully, and create an environment of shared liminality. In doing so, they enable frank and even transformative discussion that faculty participants tell us could not have occurred without the presence of a curious foreigner. Moving from writing pedagogy expert to curious listener and fellow discussant is a significant role shift for WAC consultants.

CONTINUOUS SUPPORT

Department chairs tell us that they would have been unlikely to agree to WEC if enrolling meant substantial amounts of extra work for themselves or their colleagues. When they understand that the WAC team will take care of WEC's administrative tasks, e.g., collecting writing samples, administering surveys, compiling results, summarizing meetings, putting together slides, organizing assessments data collection and reporting, their reluctance diminishes. Once a writing plan is moving through its implementation and assessment paces, members of the WAC team continue to offer support as needed, whether that means co-facilitating a requested workshop or meeting, helping report on assessment results or reviewing newly developed instructional materials. Where available, fiscal support in the form of stipends for faculty liaisons and seed money to support the implementation of writing plans is supplied to departments whose plans are deemed to merit this support. Particularly in the context of a research university, even minimal funding provides both symbolic and pragmatic support.

Sustainability

Each of the previous five features contributes to WEC's durability. The model's decentralized locations and distributed leadership roles enacted by departmental faculty members allow WEC to adapt to circumstantial disruptions and personnel changes that frequently threaten centralized WAC initiatives. Providing fiscal support for faculty-authored writing plans, plans in which the faculty outlines and justifies activities that they will take responsibility for successfully implementing and assessing, provides senior administrators with an alternative to one-size-fits-all funding for intra-department, difficult to assess, writing support. The model equips an institution's central administration with a means for granting differential and meritorious support to innovative and perpetually assessed curricular activity—just the sort of activity that is valued most institutional and collegiate accreditation agencies. In this way, the model works in an integrated bottom-up and top-down capacity. Finally, WEC's long-term process and deliberately paced scaling provides participating departments with time to pilot, assess, and revise their approaches to integrated writing instruction. Engaging departments gradually and in small cohorts has the added advantage of building community among departments who are at the same stage of programming. On my campus, as we near saturation for the undergraduate curriculum, we've begun to reach back to departments that have been implementing writing plans for ten or more years. We offer these "legacy departments" tools for testing and increasing the ongoing relevance and sustained implementation of their writing plans.

CONCLUSION

Despite the WEC approach's apparent obviousness, putting departmental faculty groups in charge of departmental writing instruction is neither a fast nor effortless business. Part of the effort WEC exacts may correspond to the changes it proposes to some familiar WAC methods. Like most WAC/WID programs, WEC aims to increase the curricular incorporation of relevant writing instruction and to graduate able communicators across majors. To achieve these shared aims, however, WEC activates shifts in *location* (from interdisciplinary and course-specific to departmental and curricular), *control* (from administration to faculty), stance (from one of expertise to one of inquiry) and pacing (from episodic to enduring). Some aspects of WEC practice—the inductive approach taken by its consultants, its incremental cycles of engagement and gradual scaling, and its insistence on scheduling activity to take place within pre-existing faculty meetings for three examples—are unusual not only in WAC/WID circles but in the world of academic initiatives more generally. Perhaps more recognizable to community organizers than to academics, these practices are taken up in support of both immediate insights—the aha! moments that enliven a meeting—and long-term changes that result from increases in a department's collective capacity for change.

WEC's contribution to WAC/WID theory is its assertion that many long-standing roadblocks to writing-infused curricula can be dismantled by surfacing and collectively discussing instructors' tacit-level assumptions about writing and writing instruction. WEC's contribution to WAC/WID practice is its model, a framework of sequenced activity that manages to balance contextual malleability with reliable stability. As the other chapters in this collection evidence, the model's expanded adoption allows for its expanded and collective investigation. I look forward the continued work of WEC's community of practice.

REFERENCES

Adams, B. & Durfee, W. (2011). *Mechanical Engineering writing style guide: Problem sets*. University of Minnesota.

Adler-Kassner, L. & Wardle, E. (Eds.). (2015). *Naming what we know: Threshold concepts of writing studies*. Utah State University Press.

Anson, C. M. (2006). Assessing writing in cross-curricular programs: Determining the locus of activity. *Assessing Writing, 11*(2), 100–112. https://doi.org/10.1016/j.asw.2006.07.001.

Anson, C. M., Carter, M., Dannels, D. & Rust, J. (2003). Mutual support: CAC programs and institutional improvement in undergraduate education. *Language and Learning Across the Disciplines, 6*(3), 13. https://doi.org/10.37514/LLD-J.2003.6.3.06.

Anson, C. M., Dannels, D., Flash, P. & Gaffney, A. H. (2012). Big rubrics and weird genres: the futility of using generic assessment tools across diverse instructional contexts. *The Journal of Writing Assessment, 5*(1).

Bean, J. C., Caruthers, D. & Earenfight, T. (2005). Transforming WAC through a discourse-based approach to university outcomes assessment. *WAC Journal, 16*, 5–21. https://doi.org/10.37514/WAC-J.2005.16.1.01.

Broad, B. (2003). *What we really value: beyond rubrics in teaching and assessing writing*. Utah State University Press.

Carter, M. (2002). A process for establishing outcomes-based assessment plans for writing and speaking in the disciplines. *Language and Learning Across the Disciplines, 6*, 4–29. https://doi.org/10.37514/LLD-J.2003.6.1.02.

Cox, M., Galin, J. & Melzer, D. (2018). *Sustainable WAC: A whole systems approach to launching and developing writing across the curriculum programs.* National Council of Teachers of English.

Department of Art History. (2015). *University of Minnesota writing plan, 2nd ed.* University of Minnesota.

Department of Mechanical Engineering. (2016). *University of Minnesota writing plan, 3rd ed.* University of Minnesota

Department of Youth Studies. (2018). *University of Minnesota writing plan, 3rd ed.* University of Minnesota.

Engstrom, Y., Miettinen, R. & Punamaki-Girai, R.-L. (1990). *Perspectives on activity theory.* International Congress for Research on Activity Theory, Lahti, Finland.

Flash, P. (2016). From apprised to revised: Faculty in the disciplines change what they never knew they knew. In K. B. Yancey (Ed.), *A rhetoric of reflection* (pp. 227–249). Utah State University Press.

Fullan, M. (2005). *Leadership & sustainability: System thinkers in action.* Corwin Press.

Goodenough, W. H. (1956). Componential analysis and the study of meaning. *Language, 32*(1), 195–216. https://doi.org/10.2307/410665.

Hall, J. (2006). Toward a Unified writing curriculum: Integrating WAC/WID with freshman composition. *WAC Journal, 17,* 5–22. https://doi.org/10.37514/WAC-J.2006.17.1.01.

Harris, M. (1976). History and significance of the emic/etic distinction. *Annual Review of Anthropology, 5,* 329–350.

Huot, B. (2002). *(Re)articulating writing assessment for teaching and learning.* Utah State University Press.

Kemmis, S., McTaggart, R. & Nixon, R. (2014). *The action research planner: Doing critical participatory action research.* Springer.

McLeod, S. H. (1995). The foreigner: WAC directors as agents of change. In J. Janangelo & K. Hansen (Eds.), *Resituating writing: Constructing and administering writing programs* (pp. 108–116). Heinemann.

Messick, S. (1989). Validity. In R. L. Linn (Ed.), *Educational measurement* (3rd ed.) (pp. 13–104). Macmillan.

Meyer, J. & Land, R. (2006). *Overcoming barriers to student understanding: Threshold concepts and troublesome knowledge—Twin Cities.* Routledge.

Nowacek, R. S. (2011). *Agents of integration: Understanding transfer as a rhetorical act.* Southern Illinois University Press.

Office of Institutional Research. (2015). *2014 SERU results for writing enriched curriculum participants.* University of Minnesota. https://wac.umn.edu/sites/wac.umn.edu/files/2019-09/seru_2014.pdf.

O'Neill, P. (2003). Moving beyond holistic scoring through validity inquiry. *Journal of Writing Assessment, 1*(1), 47–65.

Pike, K. L. (1954). *Language in relation to a unified theory of the structure of human behavior.* Summer Institute of Linguistics. http://hdl.handle.net/2027/mdp.39015041850119.

Russell. (1995). Activity Theory and its implications for writing instruction. In J. Petraglia (Ed.), *Reconceiving writing, rethinking writing instruction* (pp. 51–78). Erlbaum.

Task Force on Liberal Education. (1991, May 6). *A liberal education agenda for the 1990s and beyond on the Twin Cities campus of the University of Minnesota* (The Final Report of the Twin Cities Campus Task Force on Liberal Education). University of Minnesota.

Walvoord, B. E. F. (2000). *Academic departments: How they work, how they change.* Graduate School of Education and Human Development, the George Washington University.

Wiggins, G. & McTighe, J. (1998). *Understanding by design.* Association for Supervision and Curriculum Development.

Yancey, K. B., Davis, M., Robertson, L., Taczak, K. & Workman, E. (2018). Writing across college: Key terms and multiple contexts as factors promoting students' transfer of writing knowledge and practice. *The WAC Journal, 29,* 42–63. https://doi.org /10.37514/WAC-J.2018.29.1.02.

Yancey, K. B., Robertson, L. & Taczak, K. (2014). *Writing across contexts: Transfer, composition, and sites of writing.* Utah State University Press.

Zawacki, T. M., Reid, E. S., Zhou, Y., Baker, S. E. & Mason, G. (2009). Voices at the table: Balancing the needs and wants of program stakeholders to design a value-added writing assessment plan. *Across the Disciplines, 6* [Special Issue], 1–14. https://doi.org/10.37514/ATD-J.2009.6.1.03.

CHAPTER 2.

THE NEW GRASS ROOTS: FACULTY RESPONSES TO THE WRITING-ENRICHED CURRICULUM

Chris M. Anson
North Carolina State University

Although assessment is a crucial component of the WEC model, studies of how faculty respond to its implementation are needed, especially by outsiders who can impartially analyze its successful uptake. This chapter describes an interview-based study of eight faculty—four at a small liberal arts college and four at a large state-supported university—representing five departments all in the formative stages of WEC implementation. Analysis based on grounded theory surfaced five themes that interviewees consistently described, and that appear to be important considerations in the development of the WEC model and in the inductive learning of threshold concepts for WAC: the role of cross-curricular activities such as faculty workshops; the importance of departmental autonomy and self-directed innovation; the usefulness of lower-stakes, learning-based writing; the perception of improvement in student writing ability; and the transformative effects of WEC as a pedagogical and curricular initiative.

In the introduction to this volume, I describe the core attributes of the WEC model—collaboratively created with Pamela Flash—which are variously instantiated in the programs described throughout the chapters. Typically, an institution decides to adopt the model and sets to work with the help of writing experts, often initially recruiting two or three departments that seem the most eager to participate. Theoretically, this approach incentivizes faculty and lets them collectively determine the most appropriate ways to build or revise their curriculum, engage in faculty-development efforts, and track their progress using disciplinarily and departmentally appropriate kinds of assessment. Articulation efforts usually coordinated by the leader(s) of the WEC program help individual departments to learn from each other. Departments not yet engaged can see how WEC advantages and empowers those that are, and one by one additional departments and programs can follow their lead.

DOI: https://doi.org/10.37514/PER-B.2021.1299.2.02

As Galin explains in Chapter 5 of this volume and in Cox et al. (2018), sustainability is the lifeblood of WAC programs. If early efforts bear no fruit—if faculty or administrators resist, become complacent, or sense that the barriers are too great to continue—the lore of those experiences can soon poison the campus and subvert activity in further departments. As contributors to this collection explain, the work of WEC implementation is challenging and slow but potentially transformative in the way that writing is supported within departments that have joined the effort. However, because WEC programs are still relatively new compared with other curricular forms of WAC and WID, there has been little inquiry into how faculty feel about the model as it is being implemented—in spite of the plentiful assessment activity in established programs as departments determine how effectively their curricular revisions and innovations are affecting student writing. Of course, WEC leaders themselves, myself among them, are especially close to their own work and can speak with authority about faculty attitudes and uptake of the initiative. But by virtue of their institutional investment, they may lose some objectivity as they advocate for their efforts. Hearing directly and dispassionately from faculty at other institutions that have initiated WEC programs can help WEC leaders to anticipate challenges and adopt successful strategies.

It is also important to understand what happens in the early stages of a WEC program's development, rather than at institutions, like North Carolina State University and the University of Minnesota, that have well-established WEC programs that began many years ago and have become part of the institutional culture. How do faculty initially respond? Do views of writing within a department evolve? Do teaching practices change? Does student writing improve?

This chapter reports on an interview-based study of departments in two quite different institutions working to establish new WEC programs: a research-extensive state-supported university and a small private liberal arts and sciences college. Through interviews with faculty, it documents the consequences of implementation in several departments that were among the earliest to experiment with WEC at these institutions. An analysis of the interviews revealed several themes that emerged consistently across departments at both institutions and, while in need of further validation, appear to be important to the creation and sustenance of WEC programs and demonstrate their effectiveness in changing faculty attitudes toward writing and methods to support it.

INSTITUTIONAL BACKGROUND AND INTERVIEW DETAILS

At the time of this inquiry, both institutions were about two years into their WEC implementation process. That process began with a campus-wide agreement to adopt the WEC model, the appointment of a writing expert to help coordinate it, and an understanding that departments would take the initiative to work on their own curriculum and courses with the support of the coordinator. Several departments in each institution had engaged in faculty-development activities (including multi-day workshops) led by outside WAC experts and by the WEC campus coordinator and had made strides in articulating their goals and outcomes for student writing, studying and revising their curricula, and improving individual courses.

Pound Ridge College[1] is a small, private liberal arts and sciences college founded as a co-educational institution in the mid-nineteenth century. Located in a rural area less than an hour's drive from the nearest major city (but still primarily residential, with 85% of students living on campus), it enrolls approximately 1,600 undergraduate students and around 1,000 graduate students. It offers 35 majors, with the highest enrollments in business, sociology, and psychology. There are approximately 150 full-time faculty, almost all holding the terminal degree in their field; class size averages 15 students.

The WEC program at Pound Ridge had its genesis in a broader curricular overhaul that focused strongly on student writing. However, the version of WEC established at Pound Ridge presented departments with a choice: they could either create one or two writing-intensive (WI) courses exclusively for their majors (such as the nationally popular low-enrollment senior capstone seminar), or they could adopt a total-curriculum approach in which they would "infuse" writing into all the courses in the department. Unlike institutions that first created a writing-intensive program as a credit-bearing requirement and later supplemented that program with a WEC program designed eventually to take its place, Pound Ridge decided to give departments the freedom to discuss and choose their approach from the beginning. The writing-intensive option allowed departments to offer and control their own WI courses and enrollments without the need to serve the interests of the broader academic curriculum. The total-curriculum option provided flexibility for departments to decide how and where writing would occur across all their courses. All three departments whose faculty were interviewed had chosen the total-curriculum approach. At Pound Ridge, the appointed leader of the WEC program was a faculty member from the English Department who had a background in discipline-based writing and experience leading faculty workshops and was fully acquainted with the WEC approach.

Cowling State University is a large research-extensive university with a student enrollment of about 29,000. It has a history of writing across the curriculum

---

1   The names of both institutions are pseudonyms, as are the names of interviewees.

stretching back many years, but the effort was loosely focused on general faculty development and never achieved cross-campus legitimacy and widespread adoption. Before the establishment of the WEC program, the provost had appointed a task force to discuss concerns about student writing and oral communication and explore possibilities for a campus-wide effort, mirroring some of the processes described in Gary Blank's chapter in this collection about the history that led to the establishment of the WEC program at North Carolina State University in the late-1990s.

After much discussion, Cowling State established a new departmentally focused WEC program to strengthen students' written and oral communication abilities across the campus. This program was initially located in a division of the university that oversees general education. The titular leader of the broader WEC effort, who came from an academic department outside of English or composition, headed this division and oversaw the management and funding of the program. Plans for Cowling State's program included support for faculty development and implementation in the context of individual departments. Because the university acknowledged the need for someone with more specific expertise in cross-disciplinary communication, a coordinator with a background in composition and WAC/WID was hired to help, but only after outside WAC experts were brought to campus over the period of approximately a year to help establish the foundation for the program.

The WEC programs at both institutions were created in the spirit of the principles and operating procedures described in the Introduction to this volume: departmentally-focused, faculty-driven, bottom-up, data-enhanced, designed to draw out and make explicit the tacit disciplinary knowledge of faculty, and supported by the expertise of a campus writing coordinator acquainted with WEC-related practices such as what Sheriff, in Chapter 6 of this volume, calls "rhetorical listening."

Eight interviewees, all tenured full-time faculty with several to many years of employment at their campus, agreed to participate, four from each institution (see Table 2.1). At Pound Ridge, these represented three departments. At Cowling State, interviewees came from two departments because at the time it was not possible to recruit an interviewee from the third department that was part of the inaugural year of the program. Interviewees represented both gender and racial diversity. This study focuses entirely on the voices of the faculty and does not represent the views of the WEC coordinators on each campus. However, faculty interviewees made abundantly clear the importance of those coordinators to the successful implementation of their WEC programs.

Interviews were semi-structured (Given, 2008), based on a common set of questions I posed to participants with latitude for follow-through or clarification:

- What's the history of the WEC effort in your department?
- How specifically did you work on this initiative? What happened?
- What do you think the consequences of this effort have been in your department?
- How did faculty respond to the effort?
- What challenges did you face?
- Have you tried to assess how well the initiative is working?

Table 2.1. Interviewees and disciplines at the two institutions

Pound Ridge College	Cowling State University
Prof. Joanne Smith, political science	Prof. Harold Jones, social work
Prof. Courtney Sykes, biology	Prof. Paul White, social work
Prof. John Holcomb, chemistry	Prof. Michael Pruett, sociology
Prof. Janet Sims, political science	Prof. Dorothy Hackett, sociology

At the start, I provided a scripted overview that explained the purpose of the interviews and the fact that I was recording them; that assured anonymity (which was also important in allowing the interviewees to speak freely); and that asked participants, when it wasn't obvious, to say whether a response reflected the general feelings or experiences of the department or was a personal opinion without evidence that it was shared.

Interviews were transcribed and then analyzed using the constant-comparison method (Stern, 2008) from grounded theory (Glaser & Strauss, 1967; see also Charmaz & Bryant, 2008). In this method, pieces of data (in this case, statements or assertions in the transcripts) are continuously compared with all other pieces of data, eventually yielding theories or observations "grounded" in the data. The method involves sorting and labeling the data based on specific properties. Analysis is primarily inductive, allowing patterns or themes to "emerge out of the data rather than being imposed on them prior to data collection and analysis" (Patton, 1990, p. 390). Based on the nature of the data, it wasn't necessary to code the transcripts more formally, which would ordinarily be required in a mixed-method or quantitative study. The unit of analysis was any self-contained assertion, more than one of which could appear within a sentence or which could encompass several sentences.

Analysis yielded a number of overlapping observations, i.e., ones mentioned in similar ways by faculty in three or more departments and which therefore rose to the level of themes. In Figure 2.1, these themes are listed in order of strength (shown to the left of the figure), which refers to the number of interviewees who mentioned them at both institutions: strongest themes appear toward the bottom. Interestingly, the stronger the theme on this basis, the more likely it reflected the collective response of the department rather than the view of the individual interviewee. For this reason, a second, parallel way the themes are ordered is based on the extent to which they affected the individual faculty member or the collective interests of the department (shown to the right of the figure): themes reflecting the most faculty agreement within interviewees' departments appear toward the bottom.

The ordering process in Figure 2.1 is illustrated in a remark made by two of the interviewees from Pound Ridge College. Both said that they were incentivized to attend multi-day general faculty-development sessions, prior to starting their departmental WEC initiative, because their participation earned a modest a stipend (although both also said it was not the main reason they attended). The mention of the stipends was not entirely idiosyncratic, but also not collectively observed across the interviews; and the stipends were more individually important to the interviewees than, at least without further inquiry, to their entire department. As a result, they were not included in Figure 2.1. Of course, although this observation did not rise to the level of a theme, it still has value in WEC discussions because it highlights the possible role of extrinsic rewards for engaging in WEC-related activities, which could also include administrative recognition of participation, course release, or even the conviviality occasioned by food and refreshments (see the descriptions of stipends in Flash, Chapter 1, and Galin, Chapter 8 of this volume).

Each of the emergent themes in Figure 2.1 will be described and supported with relevant quotations from the interviews with the faculty at Pound Ridge and Cowling State (which are abbreviated PR and CS).

THE ROLE OF CROSS-DISCIPLINARY ACTIVITIES

At both Pound Ridge and Cowling State, departmental agreements to embark on WEC programs had their genesis and inspiration in higher-level planning groups as well as campus-wide faculty development opportunities (workshops, seminars, and "kick-off" presentations) led by outside experts and by the appointed director of the WEC program. On both campuses, members of different departments worked together to discuss the role of writing in their curricula and disciplines and overcome challenges the faculty perceived as they considered a stronger focus on the development of students' writing abilities. Several interviewees pointed to these experiences as important motivators to then work on writing within their own departments. As Joanne Smith (PR) explained:

> Part of it was the incentive of having [an outside WAC expert]
> come and talk to the general faculty . . . and I think that sort

of sparked people's interests. [The WAC director also] did these two-day workshops in which we used some of the materials that [the outside expert] had brought to [the Director's] attention.

Courtney Sykes (PR) pointed out that as a result of all of the Biology faculty attending the campus-wide workshops put on by the WEC director, the department then met to discuss their own curriculum. Those early discussions focused on the lack of support students were given as they completed higher-stakes assignments, and led to ideas about how the faculty could "stage [their] traditional assignments—the traditional lab reports, the end-of-the-semester paper—and break [them] down into pieces." The workshops, in other words, provided new ways for members of the Biology Department to think about students' experiences with writing, which inspired them to embark in earnest on WEC implementation. John Holcomb, in Pound Ridge's chemistry department, made a similar point: "The programs that the [director] put on really helped raise my awareness and the [outside expert's] seminar helped particularly with regard to, you don't have to be a first-year writing teacher in order to be able to do this."

Number of observations		Collective impact
Themes	**Relevance to WEC Development**	
Cross-curricular activities	Campus-wide workshops and planning groups inform and incentivize faculty prior to WEC implementation	
Autonomy and self-directed innovation	Department members study and improve their own curricula, courses, and pedagogy	
Writing to learn	Faculty discover and embrace the relationship of writing and learning	
Improvement in student ability	Prior to formal assessment, there is impressionistic evidence of stronger student writing	
Transformative effects	Collective change is seen positively	

Figure 2.1. Themes by strength and individual-to-collective impact (least to most)

Interviewees at Cowling State recounted similar experiences. Half a dozen faculty in the Department of Social Work attended a general orientation to WAC led by two outside experts. As Paul White explains it,

> The initial team that went got very excited about the possibilities that writing across the curriculum would offer to us. It would give us some common language to work with and also help us to think a little bit more about measuring the writing.

Everyone came back excited, and the next time training
became available more people wanted to attend because of the
excitement of the initial group.

Confirming this account, Harold Jones said that after participating in a
workshop, "the faculty saw right away how they could go ahead and do things
with regard to assignments and begin to implement techniques further on, and
that created some synergy." As the other faculty saw how the workshop attendees
"were embracing certain techniques, they wanted to do the same." The process
became, as Jones put it, "a little bit contagious," and the department formally
began its implementation of WEC.

Both Michael Pruett and Dorothy Hackett (CS), along with come colleagues, also participated in a two-day campus-wide workshop designed to
inspire departments to adopt the WEC approach. Pruett remarked that after
the workshop, "we realized what this could do and what the potential was and
then brought it to our department and sold our colleagues on it." Hackett also
pointed to "how useful" the two-day workshop was for subsequent departmental planning.

As Flash describes the WEC approach at the University of Minnesota in
Chapter 1 of this volume, consultations usually begin with more focused work
within departments, precipitated by the WEC leader's insertion into departmental meetings to explore instructional support for student writing. Based on
the experiences of faculty at Cowling State and Pound Ridge College, interdisciplinary, campus-wide orientations to WAC, especially at institutions that
have had little prior experience rethinking the role of writing in discipline-based
instruction, appear to be an important and valuable way to begin the effort,
incentivizing some departments to start their context-specific work. But such
experiences need to be expertly planned. A poorly coordinated workshop or an
uninspiring and ill-delivered presentation can sour departments to the prospect
of implementing a WEC program. Some institutions, of course, may have already
provided plentiful faculty-development opportunities that have "primed" the
campus for the initiation of a WEC program or may, like NC State, continuously offer those opportunities alongside departmental WEC development. The
WEC program at the University of Minnesota followed years of general faculty
development in WAC stretching back to my own ad hoc workshops there in
the late 1980s and 1990s, and the eventual creation of a full-fledged writing-
intensive program. The University of Vermont, as described by Harrington
and colleagues in Chapter 9 of this volume, historically relied on a previous
national leader in WAC to "cultivate and organize grassroots individual and
departmental attention to writing." Similarly, Galin in Chapter 8 of this volume

explains the historical importance of faculty workshops he conducted, starting in 2004, to the development of WEC at Florida Atlantic University. These histories suggest the need for further inquiry into the relationship between general cross-disciplinary faculty development in WAC (historical or contemporaneous, successful or not) and the uptake of the WEC model, as well as the relationship between intradepartmental and interdepartmental experiences.

Similar to campus-wide workshops and presentations focusing on writing, certain kinds of cross-disciplinary planning groups and task forces can also provide conceptual frameworks to inspire the beginning of WEC within departments. Two of the respondents participated in such groups prior to the establishment of the WEC program on their campus. Courtney Sykes (PR) explained that after attending meetings of the college-wide WEC planning committee, she would "come back and talk to everybody in the [biology] department about where the planning was going," which then led to critical decisions within her department. Similarly, Dorothy Hackett (CS) was a member of a task force on communication across the curriculum that considered several models before settling on WEC (similar to how the WAC committee described by Galin in Chapter 8 of this volume chose the WEC model for their QEP-inspired plan):

> We were really attracted to the departmental model, where
> different departments would in sequence implement these
> kinds of processes at the departmental level and try to think
> about, you know, spreading this idea across the curriculum
> and across the campus in that way, one department at a
> time, basically. . . . And it seemed like a good idea for me to
> volunteer my department. So we started this process as one of
> the first pilot departments for the communication-across-the-
> curriculum departmental model here.

Although interviewees described their participation in terms of its effects on their own interest in the WEC approach, their experiences appear to have influenced their colleagues as they moved forward. In light of these positive influences, one factor to consider in the creation of WEC programs, especially in their initial stages, is whether members of pilot departments are involved in broader, cross-curricular planning, where common concerns can be discussed alongside those that are specific to particular disciplines or curricula. Ideally, if more than one member of a department participates in a pre-WEC planning group, the multivocal nature of their subsequent work within their department could have stronger persuasive value. Importantly, however, such groups need to be seen as advocating for and representing faculty interests rather than those of higher-level administrators creating plans to be imposed from above.

THE ROLE OF AUTONOMY AND SELF-DIRECTED INNOVATION

The principle of autonomy plays a central role in the departmental approach. As Flash argues in Chapter 1 of this collection, WEC is a "tested strategy for putting control of writing instruction and assessment into the hands of people best positioned to make informed, locally relevant decisions—namely, a department's faculty." Buy-in comes from the freedom to do with writing what makes most sense in the context of the department, its goals for students, its curriculum, and other factors. Unconstrained by specific institutional and curricular expectations, departments articulate their goals and outcomes and design their own processes for weaving writing into their curriculum. Freedom to choose implementation and assessment methods motivates them to action because it encourages creativity and engagement in the process. This theme, clearly articulated in the interviews, focused on how departments adopted the model and took control, but acknowledged the importance of ongoing support from the WEC director, the upper administration, and others.

Having considered different approaches to implementing WAC, the interviewees tied their commitment to WEC to the opportunity for independent decision-making and self-direction. Paul White (CS) explained that he didn't think WEC would be successful "if we were trying to make this an add-on to the existing curriculum. . . . But if you develop communication objectives for every course and they are progressive, then everyone seems to be on board with that." As Harold Jones (CS) explained, it was effective for his department because "if it was a very traditional model where everyone had been in their places and all of a sudden they [the administration] are coming in and they're saying 'OK, go ahead and take this on,' I don't know how all that would have worked. Having it imposed from the top down here . . . I would have no confidence of anyone taking it seriously." Echoing Jones's sentiments, Paul White explained that in contrast to the WEC approach, creating writing-intensive courses would feel "like a real top-down kind of thing" because of the need to adhere to syllabus criteria usually imposed by a university committee or other governing group.

Similar comparisons led Dorothy Hackett (CS) to "absolutely" believe that WEC was preferable because of how it affected faculty buy-in:

> The fact that we as a department got to define what were the
> writing and speaking outcomes we wanted for our students

and then figure out how to get there—that made a big difference in terms of faculty buy-in. It wasn't just one more thing
we have to do or one more report we have to fill out. It was
really the fact that it was something that was useful to them
in a way that it wouldn't have if it had been sent down from
on high.

This sense of ownership in the process appears to have flowed across the
department; as Hackett put it, "We have very good participation across all the
different ranks of faculty." In similarly praising the WEC approach, John Holcomb (PR) described how he and his colleagues "sat down as a department,"
took control of their own curriculum, and committed to weaving writing into
every course: "We basically decided that writing ought to be something that is
across the four years, that is across the curriculum. And so we took that type of
approach in an attempt to incorporate some kind of writing in just about every
course that our majors take."

In addition to these and other positive general statements, the advantages
of departmental ownership were evidenced in the interviewees' descriptions of
their self-directed departmental activities. As Dorothy Hackett (CS) explained,
the Department of Sociology decided to collectively analyze their curriculum to
pinpoint the role of writing and oral communication in different courses:

> We've done a lot of things along the way. We have done an
> audit of all our courses by doing syllabus examination about
> what writing was actually occurring and what speaking was
> occurring in different courses. We mapped them all our
> into a great big matrix on big giant pieces of paper to try to
> see where we maybe were missing some things or where we
> had too much of certain kinds of writing. We've had several
> faculty retreats around this idea, thinking about what is it we
> really want our students to get out of communication activ-
> ities within the sociology major and within our coursework
> more generally, and really made that departmental effort over
> time to think more strategically about how we are using these
> activities.

According to Courtney Sykes, before adopting the WEC approach, the biology department at Pound Ridge thought about hiring a specialist to teach writing courses, which would increase attention to writing but relieve the rest of
the faculty of the responsibility. But with the help of the WEC coordinator and
experience in faculty workshops, she and her colleagues "sat down and looked at

all of our courses together within our bio department meetings," which led them to build significant amounts of writing into all their courses, focusing especially on "staging" the major assignments, "breaking them down into pieces." This soon led to the revision of courses for non-majors as well, so that writing "saturated" the entire biology curriculum—and removed the idea of a specialist from consideration.

The common WEC process of mapping a curriculum and analyzing the place of writing within it often reveals gaps and inconsistences in coverage and writing experience, as one of our Natural Resources departments at North Carolina State University discovered when, with our help, they found that three courses were assigning students to write a resume—a genre that does not scaffold in disciplinary complexity and therefore needs no iterations of support. Subsequently, the resume was dropped from two courses in favor of other genres, enhancing students' experience. Curricular mapping also reveals the sequence of writing throughout the major and the coordination of writing across required and elective courses. Joanne Smith (PR) explained that the WEC-focused conversations in her department led to an understanding that the existing focus on junior-level writing "was way too late in the discipline to begin to teach them how to write in the discipline. We scrapped that idea entirely and started looking at all our courses" based on more clearly defined learning outcomes. This resulted in the addition of writing where it was weakly represented and a "beefing up" of the nature of writing in courses where it was already assigned. More specific genres were developed for pre-law students, such as assignments focusing on legal reasoning; for students concentrating in public policy, such as policy briefs; and for political theory and philosophy students, such as critical and analytical essays. Similarly, the Department of Social Work at Cowling State inventoried their curriculum for the articulation of outcomes and how they were being supported. As Harold Jones (CS) put it, "We've looked at all the courses in the undergraduate curriculum. In every course, we have some kind of communication objective now. So as the student moves through the social work curriculum, they get assignments in courses that build on what was taught in previous courses, all the way through." (See also Anson & Dannels, 2009, for an example of curricular mapping in a department of food, bioprocessing, and nutrition science.)

One interesting consequence of the WEC model is the way it stimulates thinking about other aspects of instruction and curricular design. For example, in describing the effects of WEC implementation in the Department of Political Science at Pound Ridge, Janet Sims explained that the focus on writing soon opened up other possibilities for curricular innovation, such "experimentation with learning communities and interdisciplinary courses" that she and her colleagues felt improved their major:

> Each piece of the curriculum feeds the others, and all of our
> conversations are ending up with a much better final product,
> if we can call the students the final product, because we have
> a lot of discussions and debates . . . cross-fertilization, I guess
> that's the word I'm looking for. I actually think what we're
> doing with our curriculum is pretty remarkable. . . . The writ-
> ing in the disciplines is really feeding everything. The writing
> informs everything else. I actually think that with very few
> resources, we are doing some really excellent work.

Taking control of writing in their own departments also appears to affect faculty advocacy for WEC more broadly across the institution. Janet Sims explained that interdepartmental workshops put on by Pound Ridge's faculty-development office allowed members of departments implementing the WEC approach to "spread the news and encourage others to come to subsequent workshops, so it gets out there. . . . And there are a lot of conversations that also happen informally."

In discussing their self-directed work as part of the WEC initiative, it was important for most of the interviewees to recognize the role of the WEC coordinator on their campus. At the time of the interviews, for social work at Cowling State the need for support was especially acute in the process of assessment, where they were getting significant assistance from the WEC director. For sociology at Cowling State, as Dorothy Hackett explains, "having a central resource person whose specialization is in how to teach writing available to us . . . having some structure that we can fall back on when we need some additional help, has made the departmental model work well. Without that, I think we might have felt a little adrift." As the contributions to this collection all demonstrate, the role of what Flash describes in Chapter 1 as a "skilled WAC consultant, someone outside the discipline and outside the department," is a crucial component to the success of WEC programs. Those "skills," which are not the focus of this study but are described throughout this collection, should not be underestimated.

THE USE OF WRITING AS A TOOL FOR LEARNING

A strong theme to emerge across all the interviews and collectively shared within departments was how writing enhances students' learning of the discipline—how writing can, as Fulwiler and Young put it, become "a tool for discovering, for shaping meaning, and for reaching understanding" (1982, p. x). Although writing to learn has been a central part of the writing-across-the-curriculum movement from its inception (see Applebee, 1985; Britton et al., 1975; Emig,

1977; Herrington, 1981; Odell, 1980), the improvement of students' "skills" of formal academic and disciplinary writing continues to define the purpose of many programs. The importance of the relationship between writing and learning was especially apparent in interviewees' remarks about lower-stakes, "input-based" assignments (see Anson, 2017).

Before the implementation of WEC at both institutions, the faculty in the five departments in this study were not familiar with this orientation—writing was associated with papers that reflected the consequences of learning rather than as a way into learning, and that were expected to be written formally and were formally evaluated. After the interviewees participated in faculty-development workshops on both campuses, writing to learn became an important part of WEC planning and was strongly integrated into coursework and the design of departments' writing-enriched curricula. Courtney Sikes (PR) explained that lower-stakes writing was "very new" to all of the faculty and an important component in their curricular redesign. For the political science department at Pound Ridge, the idea of lower-stakes writing also had a major impact. As Joanne Smith put it, "Once we implemented [WEC], every single person in my department is using short writing exercises . . . we've seen it be enormously effective across every single class in our department." These sentiments were echoed by her colleague Janet Sims, who said that the faculty had "made great use of lower-stakes writing assignments" and described the concept of writing to learn "as a sort of revelation to all of us," leading to the widespread integration of writing-to-learn assignments across the entire department. Even in John Holcomb's chemistry department, whose curriculum "look[s] down the road to the careers students are going to occupy" and therefore focuses on the need for students "to be able to communicate their ideas in writing, orally, and visually," the faculty reconceptualized lab reports as a kind of lower-stakes writing designed to help students to learn experimental methods, causes and effects, and principles of chemistry.

The interest in writing to learn was also a manifestation of a broader conceptual change in faculty understanding of writing. As Harold Jones (CS) explained,

> In part [WEC] is about writing and communication skills.
> But more fundamentally and at the department level, it's
> about helping our students learn, and what do we want them
> to be able to do by the time they graduate, having studied
> sociology, and how can we use writing and oral communi-
> cation to get them there. It's about substance and content as
> well as skills. As soon as we started to frame our discussion in
> that way, people's initial hesitation that "oh, I'm not trained
> to teach writing, I'm not trained to teach communication and

this is one more thing I have to worry about when I grade"—
once we were able to shift that mindset to this is something
that we integrate into what we do, to let us do better, to teach
better and for our students to learn more, that really opened
it up.

This view was also evident in Dorothy Hackett's (CS) reflection on the
broader role of writing in the Sociology curriculum:

For a lot of people it's been a really nice shift to think about
writing and speaking in the classroom is not learning to write
and learning to speak, it's writing to learn. And I think that's
made a big difference in the way a lot of people approach
creating their classes. It's been really positive across the board.

IMPROVEMENT OF STUDENT PERFORMANCE

In addition to enhancing students' learning of subject matter, an important goal
of any WAC program is for students to leave their university and their department with improved communication abilities. This assumption often drives
the stated rationales or missions of WAC programs because, as Kinkead has
reminded us, writing is "one area most frequently targeted in accountability
and assessment conversations" (1997, p. 37). A key component of the WEC
model, therefore, involves continuous assessment of student writing ability, but
like the development of goals and outcomes, and the choice of specific pedagogical and curricular strategies to realize them, assessment works from the bottom
up, "based on what the *faculty* in the department believe should be the abilities
of students who graduate with a degree in that discipline" (Anson, 2006, pp.
108–109). Consequently, the means of assessment will vary. In a small department that tracks its graduates' employment carefully, alumni or even employer
surveys could be one means of assessing the effectiveness of the WEC program.
(The Department of Social Work at Cowling State, for example, gets "a lot of
community feedback" about students' writing and oral communication—how
"students need to be able to do progress notes for their patients better, students
would do better if they knew how to form an argument to advocate for a certain
policy change.") In another department whose graduates go off in a hundred
directions, such a method would be too challenging and unproductive to pursue.

At the point of the interviews, the Department of Social Work at Cowling
State was just gearing up to do "a first big assessment" of how effectively the WEC
program had worked but had not yet started. Only the biology department at

Pound Ridge had conducted any formal assessment of student writing that could gauge the effectiveness of their WEC activities (an analysis of student capstone projects, which revealed that the lower end of the scale of quality had improved significantly and that students felt "better prepared for the capstone than they used to be"). Yet the anecdotal evidence from both institutions suggested that once departments started implementing the WEC approach, improvements were noticeable in student writing, largely as a result of changes in teaching behavior. In Janet Smith's (PR) department, because of a significant increase in student writing and a strong emphasis on peer review, the writing "did get better. I mean, it was great for the students because they didn't go out of [their majors] saying 'I'm a bad writer. I know how to write now.'" Summing up the overall effects of her department's WEC-related work, Smith claimed that it "dramatically improved their writing." John Holcomb (PR) remarked that "writing has definitely improved. I've been teaching for 41 years. The papers are quite good, really. We used to get some really atrocious papers, and that doesn't happen anymore." The political science department at Pound Ridge came to the same conclusion. As Janet Sims put it, "we have actually seen improvement. We can really see the difference. . . . The students who were doing the senior seminar this year [had] pretty good projects and much more skill in writing than we had seen in previous years."

Interviewees also described the ways that their WEC programs had started to affect students' attitudes toward writing and their self-efficacy. In Dorothy Hackett's (CS) view, she and her colleagues "definitely have seen" a change in the student culture with respect to writing. For example, she soon found that students learned the value of peer review in a required core course that had been restructured as a result of the department's writing-enriched curriculum:

> I've had a number of students from that course come and
> tell me, "Now I see why we did peer review in my sopho-
> more-level class; we're going to have to do it in this class when
> we're writing these big papers and it really makes a difference."
> So they're seeing the connections across the courses, they're
> seeing different kinds of new activities in new places that they
> hadn't seen before. And they're feeling like they see how it's
> connected and how it's building in a way that we certainly
> never had before—that *we* had never thought about that way.

Although the faculty from the Department of Social Work at Cowling State were not able to say whether student writing had improved yet, both interviewees saw tangible evidence that WEC was affecting instruction. Paul White explained that their work was "making a difference in terms of how we teach." As a result, he believed that because writing was not something "added on to the courses" but integrated into them, it was "not a matter of saying that writing across the curriculum is the thing that's made the difference" in students' overall achievement. Echoing this view, Harold Jones (CS) mentioned that "In [our] culture, what I pick up on is around faculty members. They're more likely to say that embracing these techniques is all part of me becoming a better teacher and a better professor." As the department began working on appropriate assessment methods, they realized how "threaded" writing and communication were throughout the curriculum, suggesting the challenge (or questioning the wisdom) of pulling them apart from other aspects of students' learning. More tangibly, both Jones and White were seeing increased confidence in students arising from changes in faculty behaviors such as "multiple opportunities to get feedback and to assess themselves," and also as a result of writing across courses.

THE TRANSFORMATIVE EFFECTS OF WEC

The WEC approach has been described as potentially "transformative" (Anson & Dannels, 2009; Bastian, 2014; Flash, 2016; and, in this volume, Flash, Chapter 1; Yancey, Chapter 3; and Luskey & Emery, Chapter 4). As Luskey and Emery argue, a prerequisite to such transformation is the acquisition of threshold writing concepts, which they study at points of "liminality," or stages of "conceptual transition" that offer insights into the way that faculty are developing through their work on writing-enriched curricula. Liminality, they argue, "is no guarantee of transformation, [but] it is the catalyst if such a transformation is to occur." As I have claimed elsewhere, the most important threshold concepts for writing across the curriculum are that writing is shaped within disciplinary and other contexts; that it serves social and rhetorical purposes; that it can be used both to explore and to learn as well as to communicate to others; that instructionally it must rely on shared responsibilities across the disciplines; that students must to some extent "learn anew" in new communities of practice and cannot "transfer" their abilities effortlessly; and that becoming a more proficient writer is a long, developmental process (Anson, 2015).

As Sheriff points out in Chapter 6 of this volume, helping faculty in the disciplines to acquire these and other threshold concepts associated with writing may be one of the greatest challenges to change because the faculty may struggle even to "describe specific ways of writing, thinking, and researching that they expect of graduates in their majors." As evidenced in their comments, the interviewees' experience with the WEC approach in their departments appears to have inductively helped them and their colleagues to acquire these central threshold concepts associated with the principles of writing across the curriculum. Interviewees described the way that their departments had restructured their curricula and changed their courses to more accurately link writing to the work of their disciplines and view entry-level writing courses not as "inoculation" centers to "fix" student writing but as the foundation for what would follow in the disciplines. By linking writing more strongly to the goals of their disciplines, they also began creating more authentic, socially purposeful writing assignments that looked ahead to the rhetorical and informational work of their students' careers. In what some of them described as a "revelation," the interviewees pointed to their enhanced understanding of how lower-stakes writing can strengthen students' learning without creating additional evaluative burdens. They also spoke about the collective efforts of their colleagues to strengthen students' writing and pay more attention to it in their courses, without relying on outside entities to do it for them or to tell them what to do. This commitment demonstrated an understanding that writing is highly situated and that when contexts differ from each other, it becomes the responsibility of faculty in the disciplines to guide and mentor their students and help them to learn situated genres and communication practices. Finally, and perhaps most importantly, the interviews reflected an understanding that writing is not acquired once, that improvement is slow to develop, and that as a result, it needs constant practice and reinforcement across a range of settings.

In addition to the many new ways that the representative departments in this study began to rethink the nature and role of writing in their curriculum, interviewees also related the "ripple effects" of their WEC endeavors. Janet Sims, for example, pointed to the way that the WEC approach in political science at Pound Ridge led to further innovations not directly related to writing. "The writing in the discipline is really feeding everything," she remarked, including an emphasis on interdisciplinarity and the creation of learning communities. "It [the WEC approach] has actually affected everything else in the curriculum. Writing informs everything else." Similarly, Harold Jones (CS) described how WEC started to affect much more than writing and communication: "One of the most interesting and exciting parts of this is that it ended up being an opportunity for more discussions about teaching in the department." And Joanne Smith (PR) explained that "once [the faculty] were confronted with some really workable models and they started doing it," they realized the advantages to their students' learning, and even, by virtue of students' improved expression, their grading, "because you can really discern what they are learning in the discipline as opposed to, 'I know this but I can't express it.'" As Joanne Smith (PR) put it, all of the faculty bought into the approach, "miraculously so. It's been a real combination of factors."

The reciprocity of collaborative departmental work and individual faculty change also came through in some of the interviews. As a result of extensive work on their curriculum supported by the WEC director and the outside consultants, Michael Pruett (CS) pointed to the concept of "constructive alignment," developed by educational scholar John Biggs (2011). This concept refers to the extent to which goals for student learning, student-facing methods for achieving those goals, and assessment of the results are in "alignment." Courses and curricula that are not constructively aligned fail to teach or assess in ways that are aimed toward goals and outcomes. As Pruett put it,

> the notion of constructive alignment has become a part of me, not only thinking about how it influences communication across the curriculum but also how I build my courses more broadly and how my courses fit into the goals for the department as well as for education. I find myself talking in those terms and thinking in those terms in many ways. It's another example of how it's not just about communication, it's about learning and how all these things fit together. It's been really for me a beneficial process of improving my own teaching as well as how what I do fits into something bigger.

Although the process of articulating expectations for the development of students' disciplinary knowledge and abilities was one of the strongest motivations for faculty to work on their department's curriculum, some other factors also played a role. The Department of Social Work at Cowling State, for example, mentioned the importance of accreditation in their focus on writing. Harold Jones and Paul White both remarked that their accrediting body, the Council on Social Work Education, strengthened their commitment to a departmental focus on writing and oral communication. Jones explained that "the timing was right. We could fold it in to what we knew we were going to have to do anyway." Paul White further clarified that only later did the department realize that WEC could help them with their upcoming accreditation review:

> It wasn't intentional; we got the invitation to participate in [WEC] and it was afterwards that it became clear how much we needed to do in terms of curriculum redevelopment to fit with the new accreditation criteria, so they both came along right at a convenient time for us to do it. I also think that was the impetus for us to really look at WEC and what it could offer, because we already had to make substantial changes to the curriculum anyway.

These experiences were similar to what my colleagues and I have seen in some of the STEM fields at North Carolina State University, especially when the new accreditation guidelines were formulated as part of ABET 2000 (Accreditation

Board for Engineering and Technology). These standards strongly emphasized written and oral communication and shifted the focus from "what is taught to what is learned" (https://www.abet.org/about-abet/history/). As a result, ABET-accredited departments could see the advantage of our WEC model as they studied their curricula, delved more deeply into what they wanted students and faculty to achieve, and engaged in both formative and summative assessment of student ability. Interestingly, the accrediting bodies themselves can learn from the innovations at particular institutions, as Blank describes in Chapter 5 of this volume, when word of the NC State Department of Forestry's efforts influenced programs at other universities and eventually convinced the Society of American Foresters to adopt an integrated approach to writing in its new criteria and review process.

In addition to the accreditation of specific programs, broader institution-wide accreditation by the major regional bodies (MSCHE, ABET, WASC, etc.) can provide support for WEC leaders enlisting departments to join the effort. An important principle for developing WEC is to see its potential in the context of the need to showcase support for developing student communication abilities and assessment of that support. More importantly, the link to accreditation strengthens the sustainability of the WEC effort. As Paul White (CS) explained, because the WEC effort is "blended" with accreditation, "it's not going to disappear; as long as the writing and oral communication objectives remain in the syllabi—and they will because all of that is tied to our accreditation—then it's not going to disappear; it's going to be part of a continual improvement program."

CHALLENGES

The WEC model, as in any cross-curricular effort, is not a panacea, and it is confronted with its own share of struggles, oppositions, and frustrations. Unlike the collective successes and positive experiences recounted above, however, challenges mentioned in the interviews were mixed and more idiosyncratic. But one consistency emerged: interviewees positioned challenges not as impediments that forestalled implementation but as problems that their WEC program helped to *solve*. John Holcomb (PR), for example, explained the shift in his department's collective attitude toward writing:

> Initially with the writing in the disciplines, our department—
> and I think this was true in a lot of departments in the col-
> lege—viewed that as a nuisance—viewed it as, "well, we already
> have enough trouble educating our students with regard to the
> discipline; this is just something else that's in the way." But when

we got a little further with [WEC] being put into place, eventually the conviction of faculty that you need to be able to communicate, and one way of doing that is writing, has worked its way through. And I think that's what now really drives it.

Similarly, Janet Sims (PR) had difficulty identifying any significant roadblocks to her colleagues' work in political science but attributed that to being in a department that is "very innovative, always trying new things and really open to discussion." Still, if there were any frustrations among the faculty, she believed that the improvements in student' writing erased those: "In a relatively short period of time, we see much better research projects, much better senior seminar or capstone projects, and people are beginning to see the value of [WEC]." Similarly, Harold Jones (CS) expressed little concern about any defensiveness among the faculty: "Even the term 'resistance' would be a misnomer for the department. There's no resistance to it." In part, he explained, this lack of pushback owed to the existence of a least some writing prior to the implementation of the WEC program, with new ideas and methods then inspiring the faculty to innovate.

For the Department of Biology at Pound Ridge, Courtney Sikes raised a concern about some personnel turnover that required orienting the newly-hired faculty to their departmental WEC efforts—but a challenge that she also saw positively as part of faculty development. Similarly, for the Department of Chemistry at Pound Ridge, John Holcomb worried about the possible "loss of vision" and "consistency" that can come from changes in the faculty and the assignment of redesigned courses to those who had not taught them. Tied to this, he explained, is the fact that, at smaller colleges, academic freedom "has high value." The evidence at Pound Ridge suggests a remarkable level of agreement in the departments in this study for supporting student writing development and innovating the curriculum. Still, the ever-present concern about consistency suggests the need for WEC leaders to "honor the autonomy and expertise of the faculty," as Fodrey and Hassay put it in Chapter 7 of this volume, while also providing outside support and formative oversight. It also requires vigilance in follow-through, as described in Anson and Dannels (2009) and in Flash (Chapter 1 of this volume).

Another potential concern obviated by WEC implementation was shared by Harold Jones (CS). Initially, he and his colleagues feared a faculty perception (in the midst of being constantly "slammed" with work) that a WEC program would take additional time and energy. This view is related to a belief that writing will "intrude" on the coverage of course content—that it is "added on to" a course already packed with information (see Fulwiler, 1984;

and Scheurer, 2014). Interestingly, however, the WEC initiative ended up not being seen as intrusion:

> A lot of the other things are seen as sort of infringements on teaching—so you *have* to do this or you *have* to do this. But writing across the curriculum was more like, we're doing it because we thought it was important and we wanted to do it, not because we had to. And that was good. That made it a lot more palatable.

SUMMING UP: THE VALUE OF THE WRITING-ENRICHED CURRICULUM

In an analysis of how WAC programs can both respond to and effectuate changes in higher education institutions, McLeod and Miraglia argue that such changes are not linear and do not take the form of mandated policy, but involve a process in which "complexities interact and coalesce into periodic patterns that are unknowable in advance" (2011, p. 20). In reflecting on how the work of writing across the curriculum might create broader improvements in teaching and learning, they draw on Fullan's (1995) "Eight Basic Lessons for the New Paradigm of Change" (p. 21).

Table 2.3. Fullan's (1995) Lessons for Change

Lesson 1	You can't mandate what matters (the more complex the change, the less you can force it).
Lesson 2	Change is a journey, not a blueprint (change is nonlinear, loaded with uncertainty and excitement, and sometimes perverse).
Lesson 3	Problems are our friends (problems are inevitable and you can't learn without them).
Lesson 4	Vision and strategic planning come later (premature visions and planning blind us to other possibilities).
Lesson 5	Individualism and collectivism must have equal power (there are no one-sided solutions).
Lesson 6	Neither centralization nor decentralization works alone (both top-down and bottom-up strategies are necessary).
Lesson 7	Connection with the wider environment is critical for success (the best organizations learn externally as well as internally).
Lesson 8	Every person is a change agent (change is too important to leave to the experts).

This interview-based study involved a small group of faculty in several departments at two different institutions of dramatically different size, in different regions of the US, with different student populations, missions, curricula, reward systems, and organizational structures. Comments from the faculty about their respective WEC programs can't be generalized and must be seen in the context of their institutional ecologies. Not only do WEC programs vary across institutions, but their implementation in specific departments will not look the same, and the experiences of the faculty there will vary. Yet standing back from the collective experiences reflected in the interviews synthesized here, we can see the enactment of many of Fulland's principles.

Consider, for example, the idea that change cannot be mandated and that it involves a kind of journey, with unexpected twists and turns and variations in the landscape. From the perspective of simplistic ideas about writing—that students need grammar instruction, or that they need to write more papers—change may seem simple and therefore able to be mandated. But the development of writing abilities is extraordinarily complex, made more so when we consider its rhetorical and linguistic dimensions within disciplines, the need to learn particular genres and their features, or the deployment or transfer of previously learned skills or perspectives (Bazerman, 2011). In the experience of this book's contributors and clearly demonstrated in this chapter's interviews, integrating writing into departments that often have little experience explicitly considering its nature and role or that continue to act on inherited beliefs and practices is best accomplished from the bottom up with appropriate support. Although WEC as a programmatic initiative often begins at the top of an institution's hierarchy (but see Blank, Chapter 5 of this volume), its processes are not manded from there; rather, as McLeod has put it, "profound curricular and pedagogical change can come about as a result of a WAC program, but such change will not take place unless it comes from the faculty themselves" (1992, p. 4). Interviews from a humanities department, a social science department, two science departments, and one professional program at different institutions demonstrated the promise of discipline-specific, collective leadership in (re)shaping the role of writing in assignments, courses, and entire curricula.

Like the process of writing itself, cycles of continuous program review and formative improvement always loop back to the original plans and goals that generated them, because no context is stable. Early in our work at North Carolina State University, we developed such a model, shown in its basic form in Figure 2.2. Notice that the model involves a cycle of activity, but is not linear, suggesting continuous renewal: the relationship between implementation and assessment is recursive and either can be pursued first. The entire model also assumes an evolution of outcomes and what follows (consider, for example, outcomes developed before many of the affordances of the Internet).

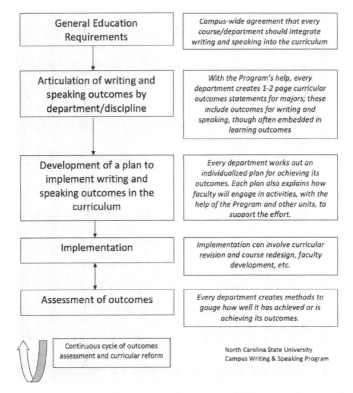

Figure 2.2 Early NC State departmental WEC model (Anson & Dannels, 2000).

At the point of the interviews in this study, departments' WEC-focused efforts were too new to inquire into sustainability or the need for continuous renewal. But experiences elsewhere show that no WEC program can be established once and let go. Departmental demographics change; student populations change; and the disciplines evolve. Consequently, WEC programs are living, evolving systems requiring a certain level of "maintenance and support" (Anson & Dannels, 2009). This will always yield continuing problems and challenges, but in the spirit of WEC, faculty embrace these as necessary to the vitality of their own programs. From this perspective, we can also imagine departments' consideration of ever more complex aspects of writing and student learning that typically (and problematically) are not the subjects of focus during the earliest stages of implementation, such as the relationship between writing assessment and implicit racial bias or dialect variation or the linguistic characteristics of L2 speakers of English (see Anson, 2012).

In the context of WAC leaders' desire to create plans for implementation, the fourth lesson may seem counterintuitive, because WEC programs—notwithstanding Blank's departmental description in Chapter 5 of this volume—are designed as campus-wide initiatives localized in departments. But in spite of the overarching planning processes at both the institutions profiled in this chapter, faculty in the departments began the process with an exploratory stage, engaging in general faculty development activities, holding retreats to discuss possibilities, and studying the status quo in their curricula to decide how to proceed. This preliminary heuristic stage, with the guidance of WEC leaders, may be a better way to begin than jumping immediately to creating plans, especially because various theoretical shifts and the weakening of entrenched views may be necessary.

Although by design the interviews here focused on faculty experiences within their departments, enough emerged about the association of their WEC work with administrative leadership to suggest the reciprocity in Lesson 6 and the relationship between departmental autonomy to work with other units in Lesson 7. In both cases, there was campus-wide agreement to pursue a WEC program, but individual faculty or small teams shuttled between committees and planning groups or other units, which precipitated broader involvement. Connection with wider environments can include other departments, first-year writing programs, writing centers, libraries, curriculum committees, technology centers, centers for teaching and learning, second-language centers, and others—as demonstrated in many of the chapters in this collection.

Throughout the interviews, it was clear that nothing would happen across the departments without collective agreements and collaboration. But that requires members of the department to see themselves individually as advocates and change agents, which McLeod and Miraglia (2011) position as the most important of the eight lessons. Throughout this study, the commitment to the interviewees' own instructional methods, to the shared vision in their departments, and to the overall effects that the WEC approach could have across their institutions was abundantly evident.

Although this study elicited feedback from department faculty involved in WEC implementation (not the local WEC directors), some further thoughts about the organizational nature of WEC programs are warranted. In particular, the approach compels us to reassess our ideology of leadership and contests our established roles as faculty developers, guides, mentors, keepers of the flame, and writing or communication experts. As several contributors to this collection point out, the WEC approach requires a delicate balance between expert consultant and naïve but interested listener. Walvoord (1999) has called this a "client-customer" relationship in which the department is free to use the WEC director's counsel within the parameters of the model. Guiding the initial departmental discussions takes considerable expertise and diplomacy—a tolerance, as Carter suggests in his Foreword to this collection, for early faculty skepticism or even resistance, and a willingness to concede, at least initially, to ideas that may seem problematic if only to let them play out, to let the faculty reach certain understandings on their own. This is where, as the interviewees pointed out, workshops and other activities can be helpful in providing new perspectives for faculty before they begin tackling tough decisions in their departments.

Finally, the WEC approach hinges in many ways on the concept of intrinsic motivation. Although programs like Florida Atlantic's (as described by Galin in Chapter 8 of this collection) provide financial support to departments, fundamentally WEC assumes that faculty care about the students in their majors and equate their success with the development of their departmental status and reputation. Over nearly 25 years of overseeing the WEC program at North Carolina State University, my colleagues and I have not found a single department that was willing to set the bar of its learning outcomes low enough to minimize their work and their attention to students' learning. Just the reverse: goals are aspirational, based on what the faculty believe to be the strongest communication abilities one might find in a graduate of their department or program. At the same time, the goals are not so challenging as to dissuade faculty from joining the effort. And when over time, department by department, an entire institution is working cooperatively to achieve localized goals, the whole institution improves.

REFERENCES

Anson, C. M. (2006). Assessing writing in cross-curricular programs: Determining the locus of activity. *Assessing Writing, 11*, 110–112.

Anson, C. M. (2012). Black holes: Writing across the curriculum and the gravitational invisibility of race. In A. B. Inoue & M. Poe (Eds.), *Race and writing assessment* (pp. 15–28). Peter Lang.

Anson, C. M. (2015). Crossing thresholds: What's to know about writing across the curriculum? In L. Adler-Kassner & E. Wardle (Eds.), *Naming what we know: Threshold concepts of writing studies* (pp. 203–219). Utah State University Press.

Anson, C. M. (2017). Writing to read, revisited. In A. S. Horning, D. Gollnitz & C. R. Haller (Eds.), *What is college reading?* (pp. 21–39). The WAC Clearinghouse; University Press of Colorado. https://doi.org/10.37514/ATD-B.2017.0001.2.01.

Anson, C. M. (2021). Introduction. In C. M. Anson & P. Flash (Eds.), *Writing-enriched curricula: Models of faculty-driven and departmental transformation*. The WAC Clearinghouse; University Press of Colorado. https://doi.org/10.27514/PER-B.2021.1299.1.3.

Anson, C. M. & Dannels, D. P. (2000). Departmental WEC model. Campus Writing & Speaking Program, North Carolina State University.

Anson, C. M. & Dannels, D. P. (2009). Profiling programs: Formative uses of assisted descriptions in the assessment of communication across the curriculum. *Across the Disciplines, 6*. https://doi.org/10.37514/ATD-J.2009.6.1.05.

Applebee, A. N. (1985). Writing and reasoning. *Review of Educational Research, 54*(4), 577–596.

Ayres, L. (2008). Semi-structured interview. In Given, L. M. (Ed.), *The SAGE encyclopedia of qualitative research methods* (pp. 811–812). Sage.

Bastian, H. (2014). Performing the groundwork: Building a WEC/WAC writing program at the College of St. Scholastica. *Composition Forum, 29*. http://composition forum.com/issue/29/st-scholastica.php.

Bazerman, C. (2011). The disciplined interdisciplinarity of writing. *Research in the Teaching of English, 46*(1), 8–21.

Biggs, J. (2011). *Teaching for quality learning at university* (4th ed.). Open University Press.

Blank, G. S. (2021). Forty years of writing embedded in forestry at North Carolina State University. In C. M. Anson & P. Flash (Eds.), *Writing-enriched curricula: Models of faculty-driven and departmental transformation*. The WAC Clearinghouse; University Press of Colorado. https://doi.org/10.27514/PER-B.2021.1299.2.05.

Britton, J., Burgess, T., Martin, N., McLeod, A. & Rosen, H. (1975). *The development of writing abilities* (11–18). Macmillan Education.

Charmaz, K. & Bryant, A. (2008). Grounded theory. In Given, L. M. (Ed.), *The SAGE encyclopedia of qualitative research methods* (pp. 375–376). Sage.

Condon, W. & Rutz, C. (2012). A taxonomy of writing across the curriculum programs: Evolving to serve broader agendas. *College Composition and Communication, 64*(2), 357–382.

Cox, M., Galin, J. R. & Melzer, D. (2018). *Sustainable WAC: A whole systems approach to launching and developing writing across the curriculum programs*. National Council of Teachers of English.

Flash, P. (2016). From apprised to revised: Faculty in the disciplines change what they never knew they knew. In K. B. Yancey (Ed.), *A rhetoric of reflection* (pp. 227–249). Utah State University Press.

Flash, P. (2021). Writing-enriched curriculum: A model for making and sustaining change. In C. M. Anson & P. Flash (Eds.), *Writing-enriched curricula: Models of faculty-driven and departmental transformation*. The WAC Clearinghouse; University Press of Colorado. https://doi.org/10.27514/PER-B.2021.1299.2.01.

Fodrey, C. N. & Hassay, C. (2021). Piloting WEC as a context-responsive writing research initiative. In C. M. Anson & P. Flash (Eds.), *Writing-enriched curricula: Models of faculty-driven and departmental transformation*. The WAC Clearinghouse; University Press of Colorado. https://doi.org/10.27514/PER-B.2021.1299.2.07.

Fullan, M. (1993). *Change forces: Probing the depth of educational reform*. Falmer.

Fulwiller, T. (1984). How well does writing across the curriculum work? *College English, 46*(2), 113–125.

Fuwiler, T. & Young, A. (Eds.). (1982). *Language connections: Writing and reading across the curriculum*. National Council of Teachers of English.

Galin, J. (2021). Theorizing the WEC model with the whole systems approach to WAC program sustainability. In C. M. Anson & P. Flash (Eds.), *Writing-enriched curricula: Models of faculty-driven and departmental transformation*. The WAC Clearinghouse; University Press of Colorado. https://doi.org/10.27514/PER-B.2021.1299.2.08.

Herrington, A. (1981). Writing to learn: Writing across the disciplines. *College English, 43*, 379–387.

Holdstein, D. (2001). "Writing across the curriculum" and the paradoxes of institutional initiatives. *Pedagogy, 1*(1), 37–52.

Kinkead, J. (1997). Documenting excellence in teaching and learning in WAC programs. In K. B. Yancey & B. Huot (Eds.), *Assessing writing across the curriculum: Diverse approaches and practices* (pp. 37–50). Ablex.

Luskey, M. & Emery, D. L. (2021). Beyond conventions: Liminality as a feature of the WEC faculty development. In C. M. Anson & P. Flash (Eds.), *Writing-enriched curricula: Models of faculty-driven and departmental transformation.* The WAC Clearinghouse; University Press of Colorado. https://doi.org/10.27514/PER-B.2021 .1299.2.04.

McLeod, S. H. (1992). Writing across the curriculum: An introduction. In S. H. McCleod & M. Soven (Eds.), *Writing across the curriculum: A guide to developing programs* (pp. 1–8). Sage.

McLeod, S. H. & Miraglia, E. (2011). Writing across the curriculum in a time of change. In S. H. McLeod, E. Miraglia, M. Soven & C. Thaiss (Eds.). *WAC for the new millennium: Strategies for continuing writing-across-the-curriculum programs* (pp. 1–27). National Council of Teachers of English.

McLeod, S. & Soven, M. (1991). What do you need to start—and sustain—a writing-across-the-curriculum program? *WPA: Writing Program Administration, 15,* 25–34.

Odell, L. (1980). The process of writing and the process of learning. *College Composition and Communication, 36,* 42–50.

Patton, M. Q. (1990). *Qualitative evaluation and research methods* (2nd ed.). Sage.

Russell, D. R. (1994). American origins of the writing-across-the-curriculum movement. In C. Bazerman & D. Russell (Eds.), *Landmark essays on writing across the curriculum* (pp. 3–22). Hermagoras Press.

Scheurer, E. (2014). What Do WAC directors need to know about "coverage"? *The WAC Journal, 26,* 7–21. https://doi.org/10.37514/WAC-J.2015.26.1.01.

Sheriff, S. (2021). Beyond "I know it when I see it": WEC and the process of unearthing faculty expertise. In C. M. Anson & P. Flash (Eds.), *Writing-enriched curricula: Models of faculty-driven and departmental transformation.* The WAC Clearinghouse; University Press of Colorado. https://doi.org/10.27514/PER-B.2021.1299.2.06.

Stern, P. N. (2008). Constant comparison. In Given, L. M. (Ed.), *The SAGE encyclopedia of qualitative research methods* (pp. 115–116). Sage.

Walvoord, B. (1997). From conduit to customer: The role of WAC faculty in WAC assessment. In K. B. Yancey & B. Huot (Eds.), *Assessing writing across the curriculum: Diverse approaches and practices* (pp. 15–36). Ablex.

White, E. M. (1990). The damage of innovations set adrift." *AAHE Bulletin, 43*(3), 3–5.

Yancey, K. B. (2021). Follow the sources: Notes toward WEC's contribution to disciplinary writing. In C. M. Anson & P. Flash (Eds.), *Writing-enriched curricula: Models of faculty-driven and departmental transformation.* The WAC Clearinghouse; University Press of Colorado. https://doi.org/10.27514/PER-B.2021.1299.2.03.

CHAPTER 3

FOLLOW THE SOURCES: NOTES TOWARD WEC'S CONTRIBUTION TO DISCIPLINARY WRITING

Kathleen Blake Yancey

Florida State University

WEC has received considerable praise for its transformation of writing curricula, its engagement of faculty, and its curricular enhancement through assessment. To date, however, the idea of the faculty writing plans as epistemological statements about disciplinary writing values and practices hasn't received as much attention—in spite of the plans' potential to show us what is valued in different contexts across a campus, what is valued in the aggregate across a campus, and what is valued in disciplinary contexts. Do parallel departments at different institutions engaging in WEC activities define their disciplinary discourses similarly, and if so, how might such activity contribute to mapping disciplinary discourses? This chapter pursues this question by drawing on WEC instantiations at three institutions—focusing on history as a kind of prototype—in order to demonstrate that an analysis of inter-institutional disciplinary WEC materials can articulate disciplinary discourses, defined as practices, texts, and values. This project thus has as a premise that WEC materials, in addition to their curricular and pedagogical value, have epistemological value; that is, they make visible disciplinary writing values, practices, and genres as expressed by faculty in those disciplines, and in so doing, they illuminate defining features of writing in specific disciplines. Moreover, through reflecting upon such patterns, assuming they do exist, we can speak more authoritatively about the nature and defining characteristics of a given discipline, in this case the discipline of history. Not least, in taking up this question, this chapter also outlines a more general process, available for use for other disciplines, of engaging in a comparative reflective review of inter-institutional departmental materials developed with a common goal of articulating writing for the same discipline. Taken together, such portraits of disciplinary writing can begin mapping the world of disparate disciplinary writing genres, practices, and values.

DOI: https://doi.org/10.37514/PER-B.2021.1299.2.03

Several years ago, I visited the University of Minnesota's writing enriched curriculum (WEC) program, in part to work with Pamela Flash and some of her colleagues, in part to attend a symposium highlighting the good work that participants in the WEC program had engaged in. At one point, after a presentation by the then-director of first-year composition (FYC), I raised a set of questions that has haunted me ever since. Given what we are seeing in this symposium about the diversity in college writing, I wondered, what if any overlaps and through lines might exist across the writing processes and texts documented in these multiple and different contexts. As the symposium presentations demonstrated, the WEC-intensive departmental investigations into disciplinary discourse revealed much about the different questions, kinds of evidence, and genres privileged in each of these different discourses; at the same time, if we read *across* them, what might they collectively point to as common processes and textual features of college-level writing? We know that there are differences, but do any common writing processes and features exist, and if so, what are they?

I began taking up these questions in a limited way in a study I completed in 2015, focusing on writing plans from three very different departments at the University of Minnesota WEC program—history, geography, and mechanical engineering—for two purposes. First, I wanted to identify the contrasting features, like observing the ethical use of visual information in geography and creating multimedia texts as members of global teams in mechanical engineering, that distinguish these three disciplinary discourses from each other. Second, based on this analysis, I also inquired into whether or not shared practices, discursive features, or values in these three very different disciplines could be observed.[1] The findings were fairly straightforward: as different as the three departments and their discourses are, there are "patterns of similarity—chiefly, an attention to writing process, a valuing of evidence, and a concern for audience . . . the writing cultures represented here are different, but they have common points of reference." Based on this analysis, my argument also was that identifying these shared values—writing process, evidence, and audience—could provide something of a through-line or pathway for college writers.[2] At the same time, a limitation of this study was that each of the disciplinary discourses was defined by only a single department in a single institution, which raises an(other) interesting

---

1   Michael Carter's Braddock-Award-winning article asks a similar question, but toward a different end: identifying discursive features and values that, he argued, constitute four meta-genres.

2   There are other ways to identify or create commonalities across disciplinary discourses as well. For an approach linking two courses through threshold concepts, see Adler-Kassner, et al. (2012). For an approach linking writing and disciplines (in this case, chemistry) through overlapping key terms, in this case influenced by the Teaching for Transfer (TFT) writing curriculum, see Green, et al. (2017).

question: do parallel departments at different institutions engaging in WEC activities define their disciplinary discourses similarly, and if so, how might such activity contribute to mapping disciplinary discourses?

The WEC approach, of course, has received considerable praise for its engagement of faculty and subsequent transformation of writing curricula, which is appropriate given that the WEC approach is understood and promoted as a curricular and pedagogical enhancement activity. At the same time, however, given the faculty conversations it facilitates—conversations that are not always natural or easy, as Anson (Chapter 2), Flash (Chapter 1), and Sheriff (Chapter 6) of this volume note—and the writing materials it creates, the WEC approach offers another rich opportunity: to examine and uncover the epistemologies of disciplinary writing values and practices, be they different or similar. More specifically, while the purpose of WEC, especially from the perspective of departments and disciplines, is curricular and pedagogical, for those interested in *studying* writing in higher education and in defining the characteristics of different disciplinary discourses, the curricular materials produced as part of the WEC process present a thus-far untapped resource.

In this chapter, I take up this question about whether or not parallel departments at different institutions engaging in WEC activities define their disciplinary discourses similarly. To pursue it, I draw on WEC instantiations at three different institutions—focusing on history as a kind of prototype—in order to demonstrate that an analysis of inter-institutional disciplinary WEC materials can articulate disciplinary discourses, defined as practices, texts, and values. This project thus has as a premise that WEC materials, in addition to their curricular and pedagogical value, have epistemological value; that is, they make visible disciplinary writing values, practices, and genres as expressed by faculty in those disciplines, and in so doing, they illuminate defining features of writing in specific disciplines. Of course, one challenge in this project is to navigate between what seem to be more general insights from the data and the particulars that are the product of specific departments with all their idiosyncratic ways of working with student writing. Still, given the shared philosophy supporting the WEC-discipline/departmentally oriented approach engaging faculty in articulating questions, genres, and kinds of evidence, it's reasonable to think that patterns will obtain. Moreover, through reflecting upon such patterns, assuming they do exist, we can speak more authoritatively about the nature and defining characteristics of a given discipline, in this case the discipline of history. Not least, in taking up this question, this chapter also outlines a more general process, available for use for other disciplines, of engaging in a comparative reflective review of inter-institutional departmental materials developed with a common goal of articulating writing for the same discipline. Taken together, such portraits of disciplinary writing can begin mapping the world of disparate disciplinary writing genres, practices, and values.

To take up this mapping task as a kind of proof of concept, I focus here on definitions of writing in the discipline of history as developed at three institutions, each with a WEC focus, but each working with somewhat different materials and taking different points of departure and rhetorical stances. Although the three departments whose work I am drawing on here are in somewhat different stages of activity, they have all taken up the same kinds of questions and have articulated historical writing curricula in response, and as the analysis shows, the three curricula express a common set of values. I begin with the Appalachian State WEC program, what I call a "coordinated translation model" program, whose primary goal is to inform students more broadly about disciplinary discourses in the context of all the campus disciplines.[3] I then turn to the North Carolina State University WEC program, which addresses disciplinary discourse through the lens of outcomes as it focuses on writing in the history major. With these two programs as context, I then consider the University of Minnesota WEC program, which takes up disciplinary writing with a somewhat wider lens, including disciplinary writing as it is made available for students in both general education and the major. I conclude by reviewing what this analysis tells us about writing in history specifically as well as about what this kind of analysis can tell us about the contribution of WEC to our knowledge of disciplinary writing more generally.

APPALACHIAN STATE UNIVERSITY: A COORDINATED TRANSLATION MODEL

The WEC program at Appalachian State University is a comprehensive program that intends to bring together multiple contexts for writing; it coordinates among those contexts, and it seeks to translate the writing in one context to others. In that sense, it is transcontextual and broadly so. Contexts include community colleges where students who will later transfer to Appalachian State first learn about college writing; the general education college composition program context, which includes a sophomore-level WAC-oriented class; and disciplinary contexts where students complete two writing in the disciplines (WID) courses at the junior and capstone levels. Taken together, these contexts are both horizontal, including general education and community colleges, and vertical,

---

3   The Appalachian State writing across the curriculum (WAC) program, although less elaborated than either the North Carolina State University or University of Minnesota WEC programs, is WEC-like in its attention to the identifying features of specific disciplines as articulated in conversations with the disciplinary faculty; its commitment is thus also to articulation of disciplinary writing by members of the disciplines themselves.

oriented to students' progression through and culmination of their academic majors. Interestingly, the sophomore-level course, which was created in 2009, is in some ways the lynchpin of the program since it provides the interface between general education writing and WID:

> The Intro to WAC course was conceived as an intersection course requiring knowledge of writing situations in the disciplines and anticipating future academic writing assignments, a natural site for continuing conversation between Composition and WID faculty. For example, a common assignment asks students to write about writing in their majors in a social studies report format using APA documentation, interviewing a student, a professor, and another professional in the discipline about writing. The cooperation of WID professors is key to the success of this assignment, and Composition faculty are allowed to gain increasing knowledge about other disciplines through their work on student projects. (Bohr & Rhodes, 2014, p. 3)

In addition, the leaders of the program, in a coordinating role, host conversations among various faculty throughout the year, deliberately bringing together composition faculty and WID faculty to talk with each other so that they might enhance their own teaching, of course, but also to contribute to three related efforts: translating what they do for a larger audience of students; building a coherent vertical writing curriculum; and contributing to a campus-wide culture of writing.

To help facilitate this coordinated approach, the WAC leaders have created what they have called "The Glossary Project," which as its title suggests, is a compilation of writing terms representing campus writing efforts. It is useful for composition faculty, allowing them "to anticipate writing tasks for students in the disciplines" while also "encourag[ing] WID faculty to refer to basic, familiar terms in new writing contexts" (Bohr & Rhodes, 2014, p. 1). The *Glossary*, created by WEC leader Dennis Bohr in consultation with disciplinary faculty, benefiting from cross-contextual campus conversations, functions as a boundary object seeking to translate into both composition and WEC disciplinary contexts. In addition, the *Glossary*'s common language, as the website explains, can contribute to students' transfer of writing knowledge and practice:

> The WAC program holds regular conversations with Writing in the Discipline teachers through its WID consultant program, workshops, class visits, and consultations, both to enrich the English 2001 Intro to WAC course with information about writing in the disciplines and to encourage WID faculty to

build on writing experiences students have had in Composition. These conversations help us to build a *common vocabulary* for writing pedagogy that strengthens the unified writing curriculum and encourages transfer of skills and genre knowledge. Therefore, in order to facilitate conversations about writing and to have a common vocabulary when we talk about writing, we have created the *WAC Glossary of Terms*. (WAC Program, Appalachian State University, *WAC Glossary of Terms*, 2021, p.1)

The *Glossary* includes eight categories of terms, among them WID terms, writing process terms, and terms related to writing assignments. In addition, the *Glossary* links to two student-oriented projects designed both to inform students about disciplinary writing generally and to introduce them to field-specific terms. The first of these projects is "Who Writes What: A Look at Writing in Your Discipline," a website listing genres and rhetorical strategies for different fields as those have been identified by disciplinary faculty. As the image in Figure 3.1 suggests, each genre is potentially available to all fields, but the display, in the context of the full university, shows how such genres and strategies vary *across* disciplines. For example, a student can see that analysis is valued by all the disciplines on campus; that case studies are included in many fields, though not in film or geology; and that briefs are used by a very few fields.

In addition, by cross-referencing this list with the *Glossary*, students can see how even a universally valued rhetorical strategy like analysis in fact refers to very different kinds of materials and procedures. As the *Glossary* explains, in business, "analysis is a systematic examination and evaluation of data or information, by breaking it into its component parts to discover interrelationships, the opposite of synthesis"; in linguistics, "analysis is the use of separate, short words and word order rather than inflection to express grammatical structure"; in literary studies, analysis "examines the elements of a novel, play, short story, or poem (such as character, setting, tone, theme, imagery), what the author wishes to achieve using those elements, and how well he/she does it"; and in mathematics, "analysis is concerned with the theory of functions and the use of limits, continuity, and the operations of calculus. Analysis is a proof of a mathematical proposition by assuming the result and deducing a valid statement by a series of reversible steps" (WAC Program, Appalachian State University, *WAC Glossary of Terms*, 2021, pp.2–3). What is apparent here, then, is that while analysis may be a strategy all fields employ, what analysis *means* in terms of materials and processes differs rather radically across disciplines, from ascertaining the intention of a literary author to mathematics' "use of limits, continuity and the operation of calculus" (WAC Program, Appalachian State University, *WAC Glossary of Terms*, 2021, p.3).

Who Writes What: A Look at Writing in Your Discipline (Majors A-Da) — Produced by Writing Across the Curriculum wac.appstate.edu	Advertising	Agribusiness	Anthropology	Apparel Design	Appalachian Studies	Art	Automotive Studies	Broadcast Journalism	Building Science	Business	Chemistry	Commercial Photography	Communication Sciences & Disorders	Communication Studies	Computer Science	Creative Writing	Criminal Justice	Culinary Arts	Dance
Analysis	X	X	X	X	X	X	X	X	X	X	X	X	X	X	X	X	X	X	X
Annotated Bib/Lit Review											X		X	X					
Argument	X		X		X	X								X	X		X	X	X
Briefs	X						X					X					X	X	
Brochures/Newsletters	X			X		X												X	
Case Studies			X		X						X		X	X			X		
Digital Pres. (e.g. PowerPoint/Prezi)								X		X		X							
Essays			X		X	X								X	X		X	X	X
Journals	X		X		X	X					X					X	X		X
Lesson Plans/IEPs													X	X	X				
Memos/Emails				X			X		X	X		X					X	X	
Narratives					X											X			
Personal Responses	X				X	X	X					X			X				X
Portfolios					X	X				X		X		X		X			
Presentations		X	X		X	X		X	X	X				X		X		X	X
Press Releases				X		X		X	X			X		X				X	

Figure 3.1. A portion of Appalachian State's genres by majors.

The second student-oriented project tapping WID faculty expertise is a set of "Writing About" Guidelines; each set of guidelines provides a quick synopsis of writing in a field, with fields ranging from advertising and agribusiness to religious studies and sociology. Each guide includes six sections functioning as a portal for all the fields: Purpose and Audience; Types (or Genres) of Writing; Types of Evidence; Conventions, which tend to be practices other than documentation; Terms; and Documentation Style. The "Writing About History Guideline," which follows this same format, outlines the contours of historical writing at Appalachian State, its primary purpose to translate them for students' use.

In the first category, General Purpose and Audience, the focus is on what historians do and who their audiences are. As the "Guideline" says,

> Historians analyze data to develop theories about past events, ideas, experiences, or movements; to explain why or how something happened; and to place events in larger contexts. They are expected to use both primary and secondary sources, to do thorough, authoritative research, and to make a clear and

concise argument in the correct format. Audiences include peers, teachers, students, and the general public.[4] (WAC Program, Appalachian State University, *Writing about History*, 2019, p.1)

As to genres, the "Guideline" identifies four—critical essays, book reviews, research papers, and historiographic essays, this last defined as a genre focusing on how history is written and including an examination of "assumptions, biases contexts, or methods of other historians" (WAC Program, Appalachian State University, *Writing about History*, p.1). The genres of writing as represented in the "Guide" are thus more specifically disciplinary than those cited in the "Who Writes What" list, which for history includes analysis, annotated bib/lit review, argument, essays, presentations, portfolios, proposals, reports/lab reports, research, and reviews/evaluations. The difference between these two accounts of historical writing seems located in identity. The "Guideline" lists genres specific to history like historiographic essays, which the faculty themselves might compose, while the "Who Writes What" lists includes genres—like portfolios—that history faculty are unlikely to write themselves, but that they may assign to students.

As to types of evidence valued in history, a distinction is made between primary sources, defined as "material from the period being studied," including government documents, public records, diaries, and maps, and secondary sources, defined as "material that analyzes, synthesizes, or evaluates an event," including books and articles (WAC Program, Appalachian State University, *Writing about History*, 2019, p.1). At the same time, the "Guide" also helpfully observes that the source types are ambiguous and that sources can be primary, secondary, or both:

Some sources, such as newspapers and magazines, can be both primary *and* secondary sources. For example, if a historian were writing about the war in Iraq, she could use a newspaper article from that period as a primary source by citing it as an example of how journalists write about the war. But if she supported her

---

4   It's worth noting that this guideline is aligned almost perfectly with the history department's description of historical method: "At the heart of history is historical method. History involves locating, evaluating and using evidence to reconstruct and understand the past. It entails asking useful questions and being critical of the evidence found—are the sources genuine and, even if they are, is the information valid? Honest answers can still be wrong. Once the credibility of evidence is determined, information must be organized into a larger whole that can be clearly communicated." See https://history.appstate.edu/students (Department of History, 2019).

paper's argument by referring to the author of that same article as an authority on the war, she would be using the newspaper as a secondary source. (WAC Program, Appalachian State University, *Writing about History*, p.1)

And as not-quite an afterthought, the significance of peer review relative to certain kinds of materials is stipulated: "*In general, newspapers and magazines don't make good secondary sources because they are not peer-reviewed*" (WAC Program, Appalachian State University, *Writing about History*, 2019, p.1).

What we learn about writing in history here from the interlocking efforts at Appalachian State—the *Glossary Project*, the Who Writes What account, and "Writing Guide to History"—includes the genres defining history as identified by faculty—critical essays, book reviews, research papers, and historiographic essays—and the two kinds of sources that historians draw on, primary and secondary. Because the materials are intended for students, more explanation is included than might otherwise be expected, for example about different kinds of analysis in different disciplines and about the ways that a primary source in history can also be drawn on as a secondary source. Put more generally, in this account of writing in history, sourcing, and primary and secondary sources in particular, are definitive of history. In addition, again because of the explanatory intent of the Appalachian State approach, we also learn about the writing that students do *in* history; such writing goes beyond historical writing to include a larger range of genres, including portfolios and presentations, that students compose in.

NORTH CAROLINA STATE UNIVERSITY: AN OUTCOMES-ORIENTED MODEL IN THE MAJOR

The North Carolina State University WEC program is located in a larger Communication across the Curriculum (CAC) program and includes both speaking and writing. The origin of this CAC program, occurring in the late 1990s, was quite different from that of Appalachian State: rather than conceive of a horizontal and vertical WAC program, NC State came to a university CAC program through outcomes-based assessment, specifically by implementing a university requirement that all departments create outcomes for their majors, which would also provide the foundation for assessment activities. Key to this approach, then, was department outcomes-based assessment, which, as Michael Carter explains in "A Process for Establishing Outcomes-Based Assessment Plans for Writing and Speaking in the Disciplines," typically seeks answers to three questions: (1) What are the outcomes—skills, knowledge, and other attributes—that graduates of the program should attain? (2) To what extent is the program enabling its graduates to attain the outcomes? and (3) How can faculty use what they learn from program assessment to improve their programs so as to better enable graduates to attain the outcomes? (Carter, 2003, p. 6)

Writing and speaking, which were included in the outcomes-based assessment activities for all departments, were supported by a new Campus Writing and Speaking Program (CWSP), whose mission was to "provide guidance to departments for assessment and . . . offer faculty and course development related to writing and speaking" (Carter, 2003, p.7). Working with departments over a five-year period to "generate writing and speaking outcomes and procedures for evaluating those outcomes," the CWSP later also "provided additional support for faculty through an extensive program of faculty development workshops, seminars, and grants" (Carter, 2003, p. 7).

In history, the departmental outcomes were presented in a two-part format: the Program Objectives provided context for the Program Outcomes, which included three categories: (1) Historical Awareness, Perspective, and Understanding; (2) Historical Research Skills; and (3) Historical Expression. As the categories suggest, the outcomes are discipline-specific, a defining feature responding directly to the kinds of questions, largely about the uniqueness of the discipline, that faculty were generally asked to consider in creating outcomes:

Imagine an ideal graduate from your program. What kinds of skills, knowledge, or other attributes characterize that graduate? What is it that attracts students to this program? What value does this program offer a student? How do you know whether your students possess the kinds of abilities, knowledge, skills, and attributes you expect of them? What kinds of assignments or other activities do people in this program use to encourage the kinds of abilities, knowledge, and skills you have identified? What is it that distinguishes this program from related programs in the university? Is there anything about your program that makes it stand out from other similar programs? . . . What sorts of speaking and writing do professionals in this field do on the job? What sorts of speaking and writing do students do in their classes? Are there any particular types of communication that people this field are expected to master? (Carter, 2003, p. 15)

Using such questions as a heuristic, faculty in history, like their colleagues in other departments, completed four steps culminating in a review and plan for improvement:

> (1) determine writing and speaking outcomes for its majors, (2) create plans for assessing those outcomes, (3) implement those assessment plans, and (4) report its assessment findings to the Council on Undergraduate Education periodically and show how those findings have led to the improvement of students' writing and speaking through changes in courses or curricula. (Anson et al., 2003, p. 29)

As important, the materials collected and methods employed for assessment purposes were diverse and rich, among them surveys of faculty, surveys of students' research skills, senior exit interviews, and portfolios of student writing.

Given the NC State WEC program's emphasis on assessable disciplinary departmental outcomes, it's probably not surprising that the objectives and outcomes for history are specifically historical and targeted to the major. The Program Objectives speak to both the student-as-major and to the department's role in contributing to the development of the student-as-major, specifically constructing this student as someone who has developed "historical awareness, perspective, and understanding"; the department's role in this model is to help majors apply "sound historical research skills" (History Department, 2001, p.1) so as to critique others' arguments and create historical arguments themselves. Here, then, the analysis in history emphasized by Appalachian State is part of a larger interest in historical argument.

The commitment to historical sources expressed by Appalachian State, however, is also one shared by NC State, in the latter case focusing quite specifically on activities writers conduct *with* sources in order to make historical knowledge. Under the heading of Historical Awareness, Perspective, and Understanding, the role of knowledge and understanding is emphasized, with graduates expected to explain the historical development of events, institutions, and social values in western and non-western cultures and to identify "historical continuities and discontinuities." Understanding is also important for Historical Research Skills, the second outcomes category, which identifies writing activities history majors will undertake:

> Graduates of the history program should understand the
> nature of historical interpretation, the variety of historical
> sources, and the structure of historical argument and be able
> to apply that understanding to answering historical questions.

Specifically, graduates should demonstrate that they can:

a. pose a significant research question about history

b. locate relevant primary and secondary sources for investigating a research question

c. critically evaluate primary and secondary sources in terms of credibility, authenticity, interpretive stance, audience, potential biases, and value for answering the research question

d. interpret the sources fairly and accurately in an answer to a research question

e. marshal the evidence from the research to support a historical argument for an answer to a research question (History Department, 2001, p. 1)

This statement about writing in history links the *significant research question about history* to *evidence*—identified here as *primary and secondary sources*—that can be *marshaled to support a historical argument for an answer to a research question*. These sources, referred to in three of the five practices, are the key materials of the research process oriented to, and culminating in, answering a significant historical question. As important, the sources need to be worked with: both *evaluated*—in terms of *credibility, authenticity, interpretive stance, audience, potential biases, and value for answering the research question*—and *interpreted* so as to *answer* a research question *accurately and fairly*. Put more generally, sourcing is important, but as important is what a student of history, as student or faculty, *does with* the sources, especially in the context of answering a significant question. Likewise, under Historical Expression, the third outcome, students are identified as "informed and critical consumers and producers of history" able to work with sources—their "quality," "the validity of the interpretations of those sources, and the soundness of the argument's use of evidence to support a historical interpretation" (History Department, 2001, p.2). In terms of genres, much like students at Appalachian State, students at North Carolina State write in genres specific to history like "the critical book review" and the "historical narrative based on sources" (History Department, 2001, p.2) as well as in more generalized classroom-texts like a summary of readings.

The history department at North Carolina State University thus expresses values closely aligned with those of Appalachian State University's history department, especially regarding sources: for both history departments, sources are critical for writing in history. It's worth noting as well that in developing his meta-genres approach to disciplinary discourse based on the WEC activity at NC State as published in a Braddock Award-winning *CCC* article, Michael Carter drew on history's commitment to sources precisely to illustrate one meta-genre, what he called "Responses to Academic Situations that Call for Research from Sources":

> The two primary distinguishing characteristics of this meta-genre are (1) the kind of research that is done, that is, not based on data gathered from independent observations but largely on sources that have their origins elsewhere; and (2) the goal of the research, which typically does not have extrinsic value, such as solving practical problems or investigating hypotheses, but value that is intrinsic to the discipline. . . . (Carter, 2007, p. 398)

In addition, the NC State History Department identifies and underscores how sources, through critical examination and evaluation, contribute to the making of knowledge in historical arguments. In other words, in more fully defining the role of sources in history-making, the NC State history program approach echoes and adds to the approach articulated by historians at Appalachian State University.

UNIVERSITY OF MINNESOTA: A DEPARTMENTALLY ORIENTED MODEL OF GENERAL EDUCATION AND DISCIPLINARY WRITING

The point of departure for the University of Minnesota writing enriched curriculum (WEC) was different yet again: an earlier writing intensive program that wasn't thriving. According to WEC Director Pamela Flash, focus groups with faculty, conducted over several years, pointed to many problems with the writing intensive program, among them that faculty resisted incorporating writing into their classes, that their definitions of writing and the teaching of writing were surprisingly narrow, and that the approach to the teaching of writing, even within the same department, was disorganized and chaotic. In this context, effective writing was defined as "clear writing," and because student ability was perceived as declining, writing instruction was defined as remedial, emphasizing "clear structures" and reducing time available for "content." In addition,

> [s]ympathy was offered to those recruited to teach the writing intensive courses, and resistance was aimed at the bureaucratic procedures required to certify them, but little consideration

was given to developing alternative methods for ensuring that students graduated as able writers. Faculty members within departments had not identified harmonious or divergent writing values or outcomes they expected students in their majors to be able to demonstrate by the time they graduated and had only the sketchiest of ideas about who was requiring what in which course down the corridor. (Flash, 2016, p. 232)

As a remedy, Flash, in developing the subsequent WEC model of WAC, "changed points of contact," focusing not on instructional practices as the earlier program had, but rather on "faculty conceptions of writing and writing instruction. These become the *trigger points for change* rather than the inevitable and ignorable *reactions to change*" (Flash, 2016, p. 232). Operationalized, the trigger points are departmentally focused, year-long reflective discussions about disciplinary writing—what its questions, evidence, and genres are—informed by multiple kinds of data documenting departmental writing efforts and perceptions of those efforts, including "meeting summaries, survey data, curricular maps, and writing samples." By the conclusion of the year-long investigation, departments create "First-Edition Writing Plans" articulating outcomes and expectations for their courses, both general education courses, much like Appalachian State University, and courses in the major, like both Appalachian State and North Carolina State University.

Like other units at the University of Minnesota, the history department has developed writing plans iteratively.[5] An early adopter of the WEC model, the department created its first plan in 2007–2008; a second plan in 2009; and as a consequence of several factors including declining funding, declining majors, and instructive assessment data, a third plan in 2014. In the 2014 plan, the department also commented on the changes between the first and third plans; in the third plan, for instance, the outcomes for general education history courses as compared to expectations for upper-level courses for the major are more clearly delineated. At both levels, as the 2014 writing plan notes, "Doing history means writing history," but both writing practices and genres also vary across this vertical curriculum.

The history department offers a "flexible" curriculum, with considerable opportunity for students to elect their courses, with each course helping "all students in history courses become well-informed and thoughtful about historical knowledge, familiar with at least the basic processes by which historical

---

5   After a year of implementation, writing plans are revised and include proposed next-step activities. Second edition plans, implemented for two years, are followed by third-edition plans and so on.

knowledge is produced, and practiced in the multiple functions of writing involved in that production" (Writing-Enriched Curriculum Program, University of Minnesota: History Writing Plan, 2019, p. 3). Interestingly, then, both historical writing processes and the functions of writing are emphasized, and much as at both Appalachian State University and North Carolina State University, the genres these students will write in include school genres as well as those specific to history: "Virtually all History courses require students to write in genres ranging from informal in-class 'free writes,' blog entries and short response papers to substantial scholarly essays based on original research" (Writing-Enriched Curriculum Program, University of Minnesota: History Writing Plan, 2019, p. 5).

The writing curriculum in history is divided into four parts: 1000-level Foundation courses; 3000-level Foundation courses; 3000-level lecture courses; and the senior research seminars. The Foundation courses are four-credit writing-intensive courses with lab or discussion sessions attached, their purpose to "combine the delivery of historical content with small group activities that expose students to the fundamentals of working as practicing historians, thereby serving as introductory courses for non-majors as well as courses that prepare majors" (Writing-Enriched Curriculum Program, University of Minnesota: History Writing Plan, 2019, p. 5). The 1000-level Foundations courses include six outcomes, two of which are conceptual—"Introduction to the concept of historical interpretation and scholarly argumentation" and "Distinction between appropriate reference to scholarship and plagiarism; concept of scholarly citation concepts and practices"; one of which is genre-oriented—"Short response papers and/or analytic essays that make an argument"; and three of which are process-oriented—"Analysis of primary sources," "Development of a thesis statement," and "Revision in response to feedback." (Writing-Enriched Curriculum Program, University of Minnesota: History Writing Plan, 2019, p. 7).

In this early-in-college model of historical writing, then, there is a mix of general and historical writing activity, much as at Appalachian State University and North Carolina State University: both majors and non-majors, for example, compose texts that are oriented to writing to learn, like fairly generic "response papers," and as part of engaging in writing processes, they revise. At the same time, however, students also begin writing as historians; in composing texts including historical interpretation and scholarly argumentation, students rely on and analyze primary sources. The University of Minnesota history outcomes for the first year, then, combine the analysis of Appalachian State with the argument of North Carolina State, but they differ from Appalachian State in their exclusive focus on primary sources.

The 3000-level Foundations and 3000-level writing intensive lecture courses share the same outcomes; when those are compared to outcomes for the 1000-level Foundations courses, the beginnings of a more sophisticated notion of historical writing, even for non-majors, appears. Seven outcomes are included, some of them repetitions of the 1000-level Foundations outcomes (e.g., revision; plagiarism), others new. For example, historical interpretation is included, as is the "Concept of historiography"; and the "Distinction between primary and secondary sources" is added to "Analysis of a primary source." Generally, the shifts in this set of outcomes, however, seem more conceptual (e.g., concept of historiography) than practice-oriented, in effect helping students *see* how history is written rather than asking them to write it themselves.

That changes with the 4000-level research seminars designed for the major. Based both on faculty experiences teaching the course and on assessment data, the history department designed a new 4000-level research seminar to replace the earlier two-semester 3000–4000 level sequence, which they also had trouble staffing and which produced assessment results that concerned them.

> The outcome of this review was the determination that the Hist 3959–Hist 4961 sequence fell short of our desired outcomes for student writing in several critical respects. In particular, the results suggested that students had problems with formulating their research question clearly, with building an argument based on multiple primary sources, and with critical engagement of the sources. (Writing-Enriched Curriculum Program, University of Minnesota: History Writing Plan, 2019, p. 10)

Eleven outcomes govern the new research seminars, six of which differ from the earlier outcomes. Some of them, like "Concept of historical interpretation, including the complexity of an author's standpoint and what can be at stake when writing history" and "Concept of evidence-based argumentation, including the varied uses of sources and the relationship between object and context in the writing of history," are more disciplinary-specific elaborations of earlier outcomes. Especially interesting here is "what can be at stake when writing history," signaling that the writing of history has consequences, and "the varied use of sources," indicating that while distinctions between primary and secondary sources are important, making an argument requires "varied [source] use." Other new outcomes stipulate historical writing processes oriented to the making of historical knowledge:

- Formulation of historical research questions that are feasible, and meaningful identification of appropriate primary and secondary sources

- Synthetic review of historical scholarship on an aspect of the seminar topic, such as an article, chapter or book summary that assesses the argument and use of evidence
- Development and writing of a historical research proposal, including a synthetic literature review, a research plan, and an annotated bibliography
- Research paper (20–30 pp.) on an issue relating to seminar topic and utilizing both primary and secondary sources

The research question here takes center stage; to write like historians, students must identify a *feasible* project that can be developed through the use of *meaningful* primary and secondary sources. Critical to the success of such writing for the University of Minnesota is working with "multiple primary sources"; indeed, the work with sources is so important that it focuses two of the four new outcomes. More generally, what this set of outcomes does, in terms of defining historical writing, is to qualify it yet again: historical projects must be *feasible*, their sources *multiple* and *meaningful*.

What successful writing in history requires, as documented across all three WEC history departments, can be defined: its critical, fundamental practice is sourcing, and the issues accompanying it. How sourcing plays out—when primary and secondary sources are introduced, for instance, as well as what practices, such as establishing credibility, sources should be subjected to—differs some across these programs, as we have seen. Both primary and secondary sources are incorporated early in a student's career at Appalachian State and North Carolina State, the purpose at North Carolina State University and the University of Minnesota to make a historical argument. In this sense, the WEC approach as engaged in by faculty in history highlights not what characterizes all college writing,[6] but rather what characterizes writing in history—sources, work with sources, and use of sources for historical argument. Also critical to success in historical writing is "formulating . . . a research question clearly" (Writing-Enriched Curriculum Program, University of Minnesota: History Writing Plan, 2019, p. 10), as identified by North Carolina State and as more clearly specified by the University of Minnesota. Historical writing, as defined by these three WEC programs, thus takes up well designed feasible research questions (UMN), relies on sophisticated analysis (Appalachian State), and makes varied use (UMN) of both primary and secondary sources (all), in order to make knowledge (UMN) typically developed through an argument (North Carolina State; UMN).

---

6   Although some historians, at least, believe that their approach to evidence has implications for the critical thinking of all college students: see Flaherty and Wineberg, et al.

CONCLUSION

Sam Wineberg, a scholar who has studied the way history is taught in high schools and colleges, identifies what he claims are the three primary research practices contributing to the making of history. Historians, he says, call on many strategies: chief among them are sourcing, contextualizing and corroborating historical information. In this chapter and drawing from Wineberg's definition, *context* for how historians in WEC programs have identified disciplinary writing features has been provided and *sources* for this interpretation cited. Continuing to think as historians, we could ask, what *corroboration* regarding the definition of historical writing provided by these three WEC programs, especially with their emphasis on sourcing as defining practice, might be available?

One source of corroboration, in fact, might be the continuing research conducted by Wineberg himself, although his primary focus targets less the writing in history, more the ways history should be taught. Looking elsewhere, we might consult organizations representing scholars in history like the American Historical Association (AHA), whose purpose is to serve as "a trusted voice advocating for history education, the professional work of historians, and the critical role of historical thinking in public life" (AHA Website). Recently, the AHA has expressed official concern about a practice important to historians, students' critical thinking skills, especially in response to some evidence indicating that history courses are not enhancing such skills.[7] In an effort to remedy this situation, the 2019 annual AHA conference highlighted several panels focused on the distinguishing features of history-making as a kind of critical thinking. In the context of the WEC discussion here, one panel in particular stands out for its corroboration of the WEC-generated conclusions about writing in history.[8] That session, "What Are We Learning? Innovative Assessments and Student Learning in College-Level History Classes," included two presentations relevant to writing in history, "'I Got It!': Primary Source Analysis and Formative Assessment in an Introductory-Level Classroom" and "Sourcing Is Damn Hard to Learn." As their titles suggest, these talks directly refer to the role of sourcing in history: what their authors say about history and the making of history aligns with the claims made about history by the WEC programs documented above.

One panelist, Augustana College professor Lendol Calder, who believes that sourcing is sufficiently important that it serves as one of history's threshold concepts, conducted a study of student sourcing with results he described

---

7   Much like perceptions of writing, which some see as universalized, perceptions of critical thinking can take similar form.

8   The information reported here on the AHA panels is synthesized from a story on the conference in *Inside Higher Ed*. See Flaherty (2019).

as "disappointing": "In general . . . students either take any historical source at face value or—when they discover it was created by a human being—dismiss it outright as 'biased'" (quoted in Flaherty. NP). To address this concern, he and his colleagues in the history department at Augustana discuss historical sourcing in "every single class." In addition, they have created something of a campaign around history-making, captured in the acronym LASER: "Love history, Acquire and analyze information, Solve difficult problems, Envision new explanations, and Reveal what you know." Panelist Catherine Denial, Bright Professor of American History at Knox College, agreed, arguing that the "invisible processes at work in learning history," including observation and careful analysis of primary source materials, need to be taught. To support students in this endeavor, she too has created a scaffolding tool, in her case "a primary source analysis template" called SOCC, which "asks students to examine a primary-source document for sourcing (its origins), to observe it, to contextualize it based on existing knowledge and draw hypotheses about its meaning, and to corroborate it with other primary and secondary materials and test their hypotheses." Denial emphasizes primary-source analysis because, as she says, "students who engage in primary-source analysis get to become historians, piecing together the past for themselves. It's tremendously empowering and gives them a new perspective on secondary sources, as well as setting them up for the research they'll do in higher-level courses."

Admittedly, the claims presented at this AHA panel address history-making, not history writing per se, but writing in history, as defined in the WEC programs profiled here, is a practice of history-making that history writing articulates and represents: history making is part and parcel of history writing. Moreover, for the WEC faculty at three institutions described here, history writing, as it is for their colleagues at AHA, *is* sourcing: a practice of working with primary and secondary sources to make historical arguments. Such sources, furthermore, provide the centerpiece for research questions framing historical arguments. The delineation of historical thinking at the three institutions profiled here, then, aligns with that presented at AHA: to write in history, one begins with and follows the sources.

As important, numerous WEC documents—among them, Writing Guides at Appalachian State University; outcome statements at, and scholarly reports emerging from, North Carolina State University; and successive writing plans at the University of Minnesota—build from the epistemology of history to articulate what successful writing in that discipline requires.

Motivated to support student writers in the field of history and supported themselves by WEC facilitators, faculty focus on what makes writing in history work, on what genres define history, on what practices historical writers engage in, and on how those practices can be scaffolded such that students write with greater nuance and sophistication. As a rhetorical strategy, argument is a centerpiece; the materials it relies on are always and already multiple—multiple sources and multiple kinds of sources that are rich, authentic, contextualized, evaluated, and interpreted. Thus, while the WEC documents expressing these practices were designed for other purposes, chiefly curricular and pedagogical, they nonetheless encapsulate the foundational principles, logic, and features of history's writing.

This chapter has explored and named the principles and features of writing in history by reading the discipline's writing practices and values as represented in different institutions hosting WEC; based on this reflective analysis, we can confidently make claims about writing in history. But this approach isn't limited to history, of course: by applying this approach to other disciplines, we can identify their principles and features as well. Put another way, as WEC leaders engage disciplinary faculty in articulating the writing in their fields for curricular purposes, they also create documents—among them, writing guides, outcomes statements, transcripts of conversations, assessment reports, and writing plans—collectively identifying and defining the key features of such writing. Through engaging in a similar inter-institutional review of each of the many disciplines as represented in such WEC documents, we can create a larger, more detailed, and more comprehensive map of various kinds of disciplinary writing, one informed by the practitioners of the disciplines themselves. Such a project is valuable in two intertwined ways: first, as a Boyer-like scholarship of discovery research project, it can document, for the first time, as exemplified here, the practices and genres of disciplinary writing as articulated by faculty constituents at different campuses; and second, it provides a mechanism to design disciplinary writing curricula and pedagogy that is important to all of us—WEC programs; faculty; students; and higher education writ large—who care about student writing.

REFERENCES

Adler-Kassner, L., Majewski, J. & Koshnick, D. (2012). The value of troublesome knowledge: Transfer and threshold concepts in writing and history. *Composition Forum, 26.* https://compositionforum.com/issue/26/troublesome-knowledge -threshold.php.

American Historical Association. https://www.historians.org/.

Anson, C. M. (2021). The new grass roots: Faculty responses to the writing-enriched curriculum. In C. M. Anson & P. Flash (Eds.), *Writing-enriched curricula: Models of faculty-driven and departmental transformation.* The WAC Clearinghouse; University Press of Colorado. https://doi.org/10.27514/PER-B.2021.1299.2.02.

Anson, C. M., Carter, M., Dannels, D. P. & Rust, J. (2003). Mutual support: CAC programs and institutional improvement in undergraduate education. *Language and Learning Across the Disciplines, 6,* 25–37. https://doi.org/10.37514/LLD-J.2003 .6.3.06.

Bohr, D. J. & Rhodes, G. (2014). The WAC glossary project: facilitating conversations between composition and WID faculty in a unified writing curriculum. *Across the Disciplines, 11*(1). https://doi.org/10.37514/ATD-J.2014.11.1.02.

Carter, M. (2003). A process for establishing outcomes-based assessment plans for writing and speaking in the disciplines. *Language and Learning across the Disciplines, 6*(1), 1–29. https://doi.org/10.37514/LLD-J.2003.6.1.02.

Carter, M. (2007). Ways of knowing, doing, and writing in the disciplines. *College Composition and Communication, 58*(3), 385–418.

Department of History. (2019). Appalachian State University. https://history.appstate .edu/students.

Flaherty, C. (2019, January 4). Grading smarter, not harder: Historians discuss efforts to evaluate learning far beyond a grade. *Inside Higher Ed,* Jan. 4. https://www. insidehighered.com/news/2019/01/04/do-historians-miss-ideals-assessment-some -have-suggested.

Flash, P. (2021). Writing-enriched curriculum: A model for making and sustaining change. In C. M. Anson & P. Flash (Eds.), *Writing-enriched curricula: Models of faculty-driven and departmental transformation.* The WAC Clearinghouse; University Press of Colorado. https://doi.org/10.27514/PER-B.2021.1299.2.01.

Flash, P. (2016). From apprised to revised: Faculty in the disciplines change what they never knew they knew. In K. B. Yancey (Ed.), *A Rhetoric of reflection* (pp. 227–249). Utah State University Press.

Green, S., Keremidchieva, Z., Zimmerman, H., Rice, A., Witus, L., Rodwogir, M. & Pardini, R. (2017). Developing students' multi-modal and transferable writing skills in introductory general chemistry. *The WAC Journal, 28*(1), 106–122. https://doi .org/10.37514/WAC-J.2017.28.1.05.

History Department, North Carolina State University: Program Review. (2001). https://web.archive.org/web/20040303114400/http://www2.chass.ncsu.edu:80 /cwsp/docs/hist_outcomes.pdf.

Sheriff, S. (2020). Beyond "I know it when I see it": WEC and the process of unearthing faculty expertise. In C. M. Anson & P. Flash (Eds.), *Writing-enriched curricula: Models of faculty-driven and departmental transformation.* The WAC Clearinghouse; University Press of Colorado. https://doi.org/10.27514/PER-B .2021.1299.2.06.

Writing-Enriched Program, University of Minnesota: History Writing Plan. (2019). http://archive.undergrad.umn.edu/cwb/pdf/history.pdf.

WAC Program: Appalachian State University. (2019). https://wac.appstate.edu.

WAC Program: Appalachian State University. (2021). *WAC Glossary of Terms: Writing-Related Terminology.* https://docs.google.com/document/d/1T6a_ueXpEjd4JVGH 0jcLklpLIqq_cVkxzu7063yifZ4/edit.

WAC Program: Appalachian State University. (2021). Writing about History. https://docs.google.com/document/d/1GwVgv3k930gDLP6MSHVAh-I0L7VOjE85MJAz-72yF80/edit.

Wineberg, S. (2001). *Historical thinking and other unnatural acts*. Stanford University Press.

Wineberg, S., Smith, M. & Breakstone, J. (2018). What is learned in college history classes? *Journal of American History, 104*, 983–993.

Yancey, K. B. (2015). Relationships between writing and critical thinking, and their significance for curriculum and pedagogy. *Double Helix, 3*, 1–14. https://doi.org/10.37514/DBH-J.2015.3.1.02.

CHAPTER 4.

BEYOND CONVENTIONS: LIMINALITY AS A FEATURE OF THE WEC FACULTY DEVELOPMENT

Matthew Luskey and Daniel L. Emery

University of Minnesota

While many colleges and universities employ writing across the curriculum (WAC) and writing in disciplines (WID) programs, the embedded and faculty-driven character of the WEC program allows for a reconsideration of faculty development activities and the roles of writing professionals. This chapter argues that the structured conversations of the WEC model both unearth tacit assumptions about disciplinary writing and student learning and often challenge persistent assumptions regarding what writing is and how it works. Much as students encounter liminality in their transitions from novice outsiders to disciplinary insiders, faculty experience their own process of change and transformation, complete with the discomfort and resistance that such transformations imply. As faculty engage each other in understanding the constitutive character of writing in shaping knowledge, they often move well beyond an interest in policing surface-level conventions. Two case studies from the University of Minnesota illustrate how faculty members in departments negotiate this transition and revise their orientations toward writing through the WEC process, and how a transformed orientation toward writing leads to engaged, thoughtful, and sustained curricular change.

Several universities can lay claim to a curricular emphasis on writing across the curriculum, from pioneers at Carleton College and Beaver College to the dozens of programs identified by the WAC Clearinghouse and taxonomized by Condon and Rutz (2012). The University of Minnesota's Writing-Enriched Curriculum (WEC) Program emerged from a Bush Foundation grant in 2007. Like North Carolina State University, it provides one of the first examples of both curricular engagement with writing and faculty-led writing interventions in undergraduate curricula. In contrast to centrally administered WAC programs that might construct writing outcomes on behalf of departments and programs, WEC puts resources into the hands of faculty members—those most capable of making and sustaining institutional change—who design and compose their own goals for undergraduate writing and their own assessment criteria used to measure students' success. While these resources do entail some financial and administrative assistance, provided by the Office of Undergraduate Education, they are primarily interpersonal. WEC succeeds due to the collective and collaborative work between faculty, graduate students, and WAC consultants.

Departments at the University of Minnesota are enticed by the fact that WEC is a funded and non-mandated program for voluntary faculty development. However, this unique structure gives rise to two central questions: How can a program founded upon multiyear, voluntary commitments from departments and colleges thrive in a research-extensive university? What sustains WEC once enacted? We believe the answers to these questions lie in the durable partnerships and collaborations between WAC consultants and faculty members within WEC departments—partnerships that develop through frank and open discussion, what one department chair has described as a "structured conversation" bolstered by the use of data and assessments.

In this chapter, we look carefully at the features of these structured conversations and the ways in which the sequence of WEC meetings unearth long-held suppositions about writing and often change them. As Anson argues in "Crossing Thresholds: What's to Know about Writing Across the Curriculum" (2015), despite their records of publication and their leadership in their disciplinary specialties, faculty rarely consider themselves masters of disciplinary writing. Their discourse knowledge is often "buried in the tacit domain," operating in a manner below the surface of awareness and reinforcing persistent views that writing is a skill students should have learned earlier and should carry with them in "every writing situation without regard for disciplinary variation or convention" (p.206). Those already acculturated to disciplinary norms and practices may take the unique features of writing in their field to be identical to "scientific writing" or "good writing." For WAC consultants who work closely with faculty through this process of (re)examining deeply held assumptions, this presents some challenges. Unexamined assumptions are laden with specific values and expectations, and these assumptions may create barriers to student success. As Anson succinctly notes, "the hard work begins in implementation" (p. 213), and "requires great sensitivity to existing (mis)conceptions of the nature of writing and the roles and purposes associated with its cross-disciplinary development" (p. 216).

To closely analyze "the hard work of implementation" that accompanies WAC work and faculty development, we extend Anson's use of threshold concepts by drawing specifically on the concept of liminality. Liminality, an often prolonged stage of conceptual transition, provides a lens for examining faculty struggle throughout the WEC process; liminality also offers us a lens for viewing our own struggles as WAC consultants along with the struggle of many undergraduate students as they attempt to meet often tacit expectations for discipline-based writing. In order to understand the threshold-crossing character of conceptual change, we think it useful to begin with a key illustration that exposes student and faculty assumptions about writing—assumptions that are often a key impetus for the structured conversations that WEC enables.

As Flash has detailed in Chapter 1 of this volume, WEC begins by engaging faculty with survey information from departmental faculty, students, and affiliates about the attitudes, values, and practices of writing within their disciplines. A question set in the surveys never fails to elicit chatter among the faculty in our first meeting: student self-assessment and faculty assessment of students' writing abilities. We ask students to consider the writing they do for courses in their major and to rate their abilities ("strong," "satisfactory," "weak," "don't know," "N/A") on fifteen common dimensions of writing, such as their ability to "use field-specific terminology, organizational formats and/or conventions," their ability to "argue a position using a central thesis or hypothesis and evidence," "analyze and/or evaluate ideas, texts, or events," "integrate and correctly cite information," and so on. Working with these same dimensions of writing, faculty answer parallel questions considering the writing students do for their courses and their impression of students' abilities. We have administered this survey to 44 departments, programs, and colleges, hundreds of faculty and instructors and thousands of students, but we have only once seen a consistent alignment between the students' rating of their abilities and the faculty's rating of their students' abilities. In that one instance, the majority of courses offered for undergraduates were staffed with instructors and graduate students, while tenured faculty taught principally in the graduate curriculum. In this department, the graduate student instructors were much like the faculty in all the other surveys who tended to take a dimmer, half-empty view of student abilities.

The examples in Table 4.1—one from a humanities discipline, one from social sciences, and one from STEM—illustrate the typical gap between students' self-assessment and the faculty's impressions of student writing. For purposes of this illustration, we present four of fifteen abilities, though the gap typically extends across all or most of the abilities. Each of the results represents the highest percentage of responses from the students and faculty.

Table 4.1. Faculty and student assessments of students' writing

A Humanities Department Rate the strength of writing done (for courses that count towards the major) in terms of the following:	Strong	Satis-factory	Weak	Don't know	N/A
Use field specific terminology and formats		Students	Faculty		
Argue a position using a thesis or hypothesis	Students	Faculty			
Analyze and/or evaluate ideas, texts, or events	Students		Faculty		
Integrate and correctly cite information	Students		Faculty		

A Social Science Department Rate the strength of writing done (for courses that count towards the major) in terms of the following:	Strong	Satis-factory	Weak	Don't know	N/A
Use field specific terminology and formats		Students	Faculty		
Argue a position using a thesis or hypothesis	Students		Faculty		
Analyze and/or evaluate ideas, texts, or events	Students		Faculty		
Integrate and correctly cite information	Students		Faculty		

A STEM Department Rate the strength of writing done (for courses that count towards the major) in terms of the following:	Strong	Satis-factory	Weak	Don't know	N/A
Use field specific terminology and formats		Faculty Students			
Argue a position using a thesis or hypothesis		Students	Faculty		
Analyze and/or evaluate ideas, texts, or events		Students	Faculty		
Integrate and correctly cite information	Students	Faculty			

Such perception gaps are likely familiar to WAC professionals. Students approach their self-assessment from the vantage point of how far they've come, whereas faculty approach their rating of students from the vantage point of how far they have to go. A quick glance might also suggest this gap is indicative of cognitive biases, or, more cheekily, of student grade inflation and faculty members' predispositions to complain. It may also reveal discourse expectations and standards reflective of the demographics and educational experience of faculty, which differ from current undergraduate populations. However, it's often the case in our first WEC meeting with faculty, when these results are discussed, that faculty perceive this gap as something more substantial—namely, an incomplete or insufficient understanding of the conventions and rigors of disciplinary discourses. This excerpt from an M1 meeting in a social science discipline is symptomatic of such a view:

> **F1:** It seems the vast majority of students think they are good writers, suggesting they are not getting accurate feedback in the first-year writing course.
>
> **WAC Consultant:** Why would that suggestion be limited to the first-year writing course? Why do you think students have a stronger opinion of their skills?
>
> **F2:** So maybe it's that we are asking them to do scientific writing when the excellent writing they were doing in the first year was just not as complicated. Students often tell me they have always been told they are good writers, and they are not. I feel they are reaching back to high school when they were top of the class.
>
> **F3:** Maybe they were doing creative writing and we are asking them to do something in a new domain here.
>
> **F4:** In my freshman class, the majority of them have never written more than five pages and they are not prepared to write a research paper at all. (WEC meeting Fall 2014)

In response to the WAC consultant's prompting question, the faculty braid two common strands. The first, voiced by Faculty 1 and more bluntly by Faculty 2, is that prior student writing has lacked critical feedback and instruction—a failure of general writing instruction. The second, expressed by Faculty 2, 3, and 4, is that students have lacked exposure to the modes and genres important to writing in the discipline—a failure of genre-specific writing instruction. Both strands might seem reductive and dismissive of students' educational backgrounds, especially the perception that prior student writing has been primarily "creative" rather than academic. Nevertheless, these sentiments, commonly voiced in early WEC conversations, speak to a persistent frustration about student writing that emerges when faculty begin the WEC process.

We begin with the WEC survey and the spirited faculty discussion it fosters in the first WEC meeting because it illustrates a crucial gap between student and faculty assessment of writing ability, and it uncovers persistent differences in attitude, outlook, and experience that accord with our understanding of the transformative character of threshold concepts. We view these initial differences as highlighting important conceptual and epistemological divisions between faculty and students, between experts and novices, indicative of those who have already been initiated in disciplinary discourses and those who have yet to experience a process of acculturation. These liminal spaces are marked by a lack of shared vocabulary, expectations, and awareness, and often engender mutually expressed frustration, leading to reductive and totalizing statements, such as the faculty member's claim that "students often tell me that have always been told they are good writers, and they are not." Alternatively, consider this representative comment from a student in a social science discipline, which appears in the open response section of the WEC survey: "There's a guessing process on what [faculty] want which is probably my most frustrating thing because I do the paper in one shot—no drafts allowed—and it's like, well, I hope that's what they wanted because that's what they're getting" (WEC student survey response, 2015).

Identifying and traversing these liminal spaces is at the heart of the University of Minnesota's WEC model. To theorize this space, we turn to the educational literature of threshold concepts, driven by the efforts of Meyer and Land (Meyer & Land, 2006; Meyer et al., 2010) and extended by Adler-Kassner and Wardle in their edited volumes, *Naming What We Know: Threshold Concepts of Writing Studies* (2015) and *(Re)considering what We Know: Learning Thresholds in Writing, Composition, Rhetoric, and Literacy (2019)*. A number of international conferences and a quickly expanding bibliography (https://www.ee.ucl .ac.uk/~mflanaga/thresholds.html) attest to the powerful allure of threshold concepts for examining complex educational processes. In working with this literature, we share Perkins' view (as cited by Land 2015) that the appeal of threshold concepts lies essentially in their heuristic value, that "threshold concepts work better when more exploratory and eclectic than categorical and taxonomic" (p. xiii). Drawing on their heuristic value, we maintain that the WEC model affords extensive and sustained opportunities for faculty, students, and WAC consultants to encounter and engage with liminal states of understanding, especially when it comes to the complex relationship between writing and conceptual and disciplinary knowledge.

Given the confines of this chapter, however, we focus primarily on the liminal features of WEC work as it applies to the faculty members in departments with whom we work. Artifacts of the WEC process, including meeting transcripts, rating reports, surveys, and sections of departmental writing plans are often laced with faculty members' bold assertions and convictions alongside genuine, open-ended questions, which are subsequently re-examined, further qualified, and often revised. We maintain that these oscillating points of view evidence the liminal state, described by Turner in *The Ritual Process* (1969) as "generative" and "speculative," that provides an opportunity for sustainable and structural change (cited in Hyde, 1998, p. 121). That is, though liminality is no guarantee of transformation, it is the catalyst if such a transformation is to occur.

We would like to acknowledge three premises that guide our argument. First, evident in our earlier reference to Anson's chapter, "Crossing Thresholds," our line of reasoning is premised on the view that those interested in the development of student writing must recognize and take seriously the distinct rhetorical situations in academic writing that cannot be blithely attributed to a student's lack of familiarity with the textual features or discursive conventions of academic writing. Indeed, our work remains deeply informed by a view shared by many other WAC practitioners that thinking and writing are both inextricable and situated. To write well in one's field, one must think well in the field; likewise, good writing reflects good thinking, not simply grammatical correctness, compliance with standard written English, or citational accuracy. Second, we, as WAC consultants, must also acknowledge that as inveterate outsiders to the disciplines and departments we work with, we often confront and negotiate our own liminal understanding of the rich and various disciplinary conventions and epistemologies that shape discursive practices. WEC imposes a productive humility on WAC consultants who, though steeped in writing pedagogy and genre theory, lack advanced training in many of the disciplines. While this chapter focuses on ways that our faculty colleagues grapple productively with liminal views of writing and conceptual knowledge, we witness this liminality from our own liminal vantage as well. As other contributors to this volume describe in their chapters, WEC work often raises questions of ethos for WAC consultants. This, in turn, leads to our third premise, which is that our own liminality with disciplinary concepts and discourses enables us to approximate students who are themselves apprenticing in their disciplinary fields. Although student writing samples drive much of the discussion throughout the WEC process, students, themselves, are rarely present in the conversation. Their voices emerge indirectly in survey responses, often quite cogently and plaintively describing their own liminal experiences with writing in their majors. Consider, for example, these two responses from students in a social science discipline:

I've found an intimidating barrier to entry in the language and presentation in the professional literature whenever I've needed to reference such resources, which brilliantly sabotages my confidence of ever completing the assignment that required their use in the first place. I understand that I am not likely the target audience for the literature and, instead, it is probably meant for real [experts]. . . .

It has been implied, if not explicitly stated, that the writing we do should be a contribution to the field. Personally, this seems impossible. Probably I am not creative enough to find a writing topic to research that anybody would consider a worthwhile contribution to [the field]. But even if I could find such a topic, I feel that my education has left me with few tools to articulate, let alone perform, a coherent analysis. (WEC student survey responses, 2013).

By proxying student perspectives in WEC meetings, we can often question faculty assumptions about students, whether innocent, dismissive, or callous. Unearthing these assumptions allows faculty members to recognize this liminal condition, unsettling their views about student work or student efficacy.

Such liminal understandings of the relationship between writing and conceptual and disciplinary knowledge influence multiple stakeholders—faculty, students and consultants—throughout the WEC process in different ways. After developing our theoretical framework for liminality, we describe how it characterizes faculty experiences throughout the WEC process, and we offer two case studies that illustrate how engagement with liminal views about conceptual knowledge and writing can produce transformative conceptual and structural changes.

BETWIXT AND BETWEEN: LIMINALITY AND WEC

Throughout the threshold concept literature (Meyer & Land, 2006; Meyer et al., 2010), liminality is a complex term used to describe a condition or space that learners move through as they acquire new conceptual understanding. As such, this movement is characterized as transitional, fraught with uncertainty, characterized by imitation, mimicry, frustration, and resistance, and marked by a sense of loss. As conceptually and ontologically unsettling as it may be, liminality is essential for sustained transformation. Drawing on anthropologists Turner (1969) and van Gennep (1960), Meyer, Land, Timmermans, and others (in Meyer et al., 2010) offer a useful vocabulary for describing stages of liminality and transformation (pre-liminal, liminal, post-liminal) in relation to conceptual learning, maintaining that such stages entail frequent oscillation among them. While examples cited in Meyer and Land (2006) like "opportunity cost," "heat transfer," or "limit," are noted for their "irreversible" effects—once learned, they are hard to unlearn—they are also characterized by the prolonged wavering in understanding that accompanies their learning. Unfortunately, awareness of and empathy for this oscillation between states of understanding can be scarce from those with conceptual mastery, due to the "integrated" and "bounded" features of threshold concepts. As Meyer and Land explain, the integrative nature of threshold concepts "exposes the previously hidden interrelatedness of something" (2006, p. 7). Furthermore, "It might be that such boundedness in certain instances serves to constitute the demarcation between disciplinary areas, to define academic territories" (Meyer & Land, 2006, p. 9). This divide between insider and outsider, expert and novice, poses a number of teaching challenges, as Ambrose et al. (2010) have shown. That is, conceptual mastery often leads to tacit understanding and an "unconscious competence" (Ambrose et al., 2010, p. 96) that can make it challenging for experts to recall how they learned their discipline—including all the gradations of evolving understanding they moved through—and, therefore, difficult to identify with the needs of learners. In her chapter in this volume, Stacey Sheriff draws on studies in social and cognitive psychology to describe this condition of unconscious competence as "the curse of knowledge, the curse of expertise, and expert blind spots."

As Flash has noted previously (2016) and in Chapter 1 of this volume, WEC work is fundamentally about surfacing and animating the characteristics, abilities, and values important to the disciplines with which we work. Through the use of surveys, samples, and curricular matrices, the WEC model fosters the loose but directed conversational interplay of agreement and disagreement among colleagues, who seldom find the opportunity to talk in sustained fashion about teaching and learning in their discipline. This conversation between disciplinary experts (our colleagues), facilitated by disciplinary outsiders (us), is primarily focused on disciplinary competencies that are often not yet realized by disciplinary novices (our students). These conversations may at times become particular (e. g., whether engineering writing demands third-person address) or dismissive (e.g., whether capitalization errors are symptomatic of reading issues), especially when differences between faculty and student perceptions emerge. Ultimately, they are in the spirit of exposing what Perkins (2006) describes as the "episteme," the "underlying game" that disciplines use to justify, explain, inquire, design, and validate their forms of knowledge.

Perkins' underlying game calls to mind other characterizations of faculty development efforts concerned with WAC/WID pedagogy, outcomes assessment, and conceptual learning and the crucial role that facilitation plays throughout the process. Consider Carter's (2003) description of work with outcomes-based assessment plans at North Carolina State, one where the "writing and speaking professional's" role is to help faculty make their "insider knowledge and expertise explicit" (p. 5), as well as Anson's characterization in the Introduction to this volume that WAC consultants must often push against faculty members' unchallenged, "tacit-level assumptions about writing and writing instruction." Similarly, Middendorf and Pace (2004) describe their productive work with faculty learning communities at Indiana University as a prolonged process of disciplinary "decoding," stimulated by the use of role-playing and interviewing where faculty from divergent fields delve "deeply into the specifics of thinking and learning in their disciplines" (p. 2). Drawing on genre theory and research and her experience directing WAC programs, Soliday (2011) argues that students learn more when they have "direct access to well-defined social situations typical of an expert's practice" (p. 68). For Soliday and her WAC colleagues, defining such practices emerges out of the negotiation between disciplinary faculty and English Studies or rhetoric experts.

Among these rich characterizations, we find Perkins' "epistemological game" when coupled with Meyer and Land's work, the most trenchant for underscoring an inextricable relationship between knowing a discipline and communicating a discipline. When previously tacit rules or insider practices are articulated through the WEC process and when these practices are described in concrete criteria and implemented into classroom and curricular interventions, then students have the chance to "play the game knowingly" (Perkins, 2006, p. 40). Students arrive in their majors with diverse educational experiences, linguistic practices, and orientations toward language and learning. For all students, learning a new epistemological game entails learning a new discourse. As Land (2015) observes, changes in conceptual understanding for students are "invariably and inextricably accompanied by changes in their own use of discourse." Likewise, a student's "encounter with an unfamiliar discourse or different uses or forms of language" can transform their "understanding of particular phenomenon" (p. xi).

For many faculty, this interrelationship between conceptual learning and conceptual discourse disrupts two interrelated pedagogical assumptions: (1) writing should be taught and evaluated distinctly from course content; and/or (2) the bulk of writing instruction should be handled by writing experts. For faculty accustomed to thinking of writing as a discrete, rule-governed and reproducible skill—something that should have been mastered by students before their class—the process of clarifying phrases like "clear writing" can be taxing or seem overly deliberative. Moreover, unearthing tacit assumptions about clear writing in chemistry, nursing, environmental science, or civil engineering requires negotiation, rethinking, and consensus-seeking collaboration, typified in this exchange from an M1 meeting in a STEM field:

> **F1:** I have noticed some correlation between those students with technical abilities and exhibiting a better way of thinking leading to better writing.
>
> **WAC Consultant:** Do others agree? (Several disagree.) So, there may be some students who are really technically savvy and may be unable to communicate their ideas?
>
> **F2:** And it is also the other way around.
>
> **F3:** But these two things are not contradictory.
>
> **F4:** To write well here means being able to demonstrate linear thinking in your prose. Being able to take an argument and work through it is the same as the way you are walking through a problem-solving solution. And I think it's what [F1] was talking about with someone who thinks clearly can see from here, to here, to here, to here. (WEC unit meeting transcripts, 2008–2019)

Though they have not yet reached consensus about the "correlation" between writing and conceptual thinking, such exchanges are productive and potentially transformative. In effect, they expose previously unspoken disagreements among faculty members who come to recognize disciplinary knowledge as contested, context-specific, and steeped in epistemological, conceptual, cultural, and genre-based assumptions.

Faculty rating and discussion of student writing samples—key artifacts of WEC's triennial assessment process, as Pamela Flash details in this volume— further underscore and potentially challenge assumptions about the relationship between writing and conceptual understanding. When faculty members identify students' struggle in writing on capstone projects, they point to symptomatic features, such as patch writing, citational pastiche, imitative discourse, and murky reasoning. Such features are aligned with a failure to realize desired writing abilities, such as summary, synthesis, and integration and use of evidence.

However, when they are pressed to diagnose those symptoms, faculty members begin to draw on a conceptual and epistemological framework:

> Students were stringing beads on a garland rather than drawing conclusions or exploring critical responses, strengths, and weaknesses.
>
> Students seemed like they slapped in a mathematical model (provided by a faculty mentor) but might not always have understood it.

> Many students made unfounded connections between given information and legislation; they leaped to these inferences and made surface statements with nothing to back them up. (WEC Rating Reports, 2008–2019)

The three comments above are culled from separate rating reports in different disciplines. Significantly, all three comments begin to unpack what a seemingly generic writing ability, such as synthesis or analysis, looks like when enacted in a disciplinary context. Breaking through a commonly presumed or tacit understanding of such writing abilities often signals a more substantial transformation.

In the case studies that follow, we elaborate on what this transformation entails for faculty grappling with the relationship between academic writing, disciplinary conventions, and epistemological beliefs. In the first case study, we describe how faculty in Agronomy and Plant Genetics wrestled productively with the effort to clarify and articulate what conceptual understanding entails, particularly in regard to the status of knowledge claims and the role of persuasion in the field. Working through their liminal understanding over the course of several WEC meetings, the faculty developed writing abilities and criteria that they have now carefully linked to disciplinary ways of knowing. This alignment by the faculty signals an important and sustainable conceptual shift that is possible when faculty engage in WEC. The second, longer case study chronicles the art history department's WEC efforts over several years, where we see how the faculty's intense engagement with WEC and the fruitful struggle to articulate student-facing writing abilities aligned with disciplinary and epistemological values. While recognizing this alignment is an end in itself, this process of understanding and making meaning explicit also fueled a structural transformation of the undergraduate experience of majors. This structural transformation entailed meaningful curricular revision, ongoing collaboration, and communication among colleagues, investigation, experimentation, and assessments of success. In an academic context where faculty work is often seen as individually conceived and achieved, the collective work of envisioning meaningful writing in the discipline reinvigorated and reinforced the commitment of the department to its students.

CASE STUDIES IN LIMINALITY AND TRANSFORMATION

A Larger Role for Writing: Agronomy and Plant Genetics' WEC Story

In developing the initial writing plan for the Department of Agronomy and Plant Genetics, a conversation about discourse conventions revealed critical, liminal features of mature disciplinary writing. In their initial WEC survey results, faculty noted that while professional affiliates and students rated persuasive writing as important modes of writing in the field, faculty and TAs emphasized descriptive, analytical, and critical writing skills as significantly more important. Faculty members observed that one key challenge among several that student writers faced was balancing the roles of scientist and advocate. While agronomy involves significant lab work, governed by the attitudes and practices of bench science, the field also involves working with stakeholders in the agriculture industry, where persuasive appeals are more common and the technical details of scientific inquiry are translated into market decisions.

Typically, a WAC practitioner might be tempted to furnish language regarding the relationship between writing conventions, purpose, and audience, leading to a predictable insistence that writers should be able to address multiple stakeholders. By contrast, the WEC consultant allows the dilemma to play out in a conversation among faculty. In accounting for differences between faculty and affiliate responses, two instructors addressed the complexity of persuasion:

> **F1**: I think "Persuasive" comes out differently in certain groups.
>
> **F2:** We are selling ideas, marketing, and promoting best practices through extension.
>
> **F1**: But "persuasive" might imply biased. We need to keep persuasion separate from critical evaluation. Their conclusions need to be more evidence- and data-based. (Agronomy meeting transcripts, 2013–2014).

For an outsider to the discipline, this razor-thin distinction between communicating conclusions drawn from critical assessment of data (unbiased) and advocating for a position or outcome (potentially biased) might be difficult to perceive. For a writing expert, the presumption of bias-free interpretation may seem naively positivist. However, for a disciplinary novice, the distinction is an important gateway into the epistemology of the field. Knowledge claims based on experimental and observational evidence held persuasive value precisely in their perceived status as discrete, measurable facts. These facts could then be marshaled as quantitative evidence in a persuasive narrative or conclusion to the degree that the can be described as rigorously as possible. This demand for technical rigor eventually emerged as a strong preference for quantitative data analysis.

The faculty member who had previously articulated caution regarding the language of persuasion in the field also expressed a potentially challenging attitude about the value of writing in the field, suggesting that less writing was often an effective measure of technical understanding. In the words of this faculty member:

> **F1:** Students should get the ideas across with as little writing as possible, using more graphics, figures, and other ways of conveying complicated ideas in a smaller space. This needs to be in the appropriate style for the purpose and audience. (Agronomy meeting transcripts, 2013–2014).

Initially, the speaker draws a clear distinction between the task of writing and the task of representing data using visuals and figures, suggesting that the former can and should be limited when figures and other representations of data provide sufficient evidence. This faculty member's conventional understanding of writing as prose sentences illuminates a division of communicative labor between visual representations of quantitative data and prose descriptions of it. This tendency to communicate data visually (rather than in prose sentences) is justified in the name of efficiency: to convey complicated ideas in a smaller space. For students who may be more familiar with elaboration as a strategy of explanation and less familiar with designing visual information, these expectations run up against conceptions of how writing works and what constitutes effective writing. Although students may have a face value understanding of concision (use fewer words), they may not yet understand how an expert writer or reader of their writing might view visual representations of data as a means of achieving brevity. The conversation turned to the types of data visualization that were typical of the field and the specific audiences to whom such visuals were directed. Faculty were comfortable generating examples and most of these were met with casual affirmation. The list was expansive and included descriptions of simple tables to complex multivariate regressions.

The WEC Consultant then turned from this list back to the questions of appropriateness and purpose, which led to a number of specific data analysis abilities. In developing their own list of student writing abilities, these discussions led to explicit attention to writing and quantitative analysis as elements of their writing plan:

- acquire, select, and manage data,
- summarize data using descriptive statistics and represent these in figures and tables,
- use basic spreadsheet functions,
- accurately describe relationships based on quantitative evidence and statistical tests,

- use quantitative data to support arguments and connect data to real world situations. (Agronomy Department meeting transcripts, 2013–2014).

At face value, the faculty member featured above seems to suggest mere concision as a virtue (using fewer words). However, the actual appeal in their quotation is to the use of different modes of written expression in the design of graphics and figures. The second sentence alludes to the rhetorical features of communicating with data. When the faculty member invokes the language of purpose and audience, and even in the description of "appropriateness" as the characteristic feature of success, the conversation begins to surface the taken-for-granted assumptions about the ways data representation and presentation demonstrate mature competence in the field. For a faculty member, the virtue of conciseness is an effect of the effective graphic representation of data, and thus the avoidance of prose as a means of conveying information.

In their M2 meeting, the attention to visual communication was deepened with explicit attention to the mechanisms by which students used quantitative reasoning to develop the charts and figures that constituted "evidence" for critical conclusions.

F4: How do quantitative skills relate to the ability to write a reasonable argument? Is this in our coursework?

F1: I don't think students are getting this in our curriculum extensively. More and more students will encounter big data sets and they will need to access the correct type of data and assess the quality before analyzing and drawing conclusions from it. This could be placed strategically, as in the survey we saw that some classes are doing this.

F2: Undergraduates can do this if you give them time to discuss it. In AGRO 1XXX we do an exercise where they have a scientific study and a series of questions to answer about the study.

F3: I think we need to be more explicit with these quantitative writing abilities. The most important is using quantitative evidence to support an argument. (Agronomy Department meeting transcripts, 2013–2014).

The explicit elaboration of these features of effective writing helped significantly in transforming faculty attitudes toward student writing. This more explicit understanding of data use was expressed later in the faculty conversation.

In our M3 conversation, this distinction between data novices and experts was expressed in developmental terms:

> **F2:** Students tend to have a black and white view of the world, and we need them to appreciate the shades of gray. Often when students find apparently conflicting data, they just don't know what to do with it. (Agronomy Department meeting transcripts, 2013–2014).

In this statement, the faculty member's generalization points more clearly to the necessary transformation of student's understanding that comes from appreciating the complexity of data analysis. While novices confronted with contradictory data are initially paralyzed, experts view contradictory data as a typical component of refining understanding. Another faculty member pointed to this initial paralysis as a liminal state and opportunity for learning:

> **F1:** Students appreciate the chance to talk about contradictory data and see data sets from multiple viewpoints. Then students can see that there are elements of different ideas that can be integrated to make a more precise point. (Agronomy Department meeting transcripts, 2013–2014).

A third faculty member extended the metaphor in the same meeting:

> **F3:** I want students to go beyond being critical about what the data says and think of some other interpretations; more than just what the data looks like—reach back in their mind to relevant concepts and experiences. (Agronomy Department meeting transcripts, 2013–2014).

Despite the initial dismissal of effective writing in agronomy as "as little writing as possible," the initial list of departmental criteria reflects a change in orientation to the role of writing in the field and the ways students developed as writers. The conversation enacted by the department began with an expansion of what counts as writing and thinking further about the relationship between text, data, and image in student writing. The turn to the persuasive authority of graphic representation underscored the need for an integrated approach to writing, quantitative reasoning, and data use. Attention to information seeking, data management, and the use of statistical tests were described as features of academic writing in agronomy, as well as research more broadly. By allowing faculty to describe the unstated assumption of the status of measurable evidence, the department was able to avoid the trap of conventional and glib attention to the audience and focus on the complex interactions of fact claims, their justifications, and their relationship to changes in attitude or action.

From Islands to an Archipelago: Structural Transformation in Art History

In art history, students, faculty, and affiliates strongly agree on the importance of writing. In heralding the centrality of writing, the stakeholders are often alike, nearly indistinguishable. Consider these responses to the WEC survey's question about the importance of writing to the discipline:

1. I cannot stress enough how important writing is in art history. Your writing needs to be strong if you want to make people read and care about art.
2. Writing is extremely important in art history. It is the medium through which we meet visual representations with texts and this is a complicated process.
3. Art history is a discipline based primarily on being able to synthesize thoughts so that they can be presented to other scholars in an effort to share and promote knowledge. Having strong writing abilities is necessary to succeed in the field.
4. To me [writing is] more important than learning about art history. (Art History survey reports, 2013)

Although it is difficult to distinguish the student from the faculty member, in these next responses, also pulled from the WEC survey, the student and the faculty perceptions are quite distinct:

1. I still don't fully know what is expected of me and I am now writing my senior paper. I am not a natural at the style of writing expected of me for art history papers, and I have no clue how to utilize bibliographic notes. It is all a bit frustrating for me.
2. Most of our students have basic writing skills, but at the same time, written assignments often seem to be thrown together at the last minute and do not reflect high levels of thinking.
3. It is late for me since I am close to graduation. Right now, it will be done through self-learning. That is very sad.
4. I have the impression that writing is a chore for students, and they do not view it as a tool or method that can help them clarify their thoughts. (Art History survey reports, 2013)

The divide separating students from faculty becomes readily apparent when respondents are asked to consider writing expectations and performance in the undergraduate Art History curricula. The liminal language of struggle, mimicry, and frustration manifest themselves in phrases, such as "I have no clue," "a bit frustrating," "seem thrown together," "very sad," "writing is a chore." During the first faculty WEC meeting, these differences were engaged head on, producing candid yet unresolved moments:

> **F1:** Students say that many professors have no patience or time; that observation is grounded in fact. There is not time for this. That feeling reflects practical concerns that are true.

> **F2**: It can be individual but not systemic. It's the structure we have to work with.

> • **F3:** Am I teaching them writing or art? Obviously, there is overlap; they are not mutually exclusive. Sometimes we forgo one for the sake of the other if students are demonstrating knowledge.

In this brief exchange, time becomes a stand-in for many pressures faculty experience in teaching students to write and to think as art historians. Whether it is an individual or a systemic issue, a lack of time becomes a *de facto* justification for the tacit. As Perkins has pointed out (2006), tacit knowledge and tacit strategies benefit experts because they are efficient. But tacit knowledge also presents keen challenges for learners, especially those who know enough—the "consciously incompetent" (Ambrose et al., 2010, p. 96)—to know they have been excluded. As students in the previous passages indicate, they experience the tacit expectations about writing in art history as a form of neglect: "I still don't know what is expected of me"; "it will be done through self-learning, that is sad."

As a number of contributors to this volume articulate, WEC is a process of making tacit practices more explicit and dynamic (Anson; Flash; Sheriff; Scafe & Eodice). This often poses challenges for faculty members who must recollect how they learned those practices and then name them. The difficulty of decoding, as Middendorf terms it, or moving from a state of unconscious to conscious competence (Ambrose et al., 2010) is apparent when faculty are asked: "What specific writing abilities should art history majors be able to demonstrate upon graduation?" The first draft of abilities generated by the art history faculty is full of insider language that assumes quite a bit from would-be learners:

> By the time they graduate, students should be able to:
> 1. Describe works of art and the experiences of art. "This painting is 10 x 2 and predominantly blue" describes what it is, but students should also be able to describe what it's like to experience that work of art, to walk around it (quantitative

description versus qualitative) while indicating their awareness of subjectivity. They should be able to navigate a lack of
Truth without sacrificing validity/accuracy.

2. Perform art history: writing is the performance of art history.
    a. Think historically and understand the historical speci-
        ficity of arguments; Understand that "art history is the
        only 'disposable' history, burden of contextualizing"
    b. Understand history through an object rather than
        applying it.

3. Write in a way that is appropriate to the art objects, with
    appropriate decorum, and recognize the different choices
    they could be making. (Art History Meeting transcript,
    2013–2019)

For many readers, as for many undergraduate art history majors, these abilities are apt to be troublesome and create more dissonance than clarity. The trouble stems from the complex nexus of concepts and actions. In order to "navigate
a lack of truth without sacrificing validity/accuracy" and "understand that art
history is the only disposable history," one must be familiar with concepts such
as "validity" and "disposable history" as well as the ways those concepts are acti-
vated by the discipline. Furthermore, it is not enough to have inert knowledge,
to know what the terms refer to; one must also know how to display "a way of
knowing" with the concepts. As first drafted, the abilities above do not signal or
describe what successful activation looks like in writing.

So, what does it look like when one writes "in a way that is appropriate to
the art objects, with appropriate decorum, and recognize the different choices
they could be making"? This is a question a WEC consultant might typically
ask in a faculty meeting—often on more than one occasion—as a way to proxy
the confusion students encounter when expectations are tacitly or elliptically
expressed. "Appropriate" and "in a way" imply tacit understanding, enforc-
ing a division between novice and expert and reinscribing the very sentiments
expressed by the students and the faculty in the survey. For the faculty, students
seem to be "throwing together ideas" or not using writing as "a tool to clarify
their thoughts." For some students, lacking access to the "appropriate decorum,"
writing remains mystifying, characterized as an independent and sad struggle.

How did art history work through this liminal stage, this negative and
self-perpetuating loop? Over the course of three subsequent meetings, the art
history faculty engaged in a number of frank discussions, frequently characterized by open-ended questions. One prominent thread of discussion concerned
the flatness of the art history curriculum, a challenge the WEC process often

exposes that extends to quite a few other disciplines in the humanities and social sciences. Because some students are enrolled in 1000-level, 3000-level or 5000-level courses *simultaneously*, and some students declare their major late in their undergraduate career, an intentional sequence of courses, a coherent curricular path, was identified as a key issue.

> **F1:** How big a problem do we think the variance at each level is? Or, does this variation reflect the nature of the things we do and can, therefore, be considered a strength in our department?

> **F2:** The diversity of our curriculum overlooks the fact that *we are all art historians.* We have a commonality of approaches but our curriculum seems more focused on the islands, our personal areas of expertise. . . . We don't have any courses that look at art historical writings in diverse fields, ways of thinking about art history, ways of writing about the visual. Maybe we should.

> **F3:** Should there be an undergraduate methods course or an undergraduate senior project that everyone takes that is focused on writing?

> **F4:** With a new class that is not required, what compels students to take it? (WEC Art History Department meeting transcripts, 2014)

This excerpt reflects the genuine inquiry and interplay of agreement and disagreement at the core of WEC work. We think, too, that it captures an important liminal scene for the faculty. Nothing here is settled, not even the decision about whether or not to make its curriculum more intentionally sequenced, or whether such options are even feasible. Yet several key ideas emerge in this conversation, ones that would spur significant and transformative action. One idea, for example, begins to germinate when the second faculty member describes the department as diverse in personal interests though potentially unified by a shared identify ("we are all art historians") and by their discipline's "commonality of approaches." These claims are coupled with the observation that there are no courses focused on "ways of writing about the visual," an acknowledgment that might lead one to ask how it would be possible for students to demonstrate the third ability above, to "write in a way that is appropriate to the art objects, with appropriate decorum, and recognize the different choices they could be making." Naming the unresolved issues—engaging with the liminal—was a necessary condition in order for the faculty to pursue three broad areas of implementation:

1. Articulating and communicating writing expectations for students
2. Developing resources to support articulated writing expectations
3. Establishing a coordinated senior capstone experience

Over the course of the first year in WEC meetings and through the drafting of its first-edition writing plan, the art history faculty returned to its initial list of desired writing abilities and significantly unpacked them. A key shift from the first draft to later versions has to do with audience. Though writing plans are often written for the benefit of the departmental faculty, art history's elaboration of its original list of abilities—the act of "translating criteria into prose," as one faculty member described it—seems especially attuned to student concerns voiced in the initial WEC survey. Here is how the first ability above ("They should be able to navigate a lack of Truth without sacrificing validity/accuracy") was articulated in the subsequent first-edition writing plan:

> Art historical writing does not simply describe what all viewers presumably see or what the writer thinks is self-evident; it works *to teach the reader how to see the work.* Moreover, such writing directs the reader's eye over a work of art as a means to assert something particular about it; as a form of knowledge. Similarly, students should be able to describe texts and artifacts—how it feels to read them, leaf through them, touch them, to be moved or changed by them; how they produce revelation or disillusionment, frustration or clarity. In keeping with this inherently subjective task, the student should combine an awareness of the lack of a single Truth about what art is or how it is experienced, what texts and artifacts are or how they may be interpreted, with a dedication to the validity and accuracy of written description and analysis (emphasis in the original). (Art History, Writing Plan, ed. 1)

The elaborated prose in this passage now offers more direction for students. It assigns a rhetorical purpose to description ("to teach the reader how to see the work"), and it names what a text does when it is effectively describing a work ("directs the reader's eye," "asserts something specific"). It also clarifies the enigmatic "navigate a lack of Truth," by providing more inclusive language about the subjective work of art history. Notice, for example, the shift away from "indicating an awareness of subjectivity" in the original to "should combine an awareness of the lack of a single truth . . . with a dedication to." In the latter passage, the "inherently subjective task" that characterizes writing in art history is contextualized, not presumed. It is more attuned to the apprentice. Ultimately, more inclusive language connects the student writer with their audience and the student writer with the discipline's affective and intellectual commitments. Just as important, this passage, as with the writing plan in general, offers more guidance to the faculty members themselves. Without abandoning the original ability, it provides more language for how one might teach the "appropriate decorum" to students. In effect, it amplifies the observation from one faculty member that a "commonality of approaches" can be useful for linking the islands of professional practice. Indeed, as the opening sentence makes clear, it is crucial to move beyond what writers (student and faculty alike) might think "is self-evident."

But words without actions are not very sustainable. The second key change to emerge from the faculty-centered WEC discussions in art history concerned the need to provide more concrete support for students in meeting the writing abilities and expectations. Though adding new courses (e.g., "ways of thinking about art history," "ways of writing about the visual") proposed in the third faculty meeting was unlikely for a unit with declining majors, the development of online resources became a strong alternative. Beginning with its first-edition writing plan and developed in subsequent ones, the faculty committed themselves to pooling and sharing resources in support of the writing abilities they articulated. Some of these resources are culled from other universities, and some are fashioned by faculty in response to student-articulated needs. For the frustrated student, who lamented that they were not "natural at the style of writing expected of me for art history papers," who had "no clue how to utilize bibliographic notes," one faculty member has created an online tutorial on effective citation practices that unpacks the rhetorical, technical, and ethical reasons that inform attribution practices along with the distinguishing features of footnotes, endnotes, and a bibliography. "Notes and bibliographies are gifts," she informs the viewer, most likely a student in art history, "accept them from and give them to others." The tutorial provides examples of common citational concerns from undergraduate projects, uses effective analogies comparing established citational practices with digital literacies (e.g., footnotes are like hyperlinks), and makes a compelling case for what might seem like obscure formatting elements by emphasizing how inconsistent, or messy formatting can function like a "dirty bathroom in a restaurant" by souring your experience of the meal. Attentive and responsive to its audience, the resource now serves as a tool used by students and other faculty.

The third change to emerge out of the WEC meetings has been consequential, and it has provided a model for other WEC departments on campus. As the excerpt from the third faculty meeting indicates, faculty were concerned students lacked systematic exposure to the methods and practices that shape research writing in art history. This lack of exposure was attributed to the "flat curriculum" and a dearth of methods-oriented courses. The discussion also raised the question of why a student would be compelled to invest more in a senior project near the end of their degree. In the fourth WEC meeting, faculty returned to this discussion; this time, they began to coalesce around the idea of a senior project that required more structure and more investment from the department itself. Again, the genesis for researching, developing, piloting, assessing, and the eventual revising of a major project course emerged out of a liminal moment, one where faculty acknowledged their current lack of investment and their need to alter their departmental culture:

> **F1:** We have all voiced some dissatisfaction with the capstone project which can sometimes feel like a capstone and sometimes like a paper revision. This might be our departmental culture that doesn't quite value it as a capstone experience so students do not know that it is a synthesis of the skills they have learned.
>
> **F2:** The current capstones are not fabulous and they come in last minute. I don't think it would take too much to show that we value these documents using prizes or outside reviewers, or even publishing them in some way.
>
> **F3:** For [students] to know that the entire audience is the full faculty, that each one of us reads their work, could be in addition to the prize idea. We could also then publish the best one on the website.
>
> **F1:** Yes, we could have a nomination system and each of us would end up reading maybe six per year.
>
> **F4:** It is great if they have a destination (the prize idea) but if they don't know how to get to the destination, they haven't worked on their writing enough, thought about their writing enough . . . [we need] something along the lines of a course, putting [students] in the same room and talking, workshopping their writing with each other, reading examples of art-historical writing.
>
> **F2:** We can really do all of this in the same step. We have this one-credit class, make them come in for an hour per week, make it more systematic on writing instruction, have external reviewers, people in the real world, have a prize, the work will be seen by others, that we as a department take it seriously. (WEC meeting 4, 2014, March 5)

At first glance, the proposed solutions focus on extrinsic rewards or pressures—prizes, publications, outside reviewers—that can be fairly easily imposed on students with little additional work from faculty. However, as the conversation progresses, the fourth faculty member acknowledges that prizes and publications can only happen after students have participated in a community of writers, "in the same room and talking, workshopping their writing with each other."

Since AY 2014–15, building and supporting a community of research and writing for undergraduate majors in art history has been a core objective for the unit and a key success. All art history majors now complete a three-credit research project that includes weekly workshops with students, facilitated by an advanced graduate student, along with structured time for each student to meet with their faculty mentors one-to-one throughout the semester. At the end of each term, students give public presentations of their work at an event attended by faculty, students, advisors, affiliates and family members. Faculty introduce the students, framing the student talk with comments and praise for efforts and insights. To attend such an event is to encounter faculty sentiments significantly different from those expressed at the outset of their WEC efforts, when some faculty members fretted about the pressures of time to address writing and research issues, and questioned openly whether a "departmental culture" would ever connect the "islands of expertise" that characterized the teaching and course options in the undergraduate curriculum. Art history's third-edition writing plan captures how this significant structural shift occurred, how the department moved through a liminal stage to enact key curricular and departmental changes.

> Students are now far more aware of our WEC-defined skills and, so also, more self-aware about their individual capabilities with them. . . . This awareness has been enhanced not only in the classroom, where, each semester, faculty and TAs are encouraged to hand out our writing criteria and use them in designing and grading assignments, but also in our advising efforts and in our new "Welcome Packets" for recently declared majors.
>
> Our end-of-semester senior capstone presentations have become widely attended events, which not only send our seniors off with a sense of accomplishment against a rigorous disciplinary benchmark, but also illustrate its value to our underclassmen. (Art History Writing Plan, ed. 3)

The case studies in agronomy and plant genetics and art history offer two distinct examples of how the WEC process engages in structured conversations that can challenge and change faculty assumptions and behaviors about teaching writing. Recognizing and understanding the liminal quality of the WEC process can fundamentally change the ways in which scholars of writing have conceived of faculty participation and buy in. These shifts in thinking can lead, in turn, to substantive course and curricular revisions within undergraduate departments, or what Scafe and Eodice in Chapter 11 of this volume describe as the vital results of co-inquiry, "the almost magical ability of work to lead people to insights that no amount of abstract discussion or lecturing could induce." The WEC process varies within departments, shaped in manifold ways by the different disciplinary cultures we work with, making it difficult to measure the precise interventions that produce conceptual shifts. Nevertheless, our review of meeting minutes and transcripts demonstrates that the WEC process creates the conditions of possibility for conceptual change.

The language of assessment often describes programmatic change idealistically as an efficient and ever-evolving process where loops are exposed and neatly closed. Despite this attractive and appealing description, it belies the liminal reality when faculty authentically confront and reconsider how they have come to know their field and how they should teach it. Not all conversations bear fruit, and not all liminal experiences lead to transformation. But a willingness to keep engaging in the dialog is how sustainable change happens. As Pamela Flash details in this volume, WEC conversations—neither purely spontaneous, nor rigidly scripted—remain the bedrock for this process. In the absence of a singular protocol or scripted exercises designed to produce conveniently shared outcomes, the consultative process—the structured conversation at the core of the WEC project—requires a variety of approaches, strategies and frequent adjustments, and it demands a willingness to pursue multiple, at times contradictory, lines of thinking as expressed by faculty participants. WEC endeavors succeed when the dialog remains open and ongoing among WAC consultants and faculty members and when it is underwritten by the consideration of undergraduate writing samples, student, faculty and stakeholder surveys, curricular matrices, and triennial ratings of capstone-level papers. Across diverse disciplines and programs, WEC conversations provide data for an evidence-based discussion of faculty and student assumptions about writing and the time and space to consider why it is that faculty and students believe what they believe.

REFERENCES

Adler-Kassner, L. & Wardle, E. (Eds.). (2015). *Naming what we know: Threshold concepts of writing studies.* Utah State University Press.

Adler-Kassner, L. & Wardle, E. (Eds.). (2019). *(Re)considering what We Know: Learning Thresholds in Writing, Composition, Rhetoric, and Literacy.* Utah State University Press.

Agronomy Department meeting transcripts. (2013–2014) Writing-Enriched Curriculum Program, University of Minnesota.

Ambrose, S. A., Lovett, M., Bridges, M. W., DiPietro, M. & Norman, M. K. (2010). *How learning works: Seven research-based principles for smart teaching.* Wiley.

Anson, C. M. (2015). Crossing thresholds: What's to know about writing across the curriculum. In L. Adler-Kassner & E. Wardle (Eds.), *Naming what we know: Threshold concepts of writing studies* (pp. 203–219). Utah State University Press.

Anson, C. M. (2021). Introduction: WEC and the strength of the commons. In C. M. Anson & P. Flash (Eds.), *Writing-enriched curricula: Models of faculty-driven and departmental transformation.* The WAC Clearinghouse; University Press of Colorado. https://doi.org/10.27514/PER-B.2021.1299.1.3.

Anson, C. M. (2021). The new grass roots: Faculty responses to the writing-enriched curriculum. In C. M. Anson & P. Flash (Eds.), *Writing-enriched curricula: Models of faculty-driven and departmental transformation.* The WAC Clearinghouse; University Press of Colorado. https://doi.org/10.27514/PER-B.2021.1299.2.02.

Art History Department meeting transcripts (2013–2019). Writing-Enriched Curriculum Program, University of Minnesota.

Condon, W. & Rutz, C. (2013). A taxonomy of writing across the curriculum programs: Evolving to serve broader agendas. *College Composition and Communication, 64*(2), 357–382.

Flash, P. (2016). From apprised to revised: Faculty in the disciplines change what they never knew they knew. In K. B. Yancey (Ed.), *A Rhetoric of reflection* (pp. 227–249). Utah State University Press.

Flash, P. (2021). Writing-enriched curriculum: A model for making and sustaining change. In C. M. Anson & P. Flash (Eds.), *Writing-enriched curricula: Models of faculty-driven and departmental transformation.* The WAC Clearinghouse; University Press of Colorado. https://doi.org/10.27514/PER-B.2021.1299.2.01.

Hyde, L. (1998). *Trickster makes this world: Myth, mischief and art.* Farrar, Straus and Giroux.

Land, R. (2015). Preface. In L. Adler-Kassner & E. Wardle (Eds.), *Naming what we know: Threshold concepts of writing studies* (pp. xi–xiv). Utah State University Press.

Meyer, J. H. F. & Land, R. (Eds.). (2006). *Overcoming barriers to student understanding: Threshold concepts and troublesome knowledge.* Routledge.

Meyer, J. H. F., Land, R. & Baillie, C. (Eds.). (2010). *Threshold concepts and transformational learning.* Sense Publishing.

Perkins, D. (2006). Constructivism and troublesome knowledge. In J. H. F. Meyer & R. Land (Eds.), *Overcoming barriers to student understanding: Threshold concepts and troublesome knowledge* (pp. 33–47). Routledge.

Scafe, R. & Eodice, M. (2021). Finding writing where it lives: Departmental relations and relations with departments. In C. M. Anson & P. Flash (Eds.), *Writing-enriched curricula: Models of faculty-driven and departmental transformation.* The WAC Clearinghouse; University Press of Colorado. https://doi.org/10.27514/PER-B.2021.1299.2.11.

Soliday, M. (2011). *Everyday genres: Writing assignments across the disciplines.* Southern Illinois University Press.

Sheriff, S. (2021). Beyond "I know it when I see it": WEC and the process of unearthing faculty expertise. In C. M. Anson & P. Flash (Eds.), *Writing-enriched curricula: Models of faculty-driven and departmental transformation.* The WAC Clearinghouse; University Press of Colorado. https://doi.org/10.27514/PER-B.2021.1299.2.06.

PART TWO. ACCOUNTS OF DEPARTMENTALLY FOCUSED IMPLEMENTATION

CHAPTER 5.

FORTY YEARS OF WRITING EMBEDDED IN FORESTRY AT NORTH CAROLINA STATE UNIVERSITY

Gary B. Blank

North Carolina State University

By design, the WEC approach works across an entire institution; a program is established and then, one by one, individual departments are enlisted to engage in the process of transforming their curriculum, faculty, and approaches to supporting student writing. In contrast, this chapter chronicles the development of a WEC program in a single department at North Carolina State many years before a campus-wide system was put in place. The success of the effort depended on the presence of a writing expert who served the role of a WEC coordinator embedded in the department and who eventually became one of its own faculty through the acquisition of a Ph.D. in the discipline. Development of the WEC approach in this single department subsequently contributed to the reformulation of the accreditation standards for the discipline and the creation of the first campus-wide WEC program in the U.S., the Campus Writing and Speaking Program.

The idea of developing an embedded writing program within North Carolina State University's Department of Forestry was born in a Douglas fir (*Pseudotsuga menziesii*) stand in northern Idaho in September 1975. When forestry technicians with whom I was working asked me what someone with a masters of arts degree in English (earned the previous spring) could do, they also mentioned that none of their forestry professors provided comments about their writing. Born during that lunchtime conversation was the idea to assist faculty to address writing in technical disciplines. A month later when hired to substitute in the English department at the University of Idaho, I began asking composition students about how much attention to their writing they received in classes outside mine. The answer then, 1975–1976, was none and I recognized a gaping hole existed in higher education.

Awareness of the writing gulf was dawning in the wider composition community, as Emig (1977) and Halloran (1978) articulated. However, typical institutional responses focused on creating writing centers housed in English departments and staffed by composition faculty, graduate students and undergraduate tutors. Sometimes such centers operated independent of English departments but the dynamics were the same: students required to write in various departments visited the "writing professionals" to have their syntax aligned and grammar adjusted. Professors in their majors were often not involved. Colleagues in the composition and communication ranks in the Department of English at NC State were aware of trends in the discipline, but the institution's response remained steadfastly insular, and no writing center or outreach to the rest of the university occurred.

This chapter chronicles the origins of a departmentally-embedded writing program at North Carolina State University that paved the way for an institution-wide WEC program. It traces how the forestry faculty embraced a proposal coming from outside their department but sensitive to compelling attributes of their discipline, following the principles described in the Introduction to this volume: faculty-owned, disciplinarily defined, data-driven, mediated by a writing expert, etc. It explores how preliminary and ongoing observations, colleagues' instructional experimentation, and the department's pedagogic flexibility enabled a realistic and unique approach, parts of which other forestry and natural resources programs would adopt. The chapter contextualizes development of forestry's writing-enriched curriculum amidst the institutional search for answers to a widespread instructional need. It recalls steps in NC State's process toward creating the institutionally unique approach that centers this volume. It demonstrates that a committed group of instructors led by an appropriately focused WAC-oriented faculty member could create something impactful despite, at that time, the lack of a systematic university program.

A FORESTRY FACULTY ENCOUNTERS AN IDEA

From 1975, fast forward through several years when I taught freshman composition at North Carolina State University, transitioned to teaching technical communication courses, and developed salient university contacts outside my employment in the Department of English. Douglas Frederick, a friend and forestry faculty member, in particular appreciated my perspective on the problem. Several forestry students electing to take my technical writing classes also encouraged my thinking. During the summer of 1978, I approached my department chair, who permitted me to make inquiries in the School of Forestry about the proposal I had been formulating since 1976. The dean of the School of Forestry and his associate dean for academic affairs listened as I laid out a scenario for addressing a problem I perceived they faced. I did not know until later that the dean possessed a letter earlier sent to him by a forest company executive complaining about inept letters he was receiving from senior forestry students seeking employment. At the end of our conversation, the dean escorted me down the hall to meet the head of the Department of Forestry who recommended we arrange a seminar during the fall semester to discuss my proposal with the faculty. Subsequently, the forestry department offered to pay part of my salary to begin working with their senior classes to improve students' ability to communicate their forestry knowledge in writing.

Thus, in the spring of 1979, I sat in the senior capstone course in a technical curriculum working alongside faculty producing the next cadre of professional foresters. I knew relatively little about their technical demands, even less about the education that preceded this capstone course or components integrated in an effective forest management plan. Pragmatists, the forestry faculty said they expected me to observe and learn before I started tinkering with the process. That is how the WEC effort in the Department of Forestry at North Carolina State University began. I started sitting in on senior forestry course lectures and going to the forest with classes to experience their culture and to learn what students needed to communicate. As other authors in this volume underscore, success in this early stage was a matter of collaboration, consulting with forestry pedagogical experts, to tweak what they were already doing and strengthen the rhetorical context students would have for what they produced. I did a few invited lectures about general principles of technical communication, in the context of whatever assignment the professor was requiring, but I avoided prescriptions and tried to take my lead from the professor's instructions. I was learning as they were leading themselves toward my way of thinking about the place of writing in their process.

Overall, the forestry faculty expected students to hit a target. Requiring a forest management plan from students in the senior planning course the last semester of their tightly structured curriculum, faculty members expected that document to demonstrate comprehensive forestry knowledge. Each student produced his or her individual document based on team effort gathering and analyzing inventory data. The plan's audience, a hypothetical landowner, would be basing decisions on recommendations provided by the plan's author. The rhetorical situation seemed straightforward. It was embedded in a complex technical problem for which four years (including an intense summer of fieldwork) in science and technical courses prepared the authors. However, as I commented years later (Blank, 1988),

> most plans were not aimed at appropriate audiences. They
> were badly worded, were expressed in forestry jargon or

> technical slang and assumed that readers (professors, of course) would understand what was omitted. Grammatical barbarisms and weak sentence structures distracted readers and made concentration on content difficult. In short, many seniors still wrote as if they were freshmen, except with technical ammunition to dispense in their ill-targeted shotgun style.

My experience teaching students in English department technical communication courses showed this was too often the case across the university.

The problem laid out before the deans and again for the forestry faculty during the seminar was the pervasive problem I had recognized in 1975. Academics assumed freshman composition could fix years of bad habits and teach an immutable set of rules to apply when writing anything. The gap between writing as then taught in English classes and the teaching practiced in technical courses, whether the subject was geology or forest genetics, remained. Focusing on forms and structure such as the argumentative essay that most composition introductory courses required did not translate well to data-driven science reports that forestry professors wanted. Writing about poems or dramas or short stories, the subject of literature-composition courses, was even farther from the communications reality that would face forestry graduates. Not knowing what to think about a poem, a first-year student would struggle writing anything; not wanting to think about a short story, most university students could not understand why they should write about it.

The main assumption I made and forestry faculty could buy was that students studying forestry would most likely care about communicating forestry they were learning and care about connecting with audiences who needed their information. Matters of style and diction pertaining to technical context changed the conversation about writing. Simple declarative sentences should dominate. Ornately sophisticated syntax caused problems for readers. Jargon needed definitions. Grammar and diction and punctuation errors should not distract from the message. In this context, I realized I needed to alter some of my own stylistic and rhetorical proclivities—learned in graduate literature courses writing papers for professors rather than practitioners outside the academy.

Note that I did not teach a writing course in the Department of Forestry, and the faculty did not add a technical writing requirement to the curriculum. In fact, for two and a half years, the Department of Forestry only paid one quarter of my salary, and I continued teaching technical communication courses in the Department of English through 1981. However, the School of Engineering asked me to help create a Writing Assistance Program (WAP) in January 1980 and bought half of my time from the Department of English. This arrangement persisted until May of 1981 when, no longer eligible for employment in English, I accepted the dean's offer to hire me in the School of Forestry and split my salary with the School of Engineering. This lectureship with split employment renewed annually until 1988 when I passed preliminary examinations to begin research for my dissertation in forestry.

FORESTRY PROGRAM DEVELOPMENT AFTER 1981

My joining the forestry faculty changed the commitment everyone had to this writing across the curriculum effort. From the first-year introductory course to the senior capstone, we agreed on the goal of preparing students to be professionals who knew how to communicate their knowledge. I had become what Flash (Chapter 1), Luskey and Emery (Chapter 4), and Scafe and Eodice (Chapter 11) in this volume variously describe as someone with "insider-outsider" status; but in this case, my "insider" status would also strengthen as I became a member of the discipline of forestry.

With a target—the management plan document mentioned above—in clear view, the matter of developing student skills to hit it effectively meant examining precursor curricular courses and rhetorical challenges appropriate to each. From the beginning, the forestry faculty agreed with my assertion that writing effectiveness develops over time. Hence, we applied simple strategies in varied courses and focused our approach on four key questions that I suggested all forestry programs might ask of themselves (Blank, 1983):

1. Does the curriculum consistently demand that students communicate their knowledge?
2. Do we create realistic report situations?
3. Do we teach students to use data and the literature effectively?
4. Do we encourage students' verbal precision and stylistic flexibility?

Emphases differed from course to course, as material covered and assignments required suited pedagogical aims. In the dendrology (woody plant identification) course, for example, students did not write reports. However, the professor required attention to correct spelling of scientific names (binomial nomenclature) on tests along with acquisition and use of proper plant physiology terms during the field labs and quizzes. Here accuracy was the standard and a significant basis for evaluation. In silvics and physiology, short reports in response to assigned topics required text-based research and assimilation of source material with proper citation methods. The silviculture course involved a field lab when teams gathered data, analyzed the implications and generated brief reports in typical scientific report format. Each forestry faculty member in most cases had already discovered which types of communication were most appropriate to the pedagogical aims in his or her course. Making connections between their individually determined aims and the broader structure of the embedded writing program became my job.

Together with forestry instructors, I developed a few innovations. In the forest management course (senior year, fall semester), a co-instructor and I discovered a way simultaneously to broaden students' exposure to relevant material and accomplish a missing piece in the span of communications situations students experienced. We created the *Forest Management Senior Symposium* in 1984 (the symposium in 2019 was the 35th annual event). The idea was to create an atmosphere resembling a professional meeting, to bring a level of formality to the talks, and to reinforce the idea that writing in the academy could be for real audiences. The current professor assigns a different topic to each student in the class, and topics cluster around a general theme such as harvesting technology, inventory and measurement strategies, and stand treatments. Students review pertinent literature and generate analyses to illustrate principles or demonstrate solutions to forest management issues. Then during the semester's last several lab periods, the students present their papers in moderated sessions attended by their classmates and as many faculty members as we can gather. We publish the schedule and use faculty evaluations of the performances as one of our measures for outcomes assessment.

In the capstone course, we transformed the experience based on preparation of the management plan and introduced an assignment requiring each student to develop a client profile. We also divided the planning process into two parts requiring students to conduct a feasibility study and to submit that document midway through the semester. This change allowed us to review students' writing and provide comments attentive to content, format, style and grammar. Much of the gathered background material in the feasibility study document reappeared in the management plan, but the midterm review suggested ways students could improve when preparing their final plan document.

We also formalized field tours at the end of the semester so students presented their management plans orally to a peer and faculty audience in the forest where the plan pertained. This two-hour excursion required each team to create a tour itinerary, review plan elements on which they wanted to focus, and consider the logistics of addressing a large group in a field setting. The experience was true to life, something many of these students would do as professionals. In fact, one graduate reported that at his first job, just a month or so after his team organized and conducted their senior field tour, his work colleagues heard they needed to prepare for a visit from company "top brass." His colleagues were frantic about how to plan such a visit and what to show their corporate bosses. Based on his recent experience, this new hire volunteered to organize the field tour and manage the event, carried it off without a hitch, and guaranteed a future with the company for which he still works. Building such confidence became central to aims of the communication program developed in the forestry curriculum.

Integrating attention to writing and speaking in courses created interesting situations and a few unanticipated tensions. One confrontation seems comical in retrospect but was a serious matter at the time. A funded research project that aimed to teach forestry students word processing so they would pay more attention to revising their drafts alarmed some faculty. Professors were concerned about allocating perceived limited resources of computer lab time to student writing. Computers, after all, were for computational work, analyzing data and generating answers to technical questions, like the effects various treatments would have on forest stand growth and yield. For a while, policy dictated that students needing "quantitative" computing time could claim priority use over students "writing and revising" papers. As a practical matter, though, students soon recognized the value of word processing as a tool to facilitate better reports, from drafting through finished submissions, and the false dichotomy between work on numerical content and verbal expression of that content evaporated.

Another development that enhanced student performance was creation of a brief reference manual, first issued as a course pack and eventually posted online for easier student access. *Communicating Natural Resources Information* (1990) addressed formats and a variety of matters, using examples from students' work. The guide focused on formats from business cover letters to memoranda to scientific paper structures required in technical courses. Subsequently several other forestry schools requested permission to use the guide for their students.

Well before that, however, news about our effort in the forestry department at NC State had affected other forestry programs (Dohaney, 1984; Wellman & McMullen, 1984). Publications in the *Journal of Forestry* (Blank, 1983, 1988) and attendance at a variety of workshops and conferences (Blank, 1986) drew attention and queries. Several programs similar to ours employed part-time "writing consultants" to tutor students and help them address their writing weaknesses. In fact, the integrated approach we were taking at NC State influenced the accrediting committee of the Society of American Foresters to revise its criteria and review process concerning communication requirements. Rather than require specific composition, public speaking, and technical communication courses, the committee recognized that the integrated development of communication skills could be a more effective way to reach the desired goal: foresters who understood how to meet audience needs in a variety of media.

After eight years of program development, we had significant results to report about integrating teaching of writing skills in technical courses (Blank,

1988). Four hundred or so students had graduated and sample documents they produced in their senior capstone course testified to the improvement in the ability to communicate sophisticated technical information. That improvement evolved through continuing practice incrementally gained over four years, as shown in Table 5.1 (derived from data reported in Blank, 1988). We calculated that students produced over 200 pages of supervised writing in forestry courses during their collegiate careers (Blank, 1988).

Table 5.1. Amounts of writing by curriculum level in Forest Management WEC Program circa 1988

Curriculum Unit	Courses	Assignments	Number of Text Pages
First Year	1	7	15
Sophomore Year	2	6	15
Summer Practicum	2	4	12
Junior Year	3	20	76
Senior Year	3	9	88
Technical Electives	6	10	60

Responding to a university-administered survey in 1992, students in the College of Forest Resources (CFR) provided evidence that the emphasis on communication development was having an impact. To the statement "my courses have helped develop effective writing skills," 86.6 percent of CFR students agreed or strongly agreed. Only students in the College of Humanities and Social Sciences responded more positively (87.7%), and the next highest group was from the (then) College of Education and Psychology (81.3%). With the statement "my courses have helped develop effective speaking skills," 66.7 percent of CFR students agreed or strongly agreed, compared to College of Veterinary Medicine students (67.5%) and students from the College of Humanities and Social Sciences (66.2%). Our reading of these results was that efforts in the College of Forest resources had changed the culture and created expectations among both students and faculty.

Moreover, in response to our reporting results (Blank, 1988), peer institutions and others in natural resources reported positive effects from integrating attention to the rhetorical context and practical work of communicating in technical courses (Daniels & Reed, 1992; Wellman et al., 1990). This movement, of course, was part of broader recognition throughout academe that the point of contact for communication pedagogy mattered, and assumptions needed to be challenged (Jones & Comprone, 1993). Writing in discrete disciplines emerged as an area needing research.

While developing the program in the NC State Department of Forestry, I was taking courses preparing to qualify for and do research to earn a Ph.D. in forestry. The dissertation research examined differentiation of communications roles among professional foresters (Blank, 1992, 1994). Employed in four professional sectors outside academe, foresters encounter varied audiences. Communication internal to their organizations dominates the roles filled by industrial foresters and foresters employed by the USDA Forest Service. Most foresters in state agencies and nearly all foresters employed as private consultants far more frequently communicate with audiences outside their organizations than do their counterparts in industrial and U.S. Forest Service positions. The results of this research confirmed the correctness of educating our graduates to be versatile communicators, alerted to the variety of communication contexts where they would find themselves engaged as professionals. As their careers evolved and the technologies of communicating changed, we expected that the basic understanding we had shared would evolve as well (Blank, 1986, 1995).

The writing program created in the Department of Forestry at NC State University was unique at the time of its creation. It came about within the larger institution that eventually awoke to realize students all across its curricula and diverse programs were writing in specific disciplinary contexts. Discussions about how to accomplish the desired support for faculty progressed, and I was engaged in those discussions. Taking a leadership role on the Council on Undergraduate Education (1992–1994), I worked alongside a variety of faculty and administrators seeking to fashion the institutional framework for improved pedagogy. Communication was always an essential component of that improvement. Figure 5.1 illustrates the process through which the communication program in forestry developed. However, such a model understanding of that process perhaps exists nowhere outside my head as, in retrospect, I considered what my faculty colleagues and I accomplished in a process analogous to writing a prescription for a forest stand. From existing tree conditions, one gathers data and defines end goals, alert to the tools and techniques potentially implemented. A model prescription results, and work ensues. Multiple factors can derail the prescription, however, and change stand development.

Parts of the process were much easier to implement than others, and collegial buy-in fostered some advances better than others. For example, having a defined target that students were expected to produce in their senior spring semester capstone course could effectively structure contributing writing experiences in earlier courses. Assignment design, however, relied upon each faculty member's particular goals. Research scientists/teachers insisting on the arcane style of peer-reviewed journal articles found the gap between students' vernacular prose and publishable aspirations daunting. Thus, negotiating acceptable reality became a collective process.

The overarching plan was to create a departmental culture engaging every student in the evolution from novice to professional and fostering appropriate communication to varied audiences and to address varied situations. Having colleagues committed to doing this I found was exceptional, and not every department is likely to have such a structured curriculum. In fact, two more recently created programs (environmental technology and environmental science) in our department impose much less structure and less clear endpoint expectations. Moreover, in those curricula, our faculty teach far fewer courses, thus have diminished effect concerning students' rhetorical development.

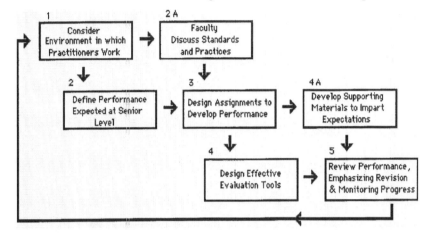

Figure 5.1. Conceptual model for developing WEC in a technical curriculum.

As a practitioner of environmental assessment and a veteran of educational problem solving, I believe this model still has validity for anyone seeking to create an embedded communication program.

THE FORESTRY MODEL AND NC STATE WEC HISTORY

Demonstrated success with the forestry faculty initiative and the School of Engineering Writing Assistance Program (WAP) (Covington et al., 1984, 1985) had prompted other advocates on campus to see prospects for writing programs in all colleges as a logical next step for NC State. However, traction outside the Department of Forestry and School of Engineering was difficult to find. Telling that story requires a bit of backtracking.

In November 1985, Dr. Carolyn Miller, recently retired SAS Distinguished Professor of Technical Communication, sent a memorandum to the Ad Hoc

Group on Writing Centers (a faculty member from English, from the College of Education, and me) about a meeting the following week. In her memorandum, she referenced a whitepaper I had prepared and circulated entitled "Writing Across the Curriculum." To her memo, she also attached Kinneavy's overview of the WAC movement published in *Profession 83* and a proposal she had created for university funding through the "State of the Future Campaign." In the memorandum, she listed a series of "attempts to raise the issue within the Department of English and SHASS" [the then School of Humanities and Social Sciences] starting in 1980 (Figure 5.2).

```
9/18/80--Proposal (six pages) to English Department's Executive Committee
         to begin long-range planning for writing center programs in each
         school, modeled on the Engineering and Forestry programs then
         recently begun.

Fall 1981--Executive Committee approves plan in principle and sets up an
           Ad Hoc Committe on Writing Centers with me as chair (Brandt,
           E. Clark, Holley, Kelton, Meyers, Moore, Pollard, M. Williams.)

spring 1981--The Ad Hoc Committee meets in March and decides to pass the
             proposal along to the Dean's Office.  In April, Acting Associate
             Dean Betty Wheeler reports to me that there is interest but that no
             action can be taken for the next year because of the transition
             between chancellors.

12/14/81--At the suggestion of the Department Head, the decision to drop
          English 200 (Composition Laboratory) is justified by the recommen-
          dation that   a network of writing centers replace it.  Memo to
          Dean Tilman from Brandt, Covington, and Miller.  No response.

spring 1984--English Department's Ad Hoc Long-Range Planning Committee
             (Williams, Harrison, Miller) submits to Dean Tilman a two-page
             proposal intended to solicit designated funds through the State
             of the Future Campaign.  John Gehrm in Foundations loves it; the
             Dean wants more detail and tables it.
```

*Figure 5.2. Schedule from C. R. Miller memorandum
11/8/1985 to AD Hoc Group on Writing Centers.*

Frustration about lukewarm administrative support for the initiative is obvious. Apparently, resource questions (space and staffing issues) stymied administrators. The $155,000 budget proposed for start-up and annual expenditure of $130,000 (see appendix) proved daunting. In hindsight, finding and sending communication "missionaries" to the rest of the technical university was a dubious agenda item for folks primarily thinking about the status quo within the institutional culture of the time. SHASS seemed and often acted isolated from the rest of the university, its administration chafing under perceived "service" roles to the professional curricula and programs. The vision articulated in the proposal would thrust SHASS into a leadership role on campus, and this was uncharted territory.

While the WEC program in the forest management program established expectations in curricula subsequently developed in the Department of Forestry, several factors prevented replication of the model in other departments or colleges at NC State. The WAP in the School of Engineering functioned in one dimension more like typical writing centers at other institutions—serving drop-in students with specific writing project questions or editorial needs. However, WAP outreach to faculty members interested in improving assignments and WAP consultations with engineering faculties about their students' overall rhetorical development moved the WAP beyond the typical writing center of the era. These latter WAP roles emulated the conceptual model the Department of Forestry was integrating. In effect, the WAP staff were missionaries, but a crucial point here is that they were missionaries the School of Engineering was paying. The problem SHASS administrators perceived but sidelined was how to pay for communication missionaries in the other schools at NC State University because the SHASS budget was not going to do it.

Out of the meetings convened in 1985–1986, a proposal developed directed to the provost. The proposal covered key elements in the initial proposal (see appendix) and identified the need for 8.5 positions to implement a Writing Assistance Program across the entire university. Positions included an overall director and secretary and coordinators in each of the schools (either full or halftime positions, depending on size of the school student population). It also called for an office in each school for these personnel, but the proposal did not include a budget or dollar amounts. In a closing section headed *Benefits*, the proposal said:

> The improvement of student writing is a widely perceived need,
> both on campus and in the industries that employ students
> after graduation. No single department can or should be made
> responsible for fulfilling that need; rather, university-wide
> cooperation and coordination are required. . . . This approach
> is effective because it treats writing not as a separate subject
> matter but as an integral part of all thinking and learning.

Nevertheless, nothing substantive came of the proposal at this point, lack of resources being the obvious impediment.

A subtler matter, never directly addressed, concerned who would champion the effort. Ad hoc committees and auxiliary initiatives by faculty members with other primary assigned duties were not getting the attention of administrative leadership. Chiefly, our institution needed a person primarily dedicated to the task defined by the proposal that had been developed. Administrators, understandably, remained reluctant to allocate resources for a nebulous idea, however ardently urged by a core of rhetoricians. Asked on several occasions if I wanted to be director of writing at North Carolina State University, I could not say. For me, several reasons precluded advancing this programmatic change across the university structure. First, I did not have tenure, in fact, was still pursuing my Ph.D. as an instructor on an annual contract. I aspired to attain the requisite degree to continue a career in the academy and was doing so in forestry—not English composition or rhetoric. Thus, I was learning requisite technical aspects of a new discipline (actually many disciplines because the subject I was engaging—forestry—encompasses varied aspects of other disciplines). That learning was feeding interests in new fields, such as environmental impact assessment. Finally, my life outside the academy included environmental consulting, a spouse and children, and several extracurricular activities (i.e., Artspace, Inc., and Capital Area Soccer League). Suffice it to say, by the late 1980s I had decided not to be the champion for WEC at NC State; instead, I had chosen to sustain an academic career by teaching in the forestry department. This choice continued my leadership of the Writing Improvement Program in the College of Forestry but, in 1988, my employment with the College of Engineering WAP ended.

Broader educational questions eventually brought attention back to WEC at NC State. Early in the 1990s the Southern Association of Colleges and Schools (SACS) started pressing for institutions to develop outcome assessment plans. In 1992, the Department of Forestry volunteered as one of the pilot programs to create an assessment process, so faculty members delivering the undergraduate program considered how to gather information to document our outcomes. Having completed my Ph.D. in the spring of 1992, I was able to lead the assessment project in forestry and was also appointed to represent the College of Forestry on the Council on Undergraduate Education (CUE). The senior capstone course appeared to provide the best opportunity to measure what our students could do and by using that experience, we engaged alumni, professors, and students in monitoring progress. The management plans produced by the senior students provided clear evidence of their written communication ability. Field tours demonstrated oral communication ability, and the questioning during these tours provided insight to depth of knowledge about the range of topics incorporated in foresters' education. These tours have been the central component for assessing forest management program outcomes for 28 years. The point here is that the forestry faculty already had accepted the fact that evaluating outcomes of an applied practice (e.g., teaching) made sense.

Attention to outcome assessment became a major concern the CUE needed to address after developing General Education Requirements (GER), as described in Carter's Foreword (this volume). The requirements were due for implementation in the fall of 1994 and grew from an extensive university self-study that included many curricular facets. Meanwhile, in tandem with developing the GER, the place of writing and speaking in all curricula became a prominent question so, once again, a new version of the Writing Center Proposal, which administrators had repeatedly kicked to the sidelines, reemerged in the context of how to implement the GER. A 22 March 1994 memorandum to the Provost from the task force chair, on behalf of the Dean for Academic and Student Affairs' *Task Force on Writing*, concerned the "Writing Center Project—Research Plan." In this memo, the chair (on behalf of task force members) challenged the need for further study and advocated moving ahead with development of college-based writing centers. The memo argued students at NC State needed writing assistance. It affirmed the efforts ongoing in the Department of Forestry and the School of Engineering but pointed out that these were efforts with limited effect because of the numbers of students reached within the total NC State population. It advocated for a writing center but acknowledged that since none existed at NC State, only results at other institutions could be used to validate the concept. The memo summary argued that further study would be complicated, that lack of writing centers on the campus would limit possibilities for research on the campus, and a study would only confirm what advocates of the writing center proposal already believed.

However, in a memorandum dated 25 August 1994, the dean charged subgroups of the Council on Undergraduate Education with several tasks. One of these tasks was to assess "impact of writing across four colleges (two with formal programs and two without) as per the provost's request." This repeated demand by the provost irked some writing-centric advocates, and his call for a study to demonstrate need for allocating resources befuddled some persons hoping to address already perceived needs. Ultimately, those of us who clearly understood the provost's desire for solid data upon which to base a commitment of considerable resources prevailed upon our colleagues. Thereafter, the Council on Undergraduate Education 1994–1995 Assessment Plan included a major emphasis on writing, with the initial focus on what was happening on campus "followed by efforts to determine what results are occurring." Efforts planned included compiling syllabi, examining results from the Riverside Base Test administered to incoming students, questioning faculty and program administrators about adherence to stated course requirements, and surveying teachers of junior-senior writing courses about incoming students' competencies. Still, the shape an institutional response should or could take remained unclear—a matter of resource allocation and an institutional culture of separate colleges each committed to its own programmatic priorities. A 23 January 1995 memo to the "Task Force on Writing" from the chair and the dean stated: "the original plan to compare writing performance across colleges was abandoned because appropriate comparison groups and conditions do not exist." Instead, the chair and dean said a reconstituted task force would "gather information from departments about current writing requirements, implementation plans for the new GERs, and resource needs." The memo also asked prior Task Force members if they wanted to continue being involved in the effort, and nine people affirmed their commitment to continue.

The Writing Work Group spent considerable attention on the question of what constituted a "major paper," because the GER required that every curriculum include a course in which a major paper was required. As a memo dated 30 March 1995 indicates, this was not easily resolved: "there is so much diversity between the 145 programs, it is difficult to determine exactly what constitutes a major paper [e.g.,] a major paper in math is very different from a major paper in history." Guidelines for length, whether written in the discipline (major), and how much grading weight it should carry in a course were some of questions to be resolved. Spotty implementation by departments was problematic. Some folks asked if computer literacy or library research were part of the major paper requirement. Others wondered whether requiring an advanced humanities or social science course in a curriculum could serve to meet the major paper requirement. A variety of other questions surfaced but, as one task force member noted, not "knowing how" hampered the true spirit of the faculty members who wanted to do more regarding writing. To address this gap, the Writing Work Group invited a consultant to campus. Art Young, Coordinator for the Communication Across the Curriculum Program at Clemson University presented a seminar in April 1995 entitled "The Writing Learning Connection." Decently attended, but still mostly by WAC and writing center advocates, the seminar signaled a galvanizing core of interest beyond the small number of folks a decade earlier. Most important, university administrators noticed and participated.

By October 1995 the Writing Work Group had developed *Guidelines for implementing the "significant writing" requirement* (Appendix B). These guidelines essentially articulated the principles behind writing-enriched curricula. Questions immediately began to emerge. Ultimately, the CUE deliberated for a year about assessment methodologies and priorities, not finding consensus concerning baseline and standardized testing methods for the variety of outcomes in the range of curricula and core demands in curricula. Attempting to find a consensus about how to address writing assessment was only part of the bigger picture in the university's mosaic of priorities during 1995. Just getting departments to embrace any level of outcomes assessment was now a chore of significant magnitude.

The Council on Undergraduate Education agenda for 26 January 1996 announced its primary focus for the spring semester was "to hold planning meetings in each college to discuss how the proposed writing-intensive course requirement can be interpreted and implemented." I do not recall attending such a meeting in the College of Forestry, though the topics of writing and the general education requirements arose frequently. Probably, the three departments in the college had already more than met expectations of the GER. We certainly had in forestry so did not see a need to participate in another round of discussions.

Nevertheless, the institutional response represented in 1996 by this expectation that every college would discuss implementation of a discipline-based communication requirement validated arduous work that had gone before. It elevated attention to writing and speaking among the priorities teaching faculties should address and formalized review of curricular outcomes in many cases. Indeed, when curricular outcome assessments were fashioned, more often than not one of the four or five stated outcomes involved the ability to communicate material obtained in pursuing the academic degree. As assessment plans evolved across the campus, the increased weight of communication's importance to the entire educational enterprise underscored the need for a central vision and leadership.

The commitment to the enhancement of communication across the NC State curriculum culminated in a proposal to establish a centralized program to coordinate the effort, headed by a recognized WAC expert and amply funded. Thus was born the first institution-wide WEC program in the US, NC State's Campus Writing and Speaking Program, designed both to provide broad, university-wide programming and to assist departments as they created writing-enriched curricula. As a national search was mounted in the fall of 1997, composition and WAC expert Michael Carter served as Interim Director and began meeting with individual departments, using the methods described in his Foreword and by other contributors to this collection to help them articulate their expectations for students' writing and oral communication and inscribing these in working documents. The national search yielded an offer in the spring of 1998 to hire Chris Anson, then at the University of Minnesota, as the new director. Unable to uproot his family in a matter of two months, he delayed his arrival until the summer of 1999 while Carter continued as interim director. The delay, however, allowed Anson to travel frequently to NC State during the 1998–1999 academic year to work with Carter, meet with faculty WEC groups, and participate as an ex officio member of the search committee for an assistant director. The person who accepted that position was Dr. Deanna Dannels, who was finishing her Ph.D. in oral communication across the curriculum at the University of Utah. Both Anson and Dannels arrived within a few weeks of each other in the summer of 1999. The CWSP has now been operating for 23 years.

UNDERSTANDINGS (NOT CONCLUSIONS)

Looking back at this history makes apparent that the idea of integrating communication throughout the curriculum could not easily translate into universal practice. The scale-up issue that often affects technological systems comes into play: what works in small and closed systems may not perform well in larger and more open systems without a full-fledged, supported program. In this case, we in forestry had an educational approach that worked on its relatively small scale. Forestry students have never constituted more than a tiny fraction of the students at NC State. The forest management curriculum has always been highly structured, and students move through their required classes together. Very few of forestry students' core curricular courses occur in multiple sections, so every student shares the experience of these courses. Students funnel through a summer practicum between their second and third years or transfer into the program with equivalent skills and then progress with the post-practicum cohort through third- and fourth-year courses, again altogether. Such features do not describe many curricula at NC State University. The cohesiveness of the curriculum and the size of the student cohorts and the cooperative commitment of the faculty involved were all exceptional. Larger and much more diverse curricula and programs did not readily embrace the model offered by the Department of Forestry until WEC became established and the university made a commitment to enhance students' communication abilities across the entire institution.

By the early 1990s, with more than a decade of experience, in forestry we expected whatever requirements the university applied regarding communication were likely to be less demanding than those self-imposed expectations the forestry faculty had applied. Thus, aspects of the CUE and broader university discussion seemed inconsequential to what the forestry faculty had already implemented. For instance, CUE discussion about a "major paper requirement" seemed irrelevant to my forestry colleagues and me. The entire debate about how much writing constituted significant writing also seemed trivial in light of 200+pages we had documented the forestry curriculum requiring (Blank, 1988). My colleagues had already, and long ago, stated their intention to integrate writing development in technical curricula. However, though a member of the Writing Work Group and of CUE, I was not inclined to push very hard for such commitment from other department faculties, having worked in three colleges with faculty across a range of academic cultures and constraints, therefore understanding the unique culture in the forestry department that had embraced me and not seeing it elsewhere.

Moreover, having piloted outcomes assessment and found it potentially helpful, we were willing to proceed. The new General Education Requirements (GER) could be accommodated reasonably easily with few alterations in the—already interdisciplinary—forestry curriculum. Within the changing culture of the university, we were no longer outliers so much as veteran pioneers in these two now-linked efforts of teaching professionals who would need to be able to communicate their acquired knowledge. The challenges that would come in the decades that followed emerged from faculty turnover, curricular evolution, various distractions that reduced vigilance concerning students' rhetorical development, and the establishment of a writing and speaking program. As curricula in the department developed and the faculty grew more discipline-diverse and younger, therefore more focused on research productivity and tenure pressures, maintaining consistent focus on teaching communication within technical contexts became harder. This challenge will forever face those advocating WEC in a research I university. Thus, having strong institutional leadership along with adequate resources and incentives to advance the ability of faculty to make the dual challenge work remains paramount, and suggests the importance of establishing and supporting centralized WEC programs such as the Campus Writing and Speaking Program and the other programs represented in this collection.

REFERENCES

Blank, G. B. (1983). Writing and the forestry curriculum. *Journal of Forestry, 81*(8), 537–538.

Blank, G. B. (1986). Forest resources students and word processing. In H. V. Wiant, D. O. Yandle & W. E. Kidd (Eds.), *Proceedings of the Forestry Microcomputer Software Symposium* (pp. 516–526). West Virginia University.

Blank, G. B. (1988). Writing in forestry: An eighth-year report. *Journal of Forestry, 86*(9), 31–35.

Blank, G. B. (1990). *Communicating natural resources information: A guide for students.* Department of Forestry, North Carolina State University.

Blank, G. B. (1992). How forestry consultants communicate. *The Consultant, 37*(4), 26–28.

Blank, G. B. (1994). Communication in the forester's workplace. *Journal of Forestry, 92*(3), 35–40.

Blank, G. B. (1995). Communications technology and foresters. *Journal of Forestry, 93*(5), 50–51.

Carter, M. (2021). Foreword. In C. M. Anson & P. Flash (Eds.), *Writing-enriched curricula: Models of faculty-driven and departmental transformation.* The WAC Clearinghouse; University Press of Colorado. https://doi.org/10.27514/PER-B.2021.1299 .1.2.

Covington, D. H., Brown, A. E. & Blank, G. B. (1984). A writing assistance program for engineering students. *Engineering Education, 74*(2), 91–94.

Covington, D. H., Brown, A. E. & Blank, G. B. (1985). An alternative approach to writing across the curriculum: The Writing Assistance Program at North Carolina State University's School of Engineering. *WPA: Writing Program Administration, 8*(3), 15–23.

Daniels, S. & Reed, M. (1992). Enhancing forestry education through writing. *Journal of Forestry, 90*(3), 221–226.

Emig, J. (1977). Writing as a mode of learning. *College Composition and Communication, 28*(2), 122–128.

Flash, P. (2021). Writing-enriched curriculum: A model for making and sustaining change. In C. M. Anson & P. Flash (Eds.), *Writing-enriched curricula: Models of faculty-driven and departmental transformation.* The WAC Clearinghouse; University Press of Colorado. https://doi.org/10.27514/PER-B.2021.1299.2.01.

Halloran, S. M. (1978). Eloquence in a technological society. *Central States Speech Journal, 29,* 221–227.

Jones, R. & Comprone, J. J. (1993). Where do we go in writing across the curriculum? *College Composition and Communication 44*(1), 59–68.

Luskey, M. & Emery, D. L. (2021). Beyond conventions: Liminality as a feature of the WEC faculty development. In C. M. Anson & P. Flash (Eds.), *Writing-enriched curricula: Models of faculty-driven and departmental transformation.* The WAC Clearinghouse; University Press of Colorado. https://doi.org/10.27514/PER-B.2021.1299.2.04.

Scafe, R. & Eodice, M. (2021). Finding writing where it lives: Departmental relationships and relationships with departments. In C. M. Anson & P. Flash (Eds.), *Writing-enriched curricula: Models of faculty-driven and departmental transformation.* The WAC Clearinghouse; University Press of Colorado. https://doi.org/10.27514/PER-B.2021.1299.2.11.

Wellman, J. D. & McMullen, J. Q. (1984). Teaching forestry students how to write. *Journal of Forestry, 82*(7), 413–416.

Wellman, J. D., McMullen, J. Q. & Hirsch, G. N. (1990). Evaluation of a writing improvement program. *Journal of Forestry, 88*(11), 24–27.

APPENDIX A. PROGRAM PROPOSAL

NCSU STATE OF THE FUTURE CAMPAIGN

PROPOSAL FOR A WRITING CENTERS PROGRAM AT NCSU

The Department of English proposes a campus-wide Writing Centers Program at North Carolina State University. Such a program would provide a mechanism for coordinating and enhancing instruction in writing at all levels and in all schools; it would also help integrate writing into student efforts in all courses. Such a program would be a major commitment to the improvement of writing throughout the university and would rely on the function of writing as a method of learning as well as a means of communicating what has been learned.

Because no such mechanism currently exists, the various writing programs on campus operate separately, without consistency in their goals and techniques. In addition, they can provide only partial and intermittent opportunities for students to progress, with the result that many students do not take writing seriously and few achieve their potential to become articulate professionals.

Program Description

AS a centralized resource of planning and expertise, a Writing Centers

Program would provide services and activities to the faculties and students within each School, according to a school-by-school assessment of needs. Such services and activities could include the following:

Writing laboratories Tutorials

Course lectures on writing assignments and problems
Training for graduate assistants who serve as graders on labs and exams Advice and assistance for faculty in designing and evaluating writing assignments

Workshops for foreign students and others with special problems
Workshops for thesis and dissertation writers

Advice on curriculum, course design, and standards to enhance student writing

This program would be based not on a principle of remediation but on integrated instruction and continual opportunity and practice; continuity is essential for the development and improvement of the complex skills required for effective written communication. On our campus, the program would need to be flexible, allowing for adaptation to the needs of each School. It should build on the well established tradition of effective programs at other institutions, such as VP!, Western Carolina, UCLA, University of Maryland, University of Michigan, Michigan Tech, Smith, George Mason, Carnegie Mellon, University of Vermont; many of these programs have been supported by major grants from the federal government as well as private corporations (for example, Buhl, Exxon, General Motors). The program should also build on the existing expertise and resources at NCSU:

The courses and programs in the Department of English
The Writing Assistance Program, School of Engineering
The Writing Improvement Program, Department of Forestry
The Academic Skills Program
The National Writing Project, School of Education
The English program for foreign students, Department of Foreign Languages

Careful planning and wide consultation would be necessary to determine the best features and design for a campus-wide program at NCSU. Such planning should include study of the occasions and purposes for writing throughout the university curriculum, the methods and resources available on campus, and evaluation of existing programs.

Benefits

The improvement of student writing is a widely perceived need, both on campus and in the industries that employ students after graduation. No single department can or should be made responsible for fulfilling that need; rather, university-wide cooperation and coordination are required. By involving faculty and students across the campus and at all levels, the Writing Centers approach would reinforce the contention that good writing is important in all classes of the University and in all aspects of professional life. This approach is effective because it treats writing not as a separate subject matter but as an integral part of all thinking and learning.

Budget

Start-up funds for a Writing Centers Program would be required to plan the program, adapt proven techniques to the NCSU environment, train faculty and staff, and purchase equipment. Beyond the planning phase, continuing funds would be necessary for a director and several staff assistants, tutors, and graduate assistants, as well as operating supplies.

Start Up	Planning (one year)	$25,000
	Visiting consultants	$10,000
	Computer laboratory	$100,000
	Training workshops	$20,000
		$155,000
Annual	Director	$30,000
	Staff for 10 Schools	$100,000
		$130,000

APPENDIX B. WRITING REQUIREMENT GUIDELINES

NCSU Writing Work Group   October 1995
Council on Undergraduate Education

Guidelines for implementing the "significant writing" requirement

A course with a "significant writing component" includes **both practice and instruction** in types of writing characteristic of a particular field or professional domain. This component of the GERs is intended to ensure that students will be introduced to the types of writing that professionals in their respective disciplines engage in, that they will receive instruction in and feedback on this writing from professionals in their major fields, and that they will thus recognize writing as integral to learning and essential for communication in all fields. Courses used to satisfy requirement (3) should provide guided **practice** in discipline-specific genres and opportunities to write for a variety of discipline-specific audiences, e.g., lab reports and research proposals in the sciences; unit plans in education; reviews and position papers in philosophy, literature, and political science; library research papers or literature reviews in anthropology, psychology, and history. Informal writing-to-learn activities would also be appropriate in these courses.

A key assumption behind this requirement is that students do not learn to write better simply by writing more. Therefore, a term paper which students work on outside of class and turn in at the end of the semester will not fulfill the goals of this requirement. Similarly, essay exams or fill-in-the-blank lab reports, while they may serve other instructional goals, do not provide opportunities for guided practice in writing. In order for students to learn how to communicate effectively in their chosen fields, instructors must introduce them to the types of writing done in those fields and must provide guidance and support for the communication tasks they assign. Such **instruction** might include discussing in class the critical features of sample proposals or position papers, analyzing audience and purpose, providing feedback on early drafts, discussing grading criteria in class, holding individual conferences with students to discuss their work in progress, and so forth.

For example, a course in which students are asked to write lab reports could be considered to have a "significant writing component" if the lab report is treated as a standalone professional document for which the instructor offers models, formative feedback, and opportunities for revision, and which is evaluated using the highest standards of professional or academic writing. Writing assignments and instructional supports should be specified in syllabi and course action forms in order to facilitate UCCC review.

APPENDIX C. WRITING AND SPEAKING REQUIREMENT REVISED RECOMMENDATIONS

NCSU Writing Work Group   October 1995
Council on Undergraduate Education

WRITING A~l> SPEAKING
Revised Recommendation

(1) Two semesters of freshman composition and rhetoric.

(2) One advanced communications course in (a) writing, (b) speech, or (c) foreign language.

(3) Two courses with significant writing components in the student's major, ideally one each in the junior and senior year. A student's major is understood to include those courses designated as major requirements (as opposed to degree requirements) on the Automated Degree Audit. Guidelines for implementing this requirement are attached.

The foregoing recommendation was developed on the assumption that the faculty and administration recognize that meeting these goals requires students to engage in writing and speaking across the curriculum and throughout their undergraduate years. In order that skills develop broadly and consistently along with the individual's increasing knowledge of subject matter, all upper-division courses offered in the university should incorporate significant communications experiences.

CHAPTER 6.

BEYOND "I KNOW IT WHEN I SEE IT": WEC AND THE PROCESS OF UNEARTHING FACULTY EXPERTISE

Stacey Sheriff
Colby College

This chapter considers a paradox at the heart of WEC and, arguably, all WAC work: the disciplinary immersion that leads to expertise makes it difficult for faculty members to articulate and pass on their knowledge of writing in the disciplines. Drawing on research in WAC/WID, psychology, and education, the chapter offers tools for WEC facilitators. First, it outlines three socio-cognitive frameworks that can help faculty become aware of their blind spots and tacit expectations. Second, it offers a heuristic to describe faculty members' key realizations about writing in their disciplines as they work to unearth disciplinary expertise. Finally, a case study from a computer science department in a small liberal arts college illustrates the application of these tools in the context of the WEC process. Implementing a WEC initiative increases faculty members' awareness of and attention to their own expertise, expectations, and potential blind spots as they articulate the characteristics, values, conventions, and forms of writing and research in their majors.

Over the last five years of leading a writing-enriched curriculum (WEC) initiative with departments at Colby College, I have found that working through the WEC process with faculty is some of the most meaningful, holistic, difficult, and transformative work I have done as a writing program administrator (WPA). Our faculty, similarly, have found that the collaborative work of articulating their disciplinary writing abilities and creating departmental writing plans to be among the most challenging and revelatory work they have undertaken as a department (see also Anson's Introduction and Chapter 2, this volume). Moreover, faculty members are often surprised and sometimes frustrated by the difficulties of WEC work. As experts in their disciplines and experienced teachers, faculty members might surmise that they could define writing and list writing-related abilities for their majors without a lot of special preparation or time.[1] But we have consistently found that this is not the case. Why is it so difficult for faculty members to conceptualize writing and writing instruction in their disciplines?

The literature in writing across the curriculum (WAC) and writing in the disciplines (WID) provides some answers to this question. Studies of the development of the disciplines have shown that faculty members typically see disciplinary content knowledge as distinct from writing and that the process of joining a discipline as an expert practitioner is usually tacit. The first holds true largely because, as David Russell argues in *Writing in the Academic Disciplines* (2002), through the development of the modern university, specialized disciplinary content came to be seen as separate from a generalized idea of academic writing. This separation has contributed to a widespread view of writing as a "transparent recording" of thoughts and physical observations rather than a rhetorical medium that shapes and helps to create knowledge in a discipline (Russell, 2002, p. 10; see also Macdonald, 1994). Moreover, as Carter argues in "Ways of Knowing, Doing, and Writing in the Disciplines," faculty members usually learn disciplinary writing "not by any direct instruction but by a process of slow acculturation through various apprenticeship discourses" (2007, p. 385). Thus, many faculty members have never thought explicitly about how they learned to write in their disciplines or even realized that they have discipline-specific assumptions, expectations, and expertise in writing in the disciplines (Moor et al., 2012).

On the contrary, faculty members often "assume that students share their perceptions and expectations about writing . . . The writing, genres, and expectations of their disciplines have become second nature" (Russell, 2001, p. 287). It is this seemingly discreet, "second nature" invisibility of their knowledge that makes it so difficult for them to articulate specific writing expectations and abilities in their disciplines. As highly educated researchers, writers, and thinkers, faculty members are immersed in specific disciplinary contexts that obscure their own awareness of their expertise and the processes by which they obtained it. Ironically, experience and time compound the problem. "Because instructors primarily teach and study within their disciplines," Joanna Wolfe et al. argue, "they come to mistake their specialized disciplinary ways of thinking and writing as universal skills" and can even come "to view their own discipline's values,

---

1   In this chapter, I use "expert" in the sense of someone who has an unusual and deep body of domain and task-specific knowledge (Hinds, 1999) upon which they draw when solving problems and responding to new situations in their fields (Dreyfus, 2006). Faculty members are typically, and reasonably, referred to as experts in this sense.

assumptions, and conventions as the norms in other disciplines" (2014, p. 43). Similarly, Adler-Kassner and Majewski, building on Lave and Wegner, explain that "the more expertise members in a community of practice have, the less visible practices associated with that community become. Instead, these practices seem like commonplaces that 'everyone knows'" (2015, p. 188). Thus, the very disciplinary acculturation and immersion that lead to disciplinary expertise can support an inaccurate view of writing as a general, transparent skill and make it difficult for faculty members to articulate and pass on their knowledge of writing in the disciplines.

As Flash and Anson establish in the opening chapters of this collection, the writing-enriched curriculum (WEC) approach is an evolution of WID that offers an iterative, faculty-driven, regularly assessed model for infusing writing into undergraduate disciplines and majors. Engaging faculty members' disciplinary knowledge, attitudes, and expertise is central to WEC work. Yet there is limited literature in WAC/WID and writing studies that delves into the dynamics of how groups of faculty come to articulate their tacit knowledge and disciplinary expectations for writing (see Flash, 2016). Research that does focus on faculty members' conceptions of disciplinary writing illuminates their assumptions, values, and beliefs about academic writing, but it is primarily based on individual interviews rather than examinations of groups or curricular systems similar to the collaborative, discursive processes at the heart of WEC (e.g., Brammer et al., 2008; Salem & Jones, 2010; Thaiss & Zawacki, 2006; Zhu, 2004). Reflecting a central philosophical tenet of the field, WAC/WID scholarship often argues that faculty members should be the ones to define the expectations for disciplinary writing and writing instruction. For example, Carter (2007) advocates that writing professionals "ask faculty" to describe disciplinary ways of doing and writing (p. 389) as the first step to creating outcomes for assessing writing. Adler-Kassner and Majewski argue that writing specialists should discuss disciplinary threshold concepts, "asking faculty about 'their own forms of evidence and ways of knowing'" to engage them through their disciplinary investments (2015, p. 187). But what if this very identification is the challenge? What if faculty members stall at "I know it when I see it" and struggle to describe specific ways of writing, thinking, and researching that they expect of graduates in their majors?

Advocating that writing professionals "ask faculty" can obscure the fact that most faculty members will need not only support but also a process like the writing enriched curriculum model to become aware that they even *have* disciplinary assumptions about writing (see also Luskey and Emery in Chapter 4 of this volume). It can also obscure the fact that reckoning with tacit expertise and disciplinary blind spots will always be part of the process of articulating expectations and teaching writing in the disciplines. Indeed, in concluding their study of a new English WID curriculum based on the *topoi* of literary analysis, Wilder and Wolfe caution that "reliance upon faculty to identify the procedural knowledge they have gained largely tacitly may prove highly difficult because faculty may be unaware of the degree to which they have internalized discipline-specific expectations for 'good writing'" (2009, p. 196). In facilitating WEC at Colby, I have found faculty members' lack of awareness and internalization, even universalization, of discipline-specific writing expectations to be common across departments. This challenge, as other chapters in this volume also illustrate, is a central and productive driver of WEC work—one that, in my opinion, WEC facilitators must recognize and embrace.

As I developed our WEC initiative, I began to think about how faculty learn to define writing and writing instruction in their disciplines and majors. What information and processes help them? What constrains them? What kind of shifts in faculty members' thinking might a WEC consultant look for through this process? Flash (Chapter 1) and Anson (Introduction and Chapter 2) in this volume outline the assumptions and processes of the WEC model and provide a compelling answer to the first question. This chapter complements that evidence and considers the questions of constraints and faculty realizations. In the sections that follow, I provide some institutional context for our WEC initiative; draw on research in WAC/WID, psychology, and education to outline three socio-cognitive frameworks that can help faculty become aware of their blind spots and tacit expectations; provide a heuristic to describe faculty members' key realizations about writing in their disciplines; exemplify with a brief case study from the Computer Science department; and conclude with implications for future study.

INSTITUTIONAL CONTEXT: WEC AT COLBY COLLEGE

It was my sense of the challenges of insider positioning as well as the inductive, faculty-driven nature of the WEC model that drew me to it. As the inaugural Director of Colby's Writing Program, I started WAC work slowly by attending department meetings, visiting classes, and holding workshops on WAC best practices and principles. In my first few years, I worked with faculty to develop dozens of new first-year, writing-intensive courses (called W1s), begin writing assessment, and integrate the Farnham Writers' Center and Writing Program. The Dean of Faculty had also asked me to "figure out what to do with upper-level writing." Our first step, working with faculty on the writing committee, was to create upper-level, writing-intensive WID course designations (called W2 and W3). We offered modest curriculum development grants and worked with faculty across departments to create these courses, which are taught by faculty across the curriculum (see Sheriff & Harrington, 2017 for more on the Writing

Program's development). These upper-level W courses were an excellent way to recognize faculty already teaching writing-intensive courses, signal the importance of writing instruction to students across the College, and bring in new faculty members interested in more intentional approaches to writing instruction.

However, as the WAC literature attests and as Anson points out in the Introduction to this volume, the benefits of writing-intensive courses can become siloed with individual courses or faculty. We needed a more systematic way to reach beyond the willing and, important in our context, to involve interested departments that could not staff capped writing-intensive courses. Chris Anson, whom I had been fortunate to bring to campus as a WAC workshop leader, recommended that I look into the University of Minnesota's WEC model. I met with Pamela Flash at the 2014 International Writing Across the Curriculum conference she chaired at Minnesota, and she agreed to partner to test the portability of the WEC model to a small-college setting. Colby was the first liberal arts college to implement the WEC model, including the data collection, structured meetings, and iterative writing plan creation and assessment cycle. Starting slowly in 2015, we are now in the fifth year of implementing a WEC initiative to enhance writing instruction in the majors.

Colby is a small liberal arts college of about 2,200 students that does not offer pre-professional or graduate degrees. It is quite different in size and scope than UMN, yet we have found that WEC approach fits Colby's culture well. At Colby, the majors are the center of gravity, and faculty members design all (or most) of their own courses and tend to know a fair amount about the details of their departments' curricula. WEC's emphasis on faculty members' ownership of writing in their majors and the process of meeting with whole departments to study the curriculum and articulate shared writing abilities suited our context. Six departments, including the largest majors on campus, have undertaken WEC initiatives and have active writing plans in first, second, and third editions. (See Flash, Chapter 1 of this volume, for more on the WEC model for developing writing plans.) These include, in order of adoption, art, computer science, biology, environmental studies, psychology, and chemistry.

In each department I've worked with, faculty members have consistently remarked upon (1) how much they have learned from their colleagues' articulation of their writing expectations and assumptions and (2) how rare and valuable it is to have such holistic conversations about their curricula.[2] These

---

2   Such comments about the value and rarity of conversations about disciplinary outcomes and concepts align with the findings of Anson's study in this volume and other writing studies scholarship, particularly that focused on faculty development and, more recently, threshold concepts (see, for instance, Adler-Kassner & Majewski, 2015; Bunnell & Bernstein, 2012; Carter, 2003; Malenczyk, 2016; Wardle & Scott, 2015).

rich conversations and the not infrequent ah-ha moments are a result of, as Flash puts it, the fact that "the WEC model takes primary aim at faculty conceptions of writing and writing instruction" (2016, p. 10). To initiate WEC, faculty members must interrogate their expertise with others, discussing and debating what is essential about research and writing in their disciplines and, ultimately, articulating their conclusions in ways that students can understand.

WRITING SCHOLARSHIP ON EXPERTISE

Expertise, particularly as it relates to knowledge acquisition and writing development, has long been of interest to scholars of rhetoric and composition, WAC, and WID. Geisler, for instance, reminds us that the "new rhetoricians" in the 1950s and 1960s—e.g., Olbrechts-Tyteca, Perelman, and Toulmin—were concerned with the rhetorical aspects of expertise and "suggested that expert practitioners in a domain employed field-specific reasoning in support of assertions about what to do and what to believe" (1994, p. 44). The cognitive study of composition typically associated with Flower and Hayes (e.g., 1981) used social scientific methods to compare novice and expert writers' behaviors, concluding that experts posed more sophisticated, rhetorically situated problems to themselves. Carter, as exigence for a theory of expertise in writing based on global (general, heuristic) and local (disciplinary, case-based) knowledge, asserts that "what we do in our writing classrooms is determined, implicitly or explicitly, by our concepts of what it means to be an expert writer and how writers attain expertise" (1990, p. 280). Given this history, I concur with Rice's recent argument that "a focus on expertise has led to pedagogical innovations like Writing Across the Curriculum (WAC) and Writing in the Disciplines (WID)" (2015, p. 120).

In *Academic Literacy and the Nature of Expertise*, Geisler argues that modern academic literacy bifurcates expertise into separate dimensions of "domain content" and "rhetorical process." (1994, p. 89). While elements of the former are conveyed through general education, the latter "more informal and tacit knowledge of rhetorical process remai[n] the more or less hidden component of advanced training" needed for professional expertise (Geisler, 1994, p. 89). In framing these two dimensions of expertise, Geisler challenges writing professionals to reveal and bridge the "great divide" that the academy, in service to the professionalization movement of the twentieth century, created between experts and the general public. In considering the political, social, and economic implications of writing instruction and programs, WAC scholarship has taken up this challenge. In delving deeply into the rhetorical conventions, genres, and activity systems of the disciplines, WID scholarship has helped to demystify and challenge the separation of domain and rhetorical process knowledge.

To this end, WID research has contributed to our understanding of disciplinary genres and purposes (e.g., Bazerman, 1988, 1997; Fahnestock & Secor, 1991; Herrington, 1985; Johns, 2002) and rhetorical and disciplinary contexts for writing (e.g., Anson, 2008; Beaufort, 2007; Johns, 2002; MacDonald, 1994). Building on this foundational work, WAC and WID scholarship has also interrogated the diverse and frequently tacit nature of faculty expectations for and definitions of "good writing" (e.g., Carter, 2007; MacDonald, 1994; Moor et al., 2012; Wilder, 2012). This literature can help new WEC facilitators increase their knowledge of other disciplines' discourse conventions, which may also help them build credibility with faculty colleagues. Yet, I would argue that the WAC/WID literature could engage more fully with Geisler's powerful theory of the academic bifurcation of expertise and its consequences, including the common view of writing as a transparent tool for communicating observations and data.[3] In addition, there is a large body of social science research (e.g., in psychology, education, and sociology) on the dynamics and constraints of expertise that can be useful to WEC facilitators. In the next section, I will briefly discuss selected concepts that can complement our understanding of the role of expertise in WAC/WID and our work with faculty as WEC facilitators.

EXPERT CURSES AND BLIND SPOTS

Research in psychology and education offers a number of socio-cognitive frameworks that are helpful to understanding the challenges of faculty members' disciplinary acculturation and expertise. This literature examines how expertise can make it difficult for faculty members to break down a problem, articulate their own process for thinking through a disciplinary issue, realize they are skipping steps, and estimate the time it takes novices to write or undertake new tasks (Hinds, 1999; Nathan & Petrosino, 2003; Nickerson, 1999). In this section, I will briefly outline three that are especially useful for writing specialists and WEC facilitators: the curse of knowledge, the curse of expertise, and expert blind spots.

Social and cognitive psychology studies of how people assess others' knowledge can help writing specialists appreciate why it can be difficult for faculty members to externalize, adjust, and unpack their own expertise. This research has shown

---

3   Some scholars have suggested that because the "compact" nature, in Toulmin's terms, of most science disciplines results in greater standardization of genres than in "diffuse" (primarily humanities) disciplines, the view of writing as transparent may be more common and appealing (Thaiss & Zawacki, 2006; Wiles, 2014). However, studies of writing in philosophy, literary studies, and first-year composition show that faculty in humanities disciplines share similar assumptions about the transparency of their disciplinary texts (Geisler, 1994; MacDonald, 1994; Wolfe et al., 2014).

that people take their own experiences and knowledge as a baseline for what they assume others know, adjusting their assumptions based on context, external cues, and repeat experiences. However, it is nearly impossible to ignore one's own knowledge, especially when that knowledge is deep and was not recently acquired—as is typically the case with experts. When experts gauge what others know or can do, they cannot help but refer to their own level of knowledge or performance (also called anchoring). They therefore fail to adequately adjust for the differences between themselves and novices, and they overestimate the ease or speed with which novices would perform (Epley et al., 2004; Kelley, 1999; Nickerson, 1999). Researchers call this phenomenon the *curse of knowledge*, "a bias in which knowledgeable people are unable to ignore information they hold that others do not" (Hinds, 1999, p. 218). Avoiding the curse of knowledge is especially difficulty for experts, like faculty members, who have a great deal of unusual or specialized knowledge that, over time, has become second nature.

In a foundational study of this concept, Hinds gave groups of experts, intermediates, and novices a variety of complex tasks (a series of cell phone tasks and a model plane assembly) and asked participants to predict the amount of time it would take novices to complete them. She found that, in keeping with the curse of knowledge, experts systematically underestimated how much time novices would need. Unexpectedly, Hinds (1999) also found that, as compared to both novices and intermediates, experts made less accurate predictions and were more resistant to "debiasing techniques," such as being prompted to remember their own learning experiences or being given a list of common problems novices encounter. Hinds coined the phrase the *curse of expertise* to describe this phenomenon of experts' particular underestimation and resistance to debiasing. This concept can help WEC facilitators appreciate why it is hard for faculty members to anticipate problems students will encounter with research and writing in their disciplines and why they may underestimate the difficulty or time students need. Learning about these concepts can help faculty realize that (in social science parlance) their expertise "curses" their ability to gauge students' knowledge accurately and may make them undervalue information that could help adjust their assessments. This knowledge may, in turn, make faculty members more open to the value of explicit scaffolding, models, and formative feedback. Moreover, given that such pedagogical techniques help make disciplinary assessment visible, WEC facilitators can also explain that WEC work and wrestling with these "curses" has the potential to make their teaching more inclusive and accessible to a diverse student body.

In the specific context of education, scholars have studied the impact of teachers' prior education and pedagogical knowledge on their approach to instruction. Nathan and colleagues developed a theory of the *expert blind spot*, which posits that educators with advanced training in an academic discipline, such as a Ph.D., "tend to use the powerful organizing principles, formalisms, and methods of analysis that serve as the foundation of that discipline" to guide their instruction rather than the level of knowledge or typical development of novice learners in that subject area (Nathan & Petrosino, 2003, p. 906). Educators with the highest level of specialized subject-area knowledge were the most likely to think through such disciplinary schemas, leading them to inaccurately assess problem difficulty level and novices' learning development (Nathan & Koedinger, 2000; Nathan & Petrosino, 2003). Thus, in a twist on the curse of knowledge, "expertise may make educators blind to the learning processes and instructional needs of novice students" while, unfortunately, also making them "entirely unaware of having such a blind spot" (Nathan & Petrosino, 2003, p. 906). WEC facilitators can help faculty become aware that they *have* expert blind spots and that their deep immersion in their subject matter causes them to think about, organize, and retrieve information differently than novice students.

Pushing awareness and conscious action into the unconscious relieves the cognitive load, but it also obscures how and when learning occurred in the first place. Faculty members may, therefore, skip steps, reason intuitively, and go too fast for less knowledgeable others, whether they be students or non-specialist colleagues. These socio-cognitive frameworks can give WEC facilitators useful language to share with faculty and a better understanding of why students may report that faculty move too quickly, skip steps, or fail to adequately explain their expectations for writing.

FACULTY'S PROCESS OF COMING TO AWARENESS OF WRITING IN THEIR DISCIPLINES

As a tool for WEC facilitators, I have synthesized insights from the literature on WAC/WID and expertise with my experience as a WEC facilitator into a descriptive heuristic (see Figure 6.1). It describes faculty members' key "realizations" in the process of unearthing their writing expectations and reckoning with the tacit dimensions and curses of disciplinary expertise. Because my institution is a small liberal arts college, some aspects may not be generalizable to other institutions. But I hope this heuristic will help WEC facilitators gauge, and perhaps even anticipate, stages in faculty members' thinking as they wrestle with describing and assessing writing in their disciplines. I have listed the realizations in an order I have often seen as a WEC facilitator, but faculty members may come to them in many different ways. Based on their fields, reflective practice, or previous experience with assessment and outcomes, some may start at the end of the list. Others may take a more circuitous path to understanding how their writing assignments and expectations instantiate tacit disciplinary conventions.

Faculty members become aware that they have . . .

- unarticulated expectations for student writing in their majors
- tacit disciplinary expertise, including unarticulated rhetorical process knowledge
- tacit assumptions that some disciplinary conventions for "good writing" are generalizable to all academic writing or are norms in other disciplines
- been assigning but not naming or teaching some departmental writing abilities
- been assuming students have knowledge of disciplinary rhetorical processes that comes with expertise
- been bringing tacit disciplinary expertise and expectations to their criteria for evaluating student writing

---

*Figure 6.1. A heuristic to describe faculty realizations
about writing in their disciplines.*

Moving through these realizations—often with recursive returns to earlier insights as new information arises—is essential to helping faculty members avoid vague or universalized notions of "good writing." But, as with any intellectual endeavor, iteration may also lead to moments of increased uncertainty as faculty members reassess prior knowledge or moments of frustration as they identify gaps in their understanding or instruction. Resisting the curses of knowledge and expertise requires intentional engagement and the support of others—fellow colleagues, WEC interlocutors, and, perhaps, students—to recognize one's disciplinary knowledge and to recalibrate expectations and instruction accordingly (Donovan & Bransford, 2005). Coming to these realizations can help faculty members open up their ideas about writing and see it as more dynamic and more dependent on audience and context than they had previously realized. Ideally, faculty members also realize that writing in their disciplines involves not just skills and conventions but also epistemologies, values, and assumptions that may (or may not) be shared with other disciplines. The end goal, in other words, is to help faculty members see that written communication in their disciplines involves, in Geisler's terms, both disciplinary domain content and rhetorical process knowledge.

For some faculty members, the experience of coming to these realizations through facilitated departmental discussion is what induces them to interrogate their disciplinary practice and expertise. For instance, I was struck by a discussion in a natural sciences department where a faculty member argued that the ability to "write concisely" was essential to good writing in their discipline but did not need to be defined. As an attribute, "concise" seemed so commonplace and clear that they doubted there was much value in describing how to evaluate it. Moreover, the evaluative criterion they initially articulated was rather circular: "concise writing uses as few words as possible without repetition." When the group discussed what "repetition" looked like in writing, it was soon evident that they were invoking a discipline-based notion of "concise" because additional knowledge of the lab report genre, assumed audience, and purpose were necessary to decide what was useful repetition versus unnecessary restatement or distracting detail. The discussion helped this faculty member realize that sometimes students struggled to write concisely because they did not have the disciplinary expertise to judge what details to include or strike. By acknowledging this, they began to "un-curse" the expertise that had obscured their rhetorical process knowledge and find a compelling reason to provide more explicit instruction in the genre conventions and audience expectations behind the concise writing they wanted to read.

Overall, the WEC process of articulating evaluative criteria for disciplinary writing helps faculty to identify the component parts and textual effects of particular writing abilities they value. This, in turn, reduces the tacitness of their expectations and, frequently, helps them connect individual writing abilities to larger disciplinary values and practices. In the next section, I will illustrate this iterative, collaborative process with examples from our WEC initiative with Computer Science.

IT'S THE CONSTANT PROCESS OF QUESTIONING: WEC IN COMPUTER SCIENCE

Computer science (C.S.) was one of Colby's two pilot WEC departments and the first to apply for an internal grant to create a writing plan and begin the WEC process. They were eager to do this work because they value writing and wanted their majors to develop strong communication skills. They felt this was especially important at a liberal arts college where a computer science major could not be as highly specialized and technically focused as might be possible in a large university context. At the same time, as a very small department—four faculty at the time, one of whom was brand new—they also felt significant time pressure from their rapidly growing major as well as the fact that most classes had over 40 students and required faculty to quickly turnaround responses to weekly projects.

The chair and faculty liaison were especially upfront about the fact that they knew little about how to teach writing but were eager to learn. In fact, it was refreshing to work with this group of faculty members because they were so open and non-territorial through detailed discussions about their teaching and curriculum. As the faculty liaison said in a later conversation, "it was nice working with you because you really respected our expertise. We may know nothing about writing, but we do know computer science!" Ultimately, however, what I came to realize was that C.S. faculty saw their expertise almost solely in terms of domain content knowledge, which obscured the fact that they *did* know a lot about and—in some cases had strong opinions on—writing and research in their discipline. This bifurcation of expertise also fostered a view of writing as a transparent, generalizable set of skills largely separate from C.S. "content."

As faculty members articulated disciplinary norms, forms, and conventions for writing in C.S., their dialogue and the facilitators' questions helped them to realize they had many unarticulated assumptions about "good writing" and their expectations for students' writing in their majors. For example, even though we had talked about the fact that "writing" could mean anything from musical notation to posters to code and cited the Minnesota WEC Program's capacious definition of writing, "visual marks that convey meaning," C.S. faculty remained focused on traditional alphabetic prose. They expressed concern over including forms that integrated text and visuals, like scientific posters, even as they articulated the importance of figures, precise descriptions of screenshots, or technical blogs when giving examples of disciplinary writing types and characteristics. Moreover, their feeling that they "should" adhere to a unimodal, generalized conception of writing continually broke down in discussions of their desired writing abilities for majors.

Take, for instance, this exchange about the three different styles of writing (their terms) they wanted C.S. majors to practice:[4]

> **FM (Faculty Member) 4**: [to FM 2] Where would a PowerPoint presentation, like for an interview talk—like FM 1's assignment, for example—fit into this? Would you consider that a fourth style?
>
> **FM 2**: I mean, I guess the question is, are we throwing things like PowerPoint presentations into the writing category?
>
> **WS (Writing Specialist) 1**: Yes.
>
> **FM 2**: 'Cause that's something that we've got that in our curriculum. And we've intentionally placed it there in a couple of different places.
>
> [Pauses to think.] It's sort of an explanatory style, but it's a very visual explanatory style.

4   The institutional review board at my institution found this study, which included citing anonymized excerpts from transcripts, to be exempt research. In accordance with standard protocols, participant names have been coded to protect their privacy. FM stands for faculty member and WS for writing specialist. In this meeting, there were two writing specialist facilitators and four faculty members present.

Though the second faculty member felt the need to ask if PowerPoint "counts" as writing, they also stated that C.S. had "intentionally placed" such multimodal communication assignments across their curriculum. Ironically, in the context of this situation, their tacit, alphabetic assumptions about "good writing" initially prevented C.S. faculty from seeing this curricular decision. Faculty members also realized that the "explanatory style" of writing they identified as important to the major did not account for the C.S. convention of integrating text and visuals to explain a process or product under consideration (e.g., in software debugging). This conversation led to a useful discussion of "concise"—a term they'd included in their list of C.S. writing characteristics but not yet defined—as particularly important to balancing text and visuals in posters and short presentations.

Another interesting example arose through dialog and self-study over the first few WEC meetings (see Pamela Flash, this volume, for details of the process). In our first meeting, faculty members brainstormed a list of characteristics of writing in Computer Science. In response, one faculty member quickly answered: "Readable. Well-organized." The other faculty members agreed. When the writing specialist asked the faculty member to clarify what they meant by these terms, she elaborated by adding speed and structure as concepts:

> **FM 1**: I think these two [readable and well-organized] are quite relevant to each other. I mean one affects the other. So, when I write a paper, I want the reviewer can scan my paper in ten seconds and understand what I'm talking about.
>
> **WS 1**: So, this is about fast comprehension? Several: Yes.
>
> **WS 2**: Which is about writing a good abstract? Or using your headings?
>
> **FM 2**: It's about having sentences at the beginning of each paragraph so that you can just read the first sentence of each paragraph and get a sense of what the paper is. I mean, in some sense, it's about fast grading.
>
> **FM 3**: Exactly, absolutely.

The comment about "fast grading" elicited agreement and some sheepish laughter. That faculty wanted students to structure their descriptive wiki "write-ups" for fast reading came up a couple of times in the first meetings. It was an admission framed as driven by the struggle to keep up with the heavy grading load, disconnected from disciplinary conventions or values.

The writing specialists continued by asking about faculty members' definition of "well organized" as a key characteristic of good writing and its connection to speed:

WS 1: So this is skimmable?

FM 3: It's not . . . I think it also means that they explicitly state the bigger picture aspects of it rather than just have the details.

WS 1: So that's the topic sentence idea of it [points to "topic sentences" on the board in the brainstorming list]. So, there's a hierarchy in the ways they're representing ideas so that you can skim quickly with these topic sentences.

FM 2: Yes, hierarchy!

FM 3: But I'm not even saying that about the topic sentences. I'm saying that the thing *above* the topic sentences is really important to have. And *that's* what might not be there. Like "The point of this project was to write a program that would *this*." Not just launch into, "I made this in class and that class and this other class." But something that's going to tell me . . . What are we [the writer and reader] doing here?

WS 1: And these [purpose for writing, topic sentences] tie back to fast comprehension.

FM 2 and 3: Yes!

As this exchange illustrates, faculty may struggle to find the language to articulate their implicit understandings of disciplinary writing. But with continued dialog and drafting, C.S. faculty realized they were bringing tacit *disciplinary* expectations and expertise to their preferences and criteria for evaluating student writing (see Figure 6.1). Faculty member 3, in moving beyond surface features like topic sentences, connected a disciplinary preference for hierarchical organization to the rhetorical expectation that these texts provide an explicit statement of the project's purpose before describing the details of implementation.

Subsequently, the first item on their writing plan's list of graduation-level writing abilities for the major pertained to the descriptive writing style C.S. faculty identified early on as important: "1. Students will be able to create precise descriptions of processes, data, and/or findings such that readers are able to quickly understand and are persuaded by the presentation." In articulating this ability, faculty decided that "precise" was more accurate than "concise," which, to them, too-simply implied shorter text. By suggesting that C.S. readers would be persuaded by precise descriptions they could "quickly understand," this ability also began to connect to discipline-based values more concrete and specific than "well organized." However, as they drafted criteria by which to evaluate this ability, the reference to speed in "quickly understand" was maintained, but the connection to organization was lost (see Table 6.1). This first draft of their criteria attempts to break down the writing ability into components, but there is no indication of how precise descriptions would lead readers to "quickly understand." Indeed, when faculty used some of these criteria to assess a writing sample, readers struggled to apply them and realized they needed more detail.

Table 6.1. Computer science draft 1 of writing ability #1[5]

Graduation-Level Writing Abilities *Students will be able to . . .*	Criteria for Assessing Writing Abilities *The text . . .*
1. Create **precise descriptions** of processes, data, and/or findings such that readers are able to **quickly understand** and are **persuaded** by the presentation.	1.1 conveys precise descriptions of processes, data, and/or findings.
	1.2 describes processes, data, and/or findings so that readers are able to **quickly understand** what was seen, done, and/or found.

Table 6.2. Revised draft of computer science writing ability #1 and evaluative criteria

Graduation-Level Writing Abilities *Students will be able to . . .*	Criteria for Assessing Writing Abilities *The text . . .*
1. Create **precise descriptions** of processes, data, and/or findings such that readers are able to **quickly understand** and are persuaded by the presentation.	1.1 is precise in that the writer provides sufficient, unambiguous information to allow the reader **to reproduce** the code/data/analysis OR **to "map out"** and **visualize the processes** while reading.
	1.2 is **organized hierarchically** to provide context (before moving into details about processes, data, and/or findings) so that the reader is able to **quickly understand** what the writer observed, tested, or found.

As the WEC facilitator, I noted that the criteria did not describe the text's desired effect(s) on readers. Faculty members, guided by those who had participated in the capstone assessment, discussed the goals and purposes of their abilities and criteria. Ultimately, they decided to define the most exigent things readers in the discipline should be able to do and understand while reading descriptive writing in C.S. The textual effects they cared about were "replication," "mapping out" (a reader's mental analogue to actually reproducing a process), and "hierarchical organization." The revised criteria for writing ability #1 (see Table 6.2) included these details and restored the reference to hierarchical

---

5   Tables 6.1 and 6.2 are based on a form licensed under a Creative Commons Attribution-NonCommercial-No Derivatives 4.0 International License. Attribution: Writing-Enriched Curriculum Program, University of Minnesota.

organization that had emerged earlier. While the iterative nature of this process means there is still room to clarify these criteria, they now invoked C.S. disciplinary values connected to the forms of writing—coding, descriptive summaries, instructions, and academic papers—faculty wanted students to learn.

While C.S. faculty could list characteristics of writing in their discipline and name writing abilities for their majors, the specific meaning and rhetorical features of many terms—like organized, concise, or descriptive—had been made invisible by tacit acquisition and the curse of expertise. Through the WEC process, faculty members realized that they had been assigning but not naming or teaching important disciplinary writing abilities (see Figure 6.1). This was a significant concern because they were committed to fostering a diverse, inclusive major and knew that such implicit expectations created an uneven playing field. Faculty members also realized they had no specific criteria for grading features of writing they expected, such as precise descriptions, an appropriate level of detail, and formatted visuals. As a first step, they revised the project grading criteria to award specific points to such features for all introductory classes.

By releasing the assumption that writing is a transparent, generalizable set of skills, C.S. faculty began to unearth tacit dimensions of their expertise and become more conscious of their expert blind spots. The process of identifying the component parts and effects of writing abilities they value reduced the tacitness of their expectations and helped faculty members connect individual writing abilities to larger disciplinary values and practices. As Faculty Member 3 put it, "It's the constant process of explaining 'in order to . . .' and asking 'Why is that important?' that helped. Bringing that stuff out explicitly has helped me to be much better at talking to students about what we want from writing." Ultimately, like the faculty interviewees in Anson's chapter in this collection, our Computer Science faculty have moved from a cheerful disavowal of writing knowledge to a more nuanced understanding of writing in their discipline and a commitment to making that knowledge visible and available to students.

IMPLICATIONS: WEC AND FACULTY DEVELOPING DISCIPLINARY AWARENESS

I have argued that implementing a WEC initiative increases faculty members' awareness of and attention to their own expertise, expectations, and potential blind spots as they articulate the characteristics, values, conventions, and forms of writing and research in their majors. The collaborative process of drafting and revising specific writing abilities and evaluation criteria—with a WEC facilitator as interlocutor—helps faculty develop a language for talking about writing that can begin to incorporate not only domain content but also rhetorical processes.

WEC facilitators need to help faculty unearth the rhetorical, communicative dimensions of expertise in their disciplines while also helping us to see that to develop expertise is to forget, to change, to think differently, and, therefore, to need to reconstruct and to reexamine one's expertise in order to more effectively share it with others.

Moving through the realizations I outline in the descriptive heuristic above (see Figure 6.1), faculty members develop a more nuanced understanding of their disciplinary writing expectations and, ideally, an increased curiosity about the writing abilities, goals, and forms other faculty value. In the long run, WEC can encourage the spread of more rich, respectful inter- and cross-disciplinary conversations about writing, learning, and research among faculty members. On our campus, new avenues of communication have opened through the process of involving faculty from "cognate" disciplines in capstone assessment readings or just from spontaneous hallway conversations about teaching shared forms, like lab reports or literature reviews.

My experience facilitating WEC and the process of helping faculty come to disciplinary awareness also suggests a few implications for facilitators beginning new WEC initiatives. First, this experience has reinforced how important it is to make space and time for faculty to unpack, discuss, and exemplify what they mean by their terms—especially common terms like "analysis" or "visualize" that seem to have meanings "everybody knows." Through the WEC process, faculty share and develop more specific concrete language for their writing expectations, which is essential and exciting. However, as a number of WAC studies have shown (e.g., Hughes & Miller, 2018; Nowacek, 2009; Schaefer, 2015; Thaiss & Zawacki, 2006), it is quite possible for faculty in the same discipline (and department) to mean different things by the same terms. Continually asking— What does that look like when you see it in writing?—is indispensable, and it is important not to short-circuit the collaborative process of discussion.

While it would be understandably tempting for a department to use language from authorities like accreditation bodies or pre-existing lists of learning objectives, it is the recursive process of articulating, questioning, parsing and revising that unearths tacit dimensions of disciplinary expertise and expectations. Moreover, to help keep a department's writing terms and expectations "live" and relevant, the WEC model includes the iterative process of faculty members' creating, over time, revised editions of their writing plans and returning, triennially, to read real student writing and reconsider their goals and criteria.

Second, it is important for facilitators to gauge how and when to bring in cross-curricular examples that can, through juxtaposition and comparison, help faculty members nuance their understanding of writing in their disciplines. Facilitators can, for instance, use comparative definitions to help faculty clarify their terms: if faculty members say they want students to "synthesize" sources in their writing, the WEC facilitator might ask: By "synthesis," do you mean citing multiple, relevant sources on the same topic in a concise summary, as in many Psychology literature reviews? Or defining two or three theoretical perspectives that will frame the arguments throughout an essay, as is common in English studies introductions? Or something else entirely? Capstone-level assessment readings can also be an opportunity to see how the same writing abilities may be enacted differently across majors. WEC facilitators and liaisons can decide, for example, to sample writing from two different types of capstones in the same department (e.g., a senior seminar with and without a lab or an art history and a studio art capstone), creating an instant cross-disciplinary reading experience that can yield rich conversation about what "integration of figures" or "source use" means.

Third, coming to disciplinary awareness and developing clear disciplinary writing criteria does not automatically mean that faculty will be able to teach these things to students. Of course, being able to articulate formerly tacit knowledge about disciplinary writing is a crucial step to developing more effective instructional activities. Moreover, as Anderson et al. (2016) found in their large study of NSSE data, providing "clear writing expectations" is one of three high-impact writing practices correlated with deep student learning. But moving from explicit knowledge and expectations to effective writing instruction also requires intentional, supported discussion, iteration, and transformation. Indeed, it strikes me this is an area of WID study that warrants continued investigation. What is the relationship between developing disciplinary awareness and one's beliefs about writing? Between changed beliefs and changed instructional practice? Fortunately, continuing our WEC initiative at Colby provides an ongoing opportunity to consider such questions, while continually learning from the process of helping faculty move beyond "I know it when I see it" to describe writing in their disciplines.

REFERENCES

Adler-Kassner, L. & Majewski, J. (2015). Extending the invitation: Threshold concepts, professional development, and outreach. In L. Adler-Kassner & E. Wardle (Eds.), *Naming what we know: Threshold concepts of writing studies* (pp. 186–202). Utah State University Press.

Anderson, P., Anson, C. M., Gonyea, R. M. & Paine, C. (2016). How to create high-impact writing assignments that enhance learning and development and reinvigorate WAC/WID programs: What almost 72,000 undergraduates taught us. *Across the Disciplines, 13*(4), 1–18. https://doi.org/10.37514/ATD-J.2016.13.4.13.

Anson, C. M. (2008). Closed systems and standardized writing tests. *College Composition and Communication, 60*(1), 113–128.

Anson, C. M. (2021). Introduction: WEC and the strength of the commons. In C. M. Anson & P. Flash (Eds.), *Writing-enriched curricula: Models of faculty-driven and departmental transformation.* The WAC Clearinghouse; University Press of Colorado. https://doi.org/10.27514/PER-B.2021.1299.1.3.

Anson, C. M. (2021). The new grass roots: Faculty responses to the writing-enriched curriculum. In C. M. Anson & P. Flash (Eds.), *Writing-enriched curricula: Models of faculty-driven and departmental transformation.* The WAC Clearinghouse; University Press of Colorado. https://doi.org/10.27514/PER-B.2021.1299.2.02.

Bazerman, C. (1988). *Shaping written knowledge: The genre and activity of the experi- mental article in science.* University of Wisconsin Press.

Bazerman, C. (1997). Discursively structured activities. *Mind, Culture, and Activity, 4*(4), 296–308.

Beaufort, A. (2007). *College writing and beyond.* Utah State University Press.

Brammer, C., Amare, N. & Sydow Campbell, K. (2008). Culture shock: Teaching writing within interdisciplinary contact zones. *Across the Disciplines, 5.* https://doi .org/10.37514/ATD-J.2008.5.1.04.

Bunnell, S. J. & Bernstein, D. L. (2012). Overcoming some threshold concepts in scholarly teaching. *Journal of Faculty Development, 26*(3), 14–18.

Carter, M. (1990). The idea of expertise an exploration of cognitive and social dimen- sions of writing. *College Composition and Communication, 41*(3), 265–286.

Carter, M. (2003). A process for establishing outcomes-based assessment plans for writing and speaking in the disciplines. *Language and Learning Across the Disciplines, 6*(1), 4–29. https://doi.org/10.37514/LLD-J.2003.6.1.02.

Carter, M. (2007). Ways of knowing, doing, and writing in the disciplines. *College Composition and Communication, 58*(3), 385–418.

Donovan, M. S. & Bransford, J. D. (2005). Introduction. In N. R. Council (Ed.), *How students learn: Science in the classroom* (pp. 1–26). The National Academies Press. https://instesre.org/NSFWorkshop/HowStudentsLearn.pdf.

Dreyfus, H. (2006). How far is distance learning from education? In E. Seliger & R. P. Crease (Eds.), *The philosophy of expertise* (pp. 196–212). Columbia University Press.

Epley, N., Keysar, B., Van Boven, L. & Gilovich, T. (2004). Perspective taking as ego- centric anchoring and adjustment. *Journal of Personality and Social Psychology, 87*(3), 327–339.

Fahnestock, J. & Secor, M. (1991). The rhetoric of literary criticism. In C. Bazerman & J. Paradis (Eds.), *Textual dynamics of the professions: Historical and contemporary studies of writing in professional communities* (pp. 76–96). University of Wisconsin Press.

Flash, P. (2016). From apprised to revised: Faculty in the disciplines change what they never knew they knew. In K. B. Yancey (Ed.), *A rhetoric of reflection.* Utah State University Press.

Flash, P. (2021). Writing-enriched curriculum: A model for making and sustaining change. In C. M. Anson & P. Flash (Eds.), *Writing-enriched curricula: Models of faculty-driven and departmental transformation.* The WAC Clearinghouse; University Press of Colorado. https://doi.org/10.27514/PER-B.2021.1299.2.01.

Flower, L. & Hayes, J. R. (1981). A cognitive process theory of writing. *College Composition and Communication, 32*(4), 365–387.

Geisler, C. (1994). *Academic literacy and the nature of expertise: Reading, writing, and knowing in academic philosophy.* Lawrence Erlbaum.

Herrington, A. (1985). Writing in academic settings: A study of the contexts for writing in two college chemical engineering courses. *Research in the Teaching of English, 19*(4), 331–359.

Hinds, P. J. (1999). The curse of expertise: The effects of expertise and debiasing methods on predictions of novice performance. *Journal of Experimental Psychology: Applied, 5*(2), 205–221.

Hughes, E. & Miller, T. (2018). WAC seminar participants as surrogate WAC consultants: Disciplinary faculty developing and deploying WAC expertise. *The WAC Journal, 29*, 7–41. https://doi.org/10.37514/WAC-J.2018.29.1.01.

Johns, A. M. (Ed.). (2002). *Genre in the classroom: Multiple perspectives.* Erlbaum.

Kelley, C. M. (1999). Subjective experience as a basis of "objective" judgments: Effects of past experience on judgments of difficulty. In D. Gopher & A. Koriat (Eds.), *Attention and performance* (Vol. 17, pp. 515–536). MIT Press.

MacDonald, S. (1994). *Professional academic writing in the humanities and social sciences* (1st ed.). Southern Illinois University Press.

Malenczyk, R. (2016). *A rhetoric for writing program administrators* (2 ed.) Parlor Press.

Moor, K. S., Jensen-Hart, S. & Hooper, R. I. (2012). Small change, big difference: Heightening BSW faculty awareness to elicit more effective student writing. *Journal of Teaching in Social Work, 32*(1), 62–77. https://doi.org/10.1080/08841233.2012.640601.

Nathan, M. J. & Koedinger, K. R. (2000). An investigation of teachers' beliefs of students' algebra development. *Cognition and Instruction, 18*(2), 207–235.

Nathan, M. J. & Petrosino, A. (2003). Expert blind spot among preservice teachers. *American Educational Research Journal, 40*(4), 905–928.

Nickerson, R. S. (1999). How we know—and sometimes misjudge—what others know: Imputing one's own knowledge to others. *Psychological Bulletin, 125*(6), 737–759. https://doi.org/10.1037/0033-2909.125.6.737.

Nowacek, R. S. (2009). Why is being interdisciplinary so very hard to do? Thoughts on the perils and promise of interdisciplinary pedagogy. *College Composition and Communication, 60*(3), 493–516.

Rice, J. (2015). Para-expertise, tacit knowledge, and writing problems. *College English, 78*(2), 117–138.

Russell, D. R. (2001). Where do the naturalistic studies of WAC/WID point? In S. H. McLeod, E. Miraglia, M. Soven & C. Thaiss (Eds.), *WAC for the new millennium: Strategies for continuing writing-across-the-curriculum programs* (pp. 259–298). National Council of Teachers of English.

Russell, D. R. (2002). *Writing in the academic disciplines: A curricular history* (2 ed.). Southern Illinois University Press.

Salem, L. & Jones, P. (2010). Undaunted, self-critical, and resentful: Investigating faculty attitudes toward teaching writing in a large university writing-intensive course program. *WPA: Writing Program Administration, 34*(1), 60–83.

Schaefer, K. L. (2015). "Emphasizing similarity" but not "eliding difference"—exploring sub-disciplinary differences as a way to teach genre flexibly. *The WAC Journal, 26*, 36–55. https://doi.org/10.37514/WAC-J.2015.26.1.03.

Sheriff, S. & Harrington, P. (2017). Colby college writing program & Farnham Writers' Center. In B. S. Finer (Ed.), *Writing program architecture: Thirty cases for reference and research*. Utah State University Press.

Thaiss, C. & Zawacki, T. M. (2006). *Engaged writers and dynamic disciplines: Research on the academic writing life*. Heinemann-Boynton/Cook.

Wardle, L. & Scott, J. B. (2015). Defining and developing expertise in a writing and rhetoric department. *Writing Program Administration, 39*(1), 72–93.

Wilder, L. (2012). *Rhetorical strategies and genre conventions in literary studies: Teaching and writing in the disciplines*. Southern Illinois University Press.

Wilder, L. & Wolfe, J. (2009). Sharing the tacit rhetorical knowledge of the literary scholar: The effects of making disciplinary conventions explicit in undergraduate writing about literature courses. *Research in the Teaching of English, 44*(2), 170–209.

Wiles, W. M. (2014). *Prompting discussion: Writing prompts, habits of mind, and the shape of the writing classroom* (Publication Number 1731) [Dissertation, The University of Louisville].

Wolfe, J., Olson, B. & Wilder, L. (2014). Knowing what we know about writing in the disciplines: A new approach to teaching for transfer in FYC. *The WAC Journal, 25*, 42–77. https://doi.org/10.37514/WAC-J.2014.25.1.03.

Zhu, W. (2004). Faculty views on the importance of writing, the nature of academic writing, and teaching and responding to writing in the disciplines. *Journal of Second Language Writing, 13*(1), 29–48.

CHAPTER 7.

PILOTING WEC AS A CONTEXT-RESPONSIVE WRITING RESEARCH INITIATIVE

Crystal N. Fodrey and Chris Hassay
Moravian College

This chapter frames WEC as a collaborative research methodology that privileges context as the primary factor in curricular revision efforts. We explain how, at our small liberal arts college, the practice of rhetorical listening with both undergraduate and graduate programs served as a catalyst to initiate WEC. A case study of our WEC pilot in the English department underscores the contextual flexibility inherent in a modified model that includes interviews/focus groups as a qualitative data component and epistemological tool meant to be placed into conversation with both writing artifacts and survey data to guide group discussion and inform the development of writing plans.

> [R]hetorical contexts should drive methods and . . . the most effective research methods in any given rhetorical situation (e.g., particular audiences and purposes) will depend on the specifics of that situation.
>
> —Broad, 2012, p. 200

One of the greatest strengths of the WEC model is that it affords practitioners the opportunity to make context-informed modifications to the methodology established by Pamela Flash at UMN that best serve campus-specific needs while maintaining underlying WEC goals: sustainable effectiveness; department-retained agency; and substantial, meaningful, goal-driven conversation about writing and the teaching of writing, all "premised on the belief faculty members situated within disciplines are positioned to offer powerful, relevant writing instruction" (Wagner et al., 2014, p. 112).

As WEC proliferates through the campus of our small liberal arts college (SLAC) in southeastern Pennsylvania—across established and developing programs in both undergraduate and graduate contexts—we as the current leaders of this initiative at Moravian College find ourselves learning alongside each academic unit with which we collaborate at every phase of the WEC process.[1] It is with this in mind, too, that we look back at the decision to frame our WEC process as research that stems from rhetorically listening to our colleagues who have shown us a faculty context that is small yet ambitious, autonomy-valuing yet highly collaborative, and desiring of strong internally sourced evidence to substantiate curricular revision.

LOCATING THE EXIGENCE FOR WEC AT MORAVIAN

The origins of WEC at our institution—both programmatically and method-ologically—begin first from an inquiry of the Writing-Intensive (WI) model that preceded WEC. Crystal, who in 2014 was the newly hired assistant professor of English and WAC Director at Moravian, inherited a program that featured WI courses positioned across almost every undergraduate major on campus. She had very little knowledge about the program's responsibilities, legacy, or reception. In order to understand this pre-existing WAC initiative and faculty perceptions of it, she met with each department over the course of a year and employed the feminist tactic of rhetorical listening described and theorized by Krista Ratcliffe (2005). Ratcliffe defines rhetorical listening as "a trope for interpretive invention and . . . as a code of cross-cultural conduct" (p. 17), making it an ideal practice to promote cross-disciplinary understanding about writing.

In action, it helped Crystal maintain a mindful stance of quiet, reflective openness—acknowledging to faculty of academic units that she came from a place where she did not yet know them or what she did not know about them (Ratcliffe, 2005, p. 73). This allowed her to position herself as an interested, non-judgmental writing specialist while she learned about the complex culture of writing at our college. Simultaneously she established important relationships across campus with the hope of fostering a shared vision of the value of writ-ing. During each meeting, Crystal asked questions like "what is a typical writ-ing assignment that a major in your department would be asked to complete, and what are the qualities of a successful piece of writing for that assignment?" Responses elicited from this early practice served as entry-points for better iden-tification with disciplinary logics and the varied definitions of "good writing"

---

1   Moravian's WEC process is broken into four phases, akin to the year-based model utilized at UMN. The major difference aside from the modifications described in this chapter is the overall timeline (i.e., phases versus years) because often the initial research process only takes a semester, and we start the research process conducted by the WEC Team (Phase 1) followed by two full unit faculty meetings and the creation of a Writing Plan by unit faculty (Phase 2), the plan's approval and implementation (Phase 3), and recurring assessment of the plan conducted by academic unit faculty (Phase 4).

that exist from department to department and sometimes even from individual to individual within those departments (as also noted by Sheriff in this volume when discussing her own experiences with WEC in a similar institutional context). The contextually situated conversations among teacher-scholars that grew out of rhetorical listening forged a pathway for Crystal to begin designing a WAC program that not only achieved her primary aim—to graduate rhetorically flexible, reflective writers—but also honored the disciplinary positionalities and contributions to writing pedagogy of those across campus. (To learn more about the overall development of the Writing at Moravian program of which WEC is a part, see Fodrey et al., 2019.)

As Bastian (2014), who explains the benefits of the practice of rhetorical listening during her initial program development of a WAC initiative at The College of St. Scholastica, suggests, "rhetorical listening allows for Writing Program Administrators (WPAs) to hear people's intersecting identifications with writing, their disciplines, and students. Moreover, this kind of listening . . . allows WPAs both to understand their colleagues' 'problems' and to collaboratively redefine those 'problems' as opportunities" (Bastian, 2014). For Crystal, rhetorical listening was an important tactic for her to use to orient her own work at Moravian for the future and discover the actual problems that faculty had so that the program she developed would be responsive to them.

Through this practice Crystal learned first and foremost that faculty across the disciplines at this private SLAC wanted a WPA who gave support but not mandates. She also learned that some faculty were dissatisfied with the WI model either because it was arbitrarily placed in the curriculum or the campus-wide outcomes were too generic to be meaningful in a given departmental context, ultimately providing the exigence to look for an alternative model to the WI system.

From Crystal's conversations with faculty, she determined that Moravian had what Carol Rutz and William Condon (2012) refer to as an "established" WAC program "focused on the pragmatic tasks of building support for WAC, inventing courses, and building an adequate resource base for the program" that she wanted to transition to "integrated," a move that brings with it "deeper, more theoretically grounded understanding of the program's role within the institution" (pp. 371–372). Crystal had relative confidence in the following: (1) WEC could provide faculty greater autonomy by decentralizing the Director of Writing's perceived and actual authority over writing in the disciplines, and (2) WEC could either serve alongside the Writing-Intensive (WI) Writing-Across-the-Curriculum course requirement in place at our institution or replace it entirely, depending on faculty reception. Her immediate goal was to continue building connections with each faculty member by helping them articulate the intersections among their values and beliefs about disciplinary writing and those of others in their unit so that decisions about the teaching and integration of writing in those units could be a collaborative effort.

While the adoption of WEC seemed a valuable albeit time-intensive direction forward for the WAC program, Crystal was concerned about the feasibility of this work in tandem with her responsibilities as a pre-tenure faculty member who was expected to develop and teach new rhetoric and writing studies courses, produce scholarship, and administer most aspects of the writing program minus the Writing Center. She also hoped to use WEC as an opportunity to conduct context-specific qualitative writing studies research that would both facilitate more conversation about writing pedagogy on our campus and afford her the opportunity to research local disciplinary knowledge production practices at play in the activity systems of various programs that opted into WEC. In theory, our WEC program could also remove the burden of "'selling' the increased and enhanced use of writing down to the level of individual teachers" that Anson suggests in the Introduction of this volume (and that Crystal first employed when arriving on campus) and replace that site of administrative effort instead with the support of faculty-driven programmatic writing curriculum development. She therefore advocated that the English Department revise their scholarship statement to consider aspects of WPA work as scholarly production. In response, the department approved the addition of language stating "administrative contributions that promote intellectual growth" could count as scholarly production toward tenure and promotion.[2] Framing WEC as research after this revision allowed Crystal to concurrently use context-specific writing studies research to apply something akin to the whole systems approach to WAC program development (Cox et al., 2018) and also provided her the opportunity to share epistemological scholarship with the field in the future.

In the spring of 2016, Crystal recruited Chris and the two received an internal summer research grant to modify the WEC methodology in place at UMN for our SLAC context. We started with the English department—which had expressed an early interest in the program and an availability to participate over the summer. The exigence, then, for framing Moravian's engagement with the WEC project as a collaborative writing research initiative first stemmed from a

---

2   A footnote in the Moravian College English Department's Scholarship Statement includes the following language to justify this addition: "As noted in the Council of Writing Program Administrators (WPA) statement on 'Evaluating the Intellectual Work of Writing Administration,' such administrative work should be 'a form of inquiry which advances knowledge and which has formalized outcomes that are subject to peer review and disciplinary evaluation' and might include work within the categories of 'Program Creation, Curricular Design, Faculty Development, Program Assessment, and Program-Related Textual Production' (http://wpacouncil.org/positions/intellectualwork.html)."

desire to honor faculty feedback in our SLAC context and from our positionalities as researchers at the time.

DEVELOPING OUR PILOT OF WEC RESEARCH WITH THE ENGLISH DEPARTMENT

In English we began by modeling our work on that of WEC at UMN, as described by Flash in Chapter 1 of this volume—adopting the materials provided on the UMN website (i.e., faculty and student surveys, WEC informational documents for faculty, etc.) and then adapting them for our context. While this initial process of studying and using UMN materials was formative, we quickly recognized just how different our institutional context was from that of Minnesota. At Moravian, our above average-sized department consisted of only nine faculty including two new hires preparing to start in the fall of 2016. These logistical concerns raised questions about the practicality of the sequence of department-wide meetings about writing in the curriculum—a key component of WEC practice at UMN. First, on a pragmatic level, the two new hires were unavailable for these conversations, making the meeting model used at UMN a poor fit within our Summer 2016 pilot. Additionally, the dynamics at play in a conversation about what department members value in writing could be somewhat difficult for pre-tenure faculty—Crystal included—in comparison to an established cohort of tenured faculty, regardless of how welcoming those tenured faculty were in this context. Instead we decided to utilize faculty interviews preceding larger department meetings as a way to gather and represent everyone's voice—which we would then share with unit faculty via anonymous representative excerpts from interview transcripts in a larger department meeting as a component of a findings report which we would produce for them.

Our interviews helped us establish connections between English faculty and the WEC process—moving into full department meetings with an idea of what each individual brings to the department and a group of faculty already aware of the areas of inquiry these WEC meetings were poised to investigate. We focused on faculty-specific writing expectations with questions modified from Crystal's initial departmental conversations the year prior. For example we asked, "describe the essential writing assignments from [name of a particular core course taught by that faculty member]," paired with the following sequence of questions: "what are the qualities of a successful piece of writing composed for that sort of assignment," and "why are these criteria particularly important?" to reveal the tacit assumptions about writing English faculty embedded within their assignments and by extension enacted across the curriculum. After compiling the full set of English data, we conducted a qualitative descriptive analysis to locate areas of emphasis related to writing-specific values. While our coding process adapts to the context and questions we are asking of faculty, we consistently organize our developed codes into code groups modeled on the knowledge domains from which successful writers draw—specifically subject matter, writing process, rhetorical, and genre knowledge (Beaufort, 2007). Through our analysis of collected writing samples, corresponding prompts, and interview transcripts from faculty across the academic unit, we identified myriad assigned genres and approaches to the teaching of writing. That process punctuated what we already suspected to be true: that each faculty member metonymically represented what could be a program or a full department at a larger institution, and these specializations[3] under the banner of English at Moravian were realized in assigned writing—often of specialized genres with respective expectations unique to a faculty member across their courses. English undergraduates echoed this discovery when participating in a focus group that supplemented our faculty interviews. Students implicitly picked up on differences in genre expectations across specific faculty emphasizing components of their experience in the curriculum by instructor instead of course title or class standing. Those genres/purposes for writing included the following, not all of which a given undergraduate English major would likely encounter given English's horizontal curriculum:

> **Thesis-driven scholarly/analytical:** literary analysis/criticism (close reading only, or contextualized with sources, or contextualized via application of theoretical lens plus sources); cultural criticism written as scholarship; stylistic analysis/craft criticism; rhetorical criticism of any communicative artifact; rhetorical historiography via archival research; empirical writing studies research; critical reflection

> **Creative:** poetry, short story, memoir, personal essay, play

> **Public Discursive:** social justice-oriented public writing; letters to editor; blogging, digital public rhetoric via video, infographics, flyers, newsletters, web design, etc.; cultural criticism written as creative nonfiction; environmental writing; documentary

> **Professional/Technical:** grant proposals, usability and feasibility reports, memos, technical documentation, project proposals, needs analysis reports, etc.

---

3   The following specializations are represented among the nine faculty in the department in Fall 2016: rhetoric and writing studies, African American literature, transatlantic modernism(s) and dramatic literature, creative writing and contemporary literature, postcolonial literature and queer studies, old and middle English and medieval saints' lives, theatre arts, and early nineteenth century British and American literature.

The findings report we produced and presented to the department at the initial department-wide Phase 2 WEC meeting shared these discoveries with faculty, who were then able to map specific genres they assigned in their courses to the larger curriculum that made up the English major. These conversations and meetings continued productively. For example, at a Spring 2017 meeting, faculty discussed the ways courses are positioned within the curriculum along with the student learning outcomes for English, ultimately noting how the expected ability levels of students play a role in defining writing pedagogy in a given course in tandem with one's disciplinary expertise and individual expectations. Department members then started conversations about how those curricular details could invite faculty to collaborate on the development of a writing plan with shared understandings and expectations for majors while still maintaining their own pedagogical identities.

In this pilot study, our findings report served as the deliverable for the department and our interviews a significant datapoint highlighted in that deliverable. As our first WEC unit, English helped us discover the ways in which the WEC process at Moravian could be designed to be most effective on our campus. These context-informed modifications, interviews, and reports that we share with faculty at our equivalent of UMN's Meeting 1 would quickly become the features of the program that were most exciting to potential WEC departments. The English pilot led us to recognize that the interview process in particular helps interviewees find both individual and collective value in the WEC process—assuaging worries that this is just another top-down initiative—and as a result improves departmental buy-in during the process and creates strong word of mouth advertising, convincing other academic units to opt in.

WEC RESEARCH METHODOLOGY AT/ FOR MORAVIAN COLLEGE

Our formative pilot study led us to conceptualize (and eventually promote) WEC at Moravian as a research initiative that privileged disciplinary participant ways of knowing and writing over our writing studies researcher interpretation. When we began implementing the WEC model, we quickly realized that in order for faculty to have a vested stake in the future of writing at Moravian, we needed to first invite them into the conversation as not merely agents through which mandated writing instruction happened but as active colleagues who were directly influencing, designing, and revising writing outcomes and pedagogical practices—an essential component of the larger WEC process. Anson (2006) highlights such sentiments when describing the WEC program he and colleagues established at North Carolina State University: "the process of negotiating and articulating [writing] outcomes leads to faculty investment by tapping into what the department cares about in student learning and achievement" (p. 109). In a similar spirit, the semi-structured interviews we conduct with faculty are positioned, first and foremost, as knowledge-producing for the departments themselves, and work towards uncovering what each faculty member cares about in their own teaching practice.

Faculty are navigating these reflective spaces with us—a collaborative movement through and across disciplinary boundaries—with which we engage in two distinct ways: as WEC practitioners *and* as researchers. We therefore see faculty both as co-researchers and research participants across two distinct aims: (1) most importantly we hope that they research their department with us as they endeavor to improve student writing, and (2) we hope that the information they provide contributes to the understanding of knowledge production both at our institution and eventually through conference presentations and the dissemination of scholarship, within and beyond the fields of writing across the curriculum and writing studies.

In the interviews we conduct, we practice rhetorical listening in similar ways to Crystal's first inquiries with departments on campus, taking a stance of what Ratcliffe (2005) calls non-identification, acknowledging the differences among what WEC research is, who we are as writing researchers, and the ideologies and tacit knowledge about writing and student writers that participants in WEC units bring to the fore. We believe that rhetorical listening provides an imperfect yet logical tactic to navigate unfamiliar yet fascinating cross-disciplinary terrain. For WEC at Moravian to work, we are creating a dialogue housed primarily in the discourse communities of the interviewee as opposed to our own—the tactic of rhetorical listening is meant to help "negotiate troubled identifications in order to facilitate cross-cultural communication about any topic" (Ratcliffe, 2005, p. 17)—and by doing interviews separately, we are able to learn about individual expectations for writing without being in a space that simultaneously must accommodate a number of additional perceptions and goals which can be, at times, overlapping and conflicting. This means placing our own disciplinary expertise outside of the conversational act (as best we can); representing ourselves as curious, active listeners; and ultimately working to table what we believe in order to be as open as possible to the perspectives of our interviewees. It also means that we listen metonymically, starting from a place where we assume that each interviewee is "associated with—but not necessarily representative of—an entire cultural group" (Ratcliffe, 2005, p. 78), in this case "cultural group" meaning discipline or academic unit. This, too, separates our work as researchers in which we produce interpretative analyses of department writing for communities outside of our campus and as WEC practitioners who work to help academic units on our campus. This work is feasible *because* we are constantly recognizing, owning, and employing these identities by focusing directly on either programmatic or research goals, depending on what we are trying to accomplish at a given point in the process.

Selfe and Hawisher (2012) describe the use of feminist research methodology in relation to their study of the digital literacy practices of U.S. citizens, noting that "intimate and richly situated information . . . emerges most productively from interviews . . . in which all participants—researchers and informants—understand that they are engaged in mutually shaping meaning and that such meaning necessarily is local, fragmentary, and contingent" (p. 36). In our context, that means asking open-ended questions like "define writing in your discipline" that invite interviewees to share knowledge from their own understanding of writing at a given point in time. We ask participants for these definitions immediately after giving the one adopted by the Writing at Moravian program as a whole: writing here is broadly defined as communication in which audio, visual, spatial, gestural, and/or textual components convey meaning (including words, sentences, tables, figures, images, video, etc.). By beginning the exchange with this definition, we move towards a state of non-identification, a concept "important to rhetoric and composition studies because it maps a place, a possibility, for consciously asserting our agency to engage cross-cultural rhetorical exchanges across both commonalities and differences" (Ratcliffe, 2005, p. 73). The stage is then set for an abstracted definition from our interviewees by showing them the breadth of writing we recognize already and encouraging them to explore the openness of this definition in their response. We provide no further emphasis on our own disciplinary values; instead we simply invite them to share their expertise. In sum, this rhetorical move allows us to work against our identities on campus as writing specialists physically located in and representative of the English department, and it disrupts a more narrow definition of writing that interviewees may bring into the space of the interview (and that they may believe is how we as writing studies scholars understand writing).

As our interviews continue, participants attempt to explain an abstract and commonly unexplored idea: what is writing in my disciplinary context? We hope that answers to this question are then productively delivered throughout our second organization of questions, which are tied to the specifics of one's pedagogy in a course: "describe the essential writing assignments from [course]" and "what are the qualities of a successful piece of writing composed for that sort of assignment, and why are they important?" and ultimately in a final sequence of questions, which ask participants to be interpretive and reflective of their larger curriculum. In every sequence we are still working towards the initial question about the definition of writing in a discipline, but as we change scopes we can approach that larger question from different entry points. In the spirit of semi-structured interviewing as described by Prior (2004), we "move between scripted questions"—those we have listed—"and open-ended conversations" (p. 188) that productively arise both from these and other academic-unit specific questions we develop with the help of a given WEC liaison and the data we have gathered to that point.

An additional layer of complexity to this process comes from the disciplines themselves and are unearthed in follow-up conversations—productive diversions embedded in our interviews that help us uncover the tacit understandings of writing that faculty bring to their academic units. As we ask faculty to rationalize and reflect on the choices that they are making, they also begin speaking about their places within the larger curriculum of an academic unit—providing their macroview which we can then place in conversation with not only what we find but also the contributions of their colleagues. This process helps us define disciplinary writing specific to contexts and the faculty who represent them within a particular academic unit.

Given that English was the first unit with which we collaboratively researched writing, the department represented the most significant development of our methods and an early example of how a specific departmental context defined the research process. For us, what initially served as a response to logistical concerns, became a recognition of the value of such small department sizes because this extra data was not only available but entirely feasible to collect.

FINDINGS REPORT AND WRITING PLAN AS WEC DELIVERABLES

Findings reports serve as culminations of the research practices utilized within a given academic unit with relevant descriptive findings triangulated from the various components of our method. Our intention is to represent the stakeholders of an academic unit as they see themselves in relation to the discipline-relevant writing they assign, placing the overlapping writing-related values and beliefs of each faculty member into conversation, and providing the occasion for faculty to look at how those conceptions of writing and student writers interact. By this point late in Phase 1 of our WEC process, we will have collected as much data as possible in order to create a holistic picture of what writing looks like at a specific point in time. Our hope is for each faculty member to see what writing looks like at a macro-level and also recognize their individual contributions. Findings reports are owned by the units for which they are produced and become important primary sources for liaisons as they construct writing plans.

These documents are oftentimes additionally used by departments to communicate with outside audiences like accreditors and potential funding sources.

As we finished our work within the English department and began to look at the initial process with that unit as a guide which could inform future WEC research, we continually returned Broad's (2012) contention that "rhetorical context should drive methods" (p. 200). Our expectation at the end of the pilot study was that the research methods used in English could be replicated across other Moravian College contexts. As of 2020, we have produced findings reports in both undergraduate programs (English, education, modern languages, chemistry and biochemistry, and mathematics) and graduate programs (education, occupational therapy, and speech-language pathology), finding that while some processes have worked across academic units others had to adapt to fit the needs of the context; as Broad (2012) suggests, "our methods choose us" (p. 202). After working with these programs we have found that the rhetorical situation oftentimes defines the ways information is communicated on our findings reports, whether that be through the inclusion of curriculum maps of writing assignments in core courses, coded transcripts of faculty dialogue with provided explanation, graphical representations of quantitative survey data, relevant scholarly research, audio clips of professional affiliates speaking on the desired writing abilities of new hires, images of student work, and much more. These findings reports, we have found, must communicate in ways that are valued by the disciplines represented in the discourse community; this makes them both accessible and actionable for the group as they begin to conceptualize (initially) the ways in which they will respond to the process in Phase 2.

After the findings report meeting occurs at the start of Phase 2, agency and expectation shifts to the academic unit faculty who begin to run their own meetings (unless we are requested to do so), and the liaison begins the process of drafting a writing plan. Writing plans at Moravian, again modified from the UMN template, are designed to address this sequence of questions (about units either at the undergraduate or graduate level):

- How can writing in this academic unit be characterized?
- What writing abilities should students demonstrate proficiency in by the time they graduate, and how do these abilities synergize with your student learning outcomes?
- How is writing instruction currently positioned in this academic unit's curriculum (or curricula), and what, if any, structural plans does this academic unit have for changing the way that writing and writing instruction are sequenced across its course offerings?
- How does this academic unit currently communicate writing

expectations to students, what do these expectations look like when they are translated into assessable criteria, and how does/will faculty in this academic unit assess that students have met these expectations?

- What does the academic unit intend to implement during the period covered by this plan, and what sorts of support do faculty need in order to achieve the optimal integration of relevant writing instruction and assess the efficacy of the plan?

During the spring 2019 semester, Moravian faculty voted in favor of adopting the WEC and writing plan approval process proposed by the Writing at Moravian Advisory Committee.

Writing plans for academic units at Moravian can exist as curricular documentation that coexists alongside or replaces pre-existing assessment structures. Units with writing-enriched curricula that are articulated in the writing plan, enacted in the unit's curriculum, and assessed by the unit faculty, have the option to remove the WI designation from core courses if they so choose. In our context, we believe giving faculty in academic units the choice to decide to either maintain their WI courses or remove them after engaging in the WEC process creates another opportunity for increased autonomy (similar to the options at Pound Ridge College in Chris Anson's chapter in this collection). As such, our proposal to faculty includes discussion on how these two can articulate together, how a group that has gone through the WEC process can apply for writing-enriched status, and how that status carries with it both opportunities for curricular change and plans for assessment moving forward. Returning to the English department who completed their writing plan two years after the initial discussion of their findings report, the group has begun implementing components of both the report and writing plan into their curriculum. For example, English is redesigning 100-level literature courses, developing a better articulation between 200 level-gateway courses and the English major capstone, updating the direct-assessment method for the department focused on mutual understanding across faculty, and discussing the potential removal of the WI label from certain English courses.

THE FUTURE OF WEC AT MORAVIAN

We have been asked before "why not just use the descriptions of discipline-relevant writing characteristics and abilities from writing plans available on UMN's website?" Our answer is that we, and increasingly our colleagues, find it of utmost importance to understand writing within the local context of academic units at Moravian College because only then can WEC liaisons develop writing plans that speak to their department's culture and writing values, not simply impose context-specific writing standards of another campus into our specific SLAC context.

Our adoption of WEC recognizes a critical feature of what Gladstein and Regaignon (2012) describe in *Writing Program Administration at Small Liberal Arts Colleges*: "Small college faculty are simultaneously autonomous agents and expected to dedicate significant time to the institution, its policies, and its future" (p. 21). For us as WEC practitioners, the goal is to honor the autonomy and expertise of the faculty at our SLAC while supporting them with our expertise as well.

WEC at Moravian works because we are able to capitalize on our small campus size and collaborative faculty culture. Each academic unit carries with it a set of (often overlapping) disciplinary ways of knowing and doing, and it is through our engagement with these shared contexts and the experiences of the faculty, students, and affiliated professionals informing the writing that happens in each academic unit, that WEC at Moravian continues to refine our methods and the methodology informing them. Through a rhetorical listening framed interview practice, we found we are able to take the varied individual perspectives in an academic unit and present them back to the larger group in ways that recognize the importance of every stakeholder a liaison puts us in contact with. Our conversations with faculty of an academic unit, then, begin not at "how is writing defined in this discipline" but rather, "let us look at how the stakeholders of this unit define writing" because of the interview data we collect. This allows the unit faculty to work toward a unified yet multifaceted definition with these individual perspectives outlined on the findings report. These modifications are emblematic of a larger trend toward locally informed design in both WEC and other WAC initiatives. Simply put, WEC at Moravian stems from both our critical reflections as members of the Moravian community and our disciplinary positionalities as writing across the curriculum scholars. While we have found situating WEC as a research initiative to be productive at Moravian, we recognize that this will not work as well in every context and advocate for WEC models that are informed by not only successful implementations of similar models by others but also responsive to the nuanced details of each individual institutional context.

REFERENCES

Anson, C. M. (2006). Assessing writing in cross-curricular programs: Determining the locus of activity. *Assessing Writing, 11*, 100–112. https://doi.org/10.1016/j.asw.2006.07.001.

Anson, C. M. (2021). The new grass roots: Faculty responses to the writing-enriched curriculum. In C. M. Anson & P. Flash (Eds.), *Writing-enriched curricula: Models of faculty-driven and departmental transformation.* The WAC Clearinghouse; University Press of Colorado. https://doi.org/10.27514/PER-B.2021.1299.2.02.

Bastian, H. (2014). Performing the groundwork: Building a WEC/WAC writing program at The College of St. Scholastica," *Composition Forum, 29.* http://composition forum.com/issue/29/st-scholastica.php.

Beaufort, A. (2007). *College writing and beyond: A new framework for university writing instruction.* Utah State University Press.

Broad, B. (2012). Strategies and passions in empirical qualitative research. In L. Nickoson & M. P. Sheridan (Eds), *Writing studies research in practice: Methods and methodologies* (pp. 197–209). Southern Illinois University Press.

Condon, W. & Rutz, C. (2012). A taxonomy of writing across the curriculum programs: Evolving to serve broader agendas. *College Composition and Communication, 64*(2), 357–382. https://www.jstor.org/stable/43490756.

Cox, M., Galin, J. & Melzer, D. (2018). *Sustainable WAC a whole systems approach to launching and developing writing across the curriculum programs.* National Council of Teachers of English.

Flash, P. (2016). From apprised to revised: Faculty in the disciplines change what they never knew they knew. In K. B. Yancey (Ed.), *A rhetoric of reflection* (pp. 227–249). Utah State University Press.

Fodrey, C. N., Mikovits, M., Hassay, C. & Yozell, E. (2019) Activity theory as tool for WAC program development: Organizing first-year writing and writing-enriched curriculum systems. *Composition Forum 42.* https://compositionforum.com/issue/42/moravian.php.

Gladstein, J. M. & Regaignon, D. R. (2012). *Writing program administration at small liberal arts colleges.* Parlor Press.

Ratcliffe, K. (2005). *Rhetorical listening: Identification, gender, and whiteness.* Southern Illinois University Press.

Selfe, C. L. & Hawisher, G. E. (2012) Exceeding the bounds of the interview: Feminism, mediation, narrative and conventions about digital literacy. In L. Nickoson & M. P. Sheridan (Eds.), *Writing studies research in practice: Methods and methodologies* (pp. 36–50). Southern Illinois University Press

Sheriff, S. (2021). Beyond "I know it when I see it": WEC and the process of unearthing faculty expertise. In C. M. Anson & P. Flash (Eds.), *Writing-enriched curricula: Models of faculty-driven and departmental transformation.* The WAC Clearinghouse; University Press of Colorado. https://doi.org/10.27514/PER-B.2021.1299.2.06.

Wagner, H. E., Hilger, P.A. & Flash P. (2014). Improving writing skills of construction management undergraduates: Developing tools for empirical analysis of writing to create writing-enriched construction management curriculum. *International Journal of Construction Education and Research, 10*(2), 111–125, https://doi.org/10.1080/15 578771.2013.852146.

WPA Executive Committee. (1996). Evaluating the intellectual work of writing program administrators: A draft. *Writing Program Administration,* 20(1/2), 92–103. http://associationdatabase.co/archives/20n1-2/20n1-2intellectual.pdf.

CHAPTER 8.

THEORIZING THE WEC MODEL WITH THE WHOLE SYSTEMS APPROACH TO WAC PROGRAM SUSTAINABILITY

Jeffrey R. Galin

Florida Atlantic University

When administration of WAC programs is discussed in WAC literature, program description and advice are typically emphasized rather than building a theory of administering and building WAC programs. Such a framework with roots in multiple disciplines that overlap enables WAC administrators and oversight committees to examine WAC programs systematically, even when they have developed organically over time. This chapter highlights ways that a WEC model can address threats to WAC programs' sustainability, i.e., the complexities of higher education programs as they relate to administrative structures and leadership. The story of developing the WEC component of FAU's twelve-year old WAC program is one of slow development, broad stakeholder participation, manageable growth, and limited scope. But it is also the story of an institution working through a systematic process of program building that is grounded in what Cox et al. (2018) call the whole systems approach to WAC program sustainability. This chapter traces FAU's process as the first WAC program in the country to implement sustainability indicators as the basis for its formative self-assessment to track all facets of its WAC program. It also demonstrates how other such programs can draw on the whole systems approach for WEC program implementation.

As one of the most systematic and comprehensive models for writing across the curriculum, whole department approaches to WAC such as writing enriched curriculum (WEC) initiatives are more likely to be sustainable over time than many other WAC initiatives. However, the very complexity of WEC with its intensive planning year meetings, seven-year timeline for each participating department, ongoing assessment support, and financial commitment to support curricular reforms poses its own challenges for program longevity. North Carolina State University and the University of Minnesota have done an extraordinary job of securing necessary resources and marshalling campus support to scale their programs over time. For any institution that hopes to match these successes, there are a number of challenges to address from university buy-in and sufficient funding to strategies for leading departmental meetings and managing assessment processes. Like any university-wide curricular initiative, these challenges are manageable with sufficient groundwork, planning, support, leadership, and tracking. It is important to note further that such complex programs build gradually. Department by department success may move forward then slow before advancing further because of the typical five- to seven-year timeframe for departmental participation. At the higher scales of the institution, across colleges, divisions, and within the upper administration, WEC programs face other types of challenges.

Programs that commit to departmental funding for each WEC proposal and revision need to establish a fiscal model from the start that will be sustainable over time, making sure not to overcommit and leaving room to scale program growth across multiple departments at a time. Similarly, human capital needs to be considered carefully. A director who also serves other administrative roles as well as faculty responsibilities within a department will want to start slowly, perhaps piloting with one department at a time for a couple of years to develop effective strategies managing full-department discussions and building out the tracking systems to ensure departments progress over time. If additional staff are available, then faster growth may be possible. There is a rather high learning curve for any director starting a WEC program, even for someone who has been leading other WAC initiatives over the years because of the level of detail and engagement. Administrators want to see concrete results of their investments, so an integrated, department-specific assessment program is important early on. This assessment process helps drive the credibility and impact of the program. It also contributes to the important threshold shift from pilot to program—the period during which a critical mass of faculty and departments forms to drive campus-wide momentum. As more departments get engaged and come to value the discussions about teaching writing and identifying the abilities and characteristics of successful graduates in their majors, other departments will want to get on board. This period is arguably the most crucial time frame for a WEC program to determine its longevity, which is why this chapter is mostly concerned with these formative years.

Drawing from the whole systems approach (WSA) discussed in *Sustainable WAC* (Cox et al., 2018), this chapter demonstrates how Sustainability Indicators

(SIs) that are tied to program mission and goals can be tracked systematically for signs of success and distress through and beyond these formative years of WEC initiatives to clarify program outcomes and anticipate challenges and long-term growth. In writing that book, Cox, Melzer, and I drew from five theoretical frameworks from various disciplines to develop the whole systems approach (WSA) and vignettes of WAC programs from across the country. At that time, no WAC program, including any WEC initiatives, had implemented the process of determining Sustainability Indicators. Since that time, Florida Atlantic University has undergone this process, which has enabled me to hone and develop it further. Using some brief examples from Florida Atlantic University's creation of a WEC program, this chapter provides an overview of the way that SIs can be utilized as part of the sustainability model at other institutions across the country as they work through the early stages of WEC program development to ensure program sustainability.

FAU'S WAC PROGRAM CONTEXT

FAU's WAC program was well established before WEC was introduced. Since I offered the first workshop in the summer of 2004 and enough courses were certified to launch the official program in 2007, WAC training has become mandated for all WAC faculty. We established an annual assessment process, a three-year cycle for WAC-course recertification, a significant celebration for the National Day on Writing, a student recognition ceremony for published work, and a need for enhancing support for writing in the upper division. While my 40% administrative appointment is dedicated to directing the writing center, WAC program, and community writing center, I have half-time assistant directors for the writing center and WAC respectively, and a manager for the Community Center for Excellence in Writing who works when resources are available but will scale as the organization grows. These institutional realities determine to a large degree what will be possible moving forward.

WEC was first proposed as a QEP initiative that lost out to a broad mandate for undergraduate research that received the lion's share of curricular development funding on campus for the past six years. Hence, from its inception, the WEC initiative was not a funded mandate, but rather a pilot program started with repurposed WAC money from a previous departmental grant initiative that was already part of my annual budget.

The WAC committee spent a semester researching initiatives to enhance writing in upper division courses. After several models were discussed, the committee agreed on WEC because it was a systematic approach that was specifically geared to enhance writing in the majors. FAU was not in a position to mandate new courses in the upper division or require departments to establish writing infused capstone courses for their majors. WEC offered a proven alternative. This groundwork helped us gauge campus interest and develop some buy-in before we started. It also raised the profile of the pilot as I visited each college chair's meetings to introduce the idea and invite participation.

The first pilot department was Languages, Linguistics, and Comparative Literatures (LLCL), whose chair had participated in a year-long learning community I hosted to explore the WEC model. Before the first departmental meeting, Pamela Flash visited our campus to discuss the WEC model and provide documents from the University of Minnesota's program, including a template presentation that I used to develop our first presentation to LLCL based on the survey data to students, faculty, and external departmental stakeholders. We followed up online a couple times as questions arose. In addition to providing an effective design and example of the kinds of data and slides to include, the adaptable template (see Figure 8.1) demonstrated effective uses of data from the student, faculty, and affiliate surveys, strategies for talking about student abilities and characteristics, and the types of student samples useful for facilitating the faculty discussion for the first of four department-wide meetings on WEC.

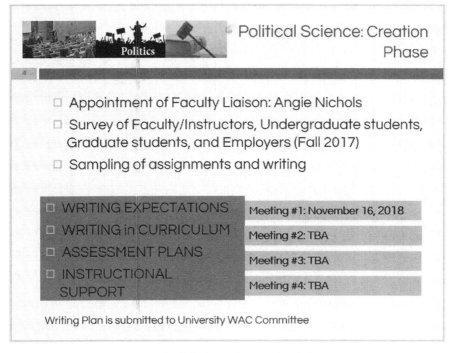

Figure 8.1. Sample slide from the Google Slides presentation for Political Science at Florida Atlantic University

As a result, I learned to facilitate the conversations by trial and error. It became clear quickly that I needed to develop a new set of skills to manage the complex interactions during these department-wide meetings to keep the conversation on track. I also had to realize that a single meeting would not enable us to formulate all student abilities criteria in final form. With each new department and each new meeting, I gained more confidence and got more effective at guiding these conversations. By the time I started the third department, I was comfortable with the system we had developed and felt confident in our process.

SUSTAINABILITY

Those first few years of the WEC program were designed as a pilot process, which I recommend to any new program just getting started. I could not have begun a WEC initiative with several departments at the same time, especially considering number of commitments I have with other administrative and faculty responsibilities and the range of challenges we faced working with our first department. It had multiple majors across numerous languages and a complex leadership concern that emerged halfway through the year that had nothing to do with the WEC initiative.

After the third department submitted its writing plan, I approached the undergraduate dean to discuss scaling the program to two or three departments a year. I also set up a meeting with the undergraduate dean and an associate provost to solicit upper administration buy-in. Based on those conversations, it became clear that we would not be scaling any time soon.

This scaling question is important for all new WEC initiatives to consider from the outset. Some programs may never attempt to start more than one new department a year. Yet, at a mid-sized state institution, for example, one program a year does not seem practical. A consideration of institutional circumstances may require a WAC leader to moderate expectations for expansion. That person's other responsibilities and levels of additional support will determine to a large degree how many departments can reasonably participate at one time. If new programs struggle to get additional departments involved, then growth can also be limited. If assessment procedures are not in place early in the program, then the program may not be able to demonstrate to the upper administration the impact of the program. If a new program sets funding levels for participating departments at the most desirable levels, it faces the possibility of not being able to scale over time. If it starts at lower levels, it may face the uphill battle of defending a need to increase stipends across the board.

All of the above indicators have proven important factors for FAU, but the financial concerns are the easiest to demonstrate. We repurposed enough funds to establish a version of Minnesota's funding model, but we did not consider the impact of trying to scale up and could not have anticipated how funding would change state-wide for higher education. Minnesota provides up to $25k for each proposal and two revisions and $5k, $3k, and $3k respective liaison stipends. FAU started with up to $20k for a first proposal and $5k for the liaison. We chose to scale down support for proposal revisions to $10k and $5k respectively so we could gradually transfer costs to each department but leave liaison stipends the same. This meant that after five years of the program with proposal revisions every two years and with each level of funding active (department $20k, $10k, $5k + liaison $5k, $3k, $3k), our standing cost was $46k a year. In our fourth year, we secured an additional $20k in performance funding. Even though we were about $6k shy of full support of the model, we have had little difficulty each year making up the additional $6k in surplus funds from the writing center, which I also manage. The difficulty arose in scaling to the next level. In order to grow from 1 department a year to 2, we would need more than double our current funding to provide for staff support.

It is important, then, for any WEC program to decide how or whether it will develop a funding model (not all WEC programs provide direct funds to departments; see, for example, Anson, Chapter 2 in this volume). The funding model we chose from the outset limited our ability to grow. Even though we had mapped out the costs of scaling the model up to four departments a year when we first devised these stipends, we did not anticipate the impact of a metrics-based approach that the Florida legislature enacted the first year we started the WEC initiative. Each school is pitted against the others for a finite amount of performance funding. The three schools at the bottom of the rankings each year have money taken away. The schools at the very top get significant performance increases. And the rest get smaller performance increases, money that is not automatically recurring funding. The system is designed to support the large state research institutions. Even though we typically rank in the middle of the pack of the 11 state schools, our performance funding increases have not been sufficient to scale our program, and the money is not guaranteed year over year.

Financial instability need not be a primary indicator of distress for WEC initiatives because there is no mandate that funding be offered for departmental proposals. Yet, without incentive, getting the program to a sustainable level university-wide might be difficult. After the first few departments willingly participate, the challenge is to encourage other departments to sign on. If a WEC start-up decides to use departmental grants, then tracking sufficiency of funding should serve as one of the Sustainability Indicators. FAU tracks a set of six SIs, each of which provides more nuanced information on long-term viability.

METHODOLOGY INFORMING SIS

In "Tracking the Sustainable Development of WAC Programs Using Sustainability Indicators" (Cox & Galin, 2019), the concept of SIs is derived from sustainable development theory and practice. Sustainable development was first defined by The United Nations World Commission report of 1987 as "development that meets the needs of the present without compromising the ability of future generations to meet their own needs" so that this "future is more prosperous, more just, and more secure" (p. 43). This ambitious political agenda requires buy-in from stakeholders at every level of the system as well as clear guidelines for building consensus and introducing and assessing change.

Cox and I note further that SIs are the tools used to assess this change (p. 6). As Bell and Morse (2008) argue, sustainability itself cannot be measured, only the parameters of sustainability—indicators of whether a project will continue to be viable. They explain further that indicator species used to test the status of ecological environments first stimulated the idea of SIs and have since evolved to include a range of factors that indicate longevity, including those related to social and economic systems. SIs have been used at multiple scales within complex systems, from private corporations to towns and cities to countries and regions and even globally (Hardi & Zdan, 1997). To understand how FAU's WAC committee arrived at the necessary but sufficient set of indicators, I first turn to the methodology of the whole systems approach, a description of Sustainability Indicators, and several strategies to facilitate the process.

Building a sustainable program (or any new project within the program) works through a four-step process, starting with a careful understanding of the campus context, a planning process that sets goals and gathers support, a development stage of implementing program initiatives (or projects), and a lead stage that manages growth, change, assessment, and revision (for more information, see Chapter 3 of *Sustainable WAC*, pp. 51-76). Figure 8.2 represents this cyclical four-stage process.

While the book offers the theoretical framework for deriving the whole systems approach (WSA), 10 principles that govern it, and each of the strategies listed in the white text boxes in Figure 8.1 (see also Cox, Galin & Melzer, 2018, p. 76), this chapter applies and demonstrates the methodology for developing and tracking SIs within the context of FAU's WEC initiative on the occasion of FAU's 10th year WAC program self-evaluation.

At the beginning of fall 2017, after three years of WEC implementation, the WAC committee decided to undertake a multi-year program-wide self-assessment using the WSA as its framework. But, as noted above, the first stage, *understanding*, had taken place the previous two years as the WAC committee explored the most viable models for supporting upper division writing at FAU, consulted with Pamela Flash, and hosted a year-long Faculty Learning Community on WEC. As a prerequisite for starting the program, the Dean asked me to gather support across campus for the initiative, so I also spent time meeting with chairs across campus and compiling a list of departments interested in participating. I knew at that time that I would be repurposing money from the existing WAC program for the pilot stage but anticipated that money would eventually be available once we could present data to the university to demonstrate what we have accomplished. Also, having served as the WAC director at FAU for 14 years and developed program mapping strategies in 2007, I had already mapped our program to visualize the nodes and hubs supporting writing on campus. I also had a clear understanding of the writing ideologies on campus concerning WAC work, but the emails to deans and chairs helped me identify eleven departments that expressed interest.

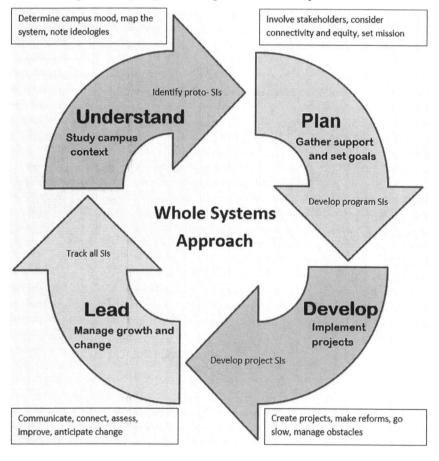

Figure 8.2. The Whole Systems Approach (adapted from Cox & Galin, 2018, p. 55)

During the *planning stage* (see Figure 8.2), we reconstituted the WAC Committee to be more representative of the colleges, rewrote the entire WAC program mission, and provided clear goals so we could establish SIs for the entire program. I had cobbled together our initial mission from other WAC programs in 2004 without input from others, which I realized was problematic as we were writing *Sustainable WAC* because a program mission statement and goals need broad stakeholder input. Starting our 10th-year program self-evaluation with mission revision gave us the opportunity to re-envision our program with the new WEC initiative in mind and establish the goals for each facet of the program that would be tracked with SIs.

The value of this exercise was immediately apparent when we focused on issues of equity and connectivity during the planning process for WEC because the existing WAC program was built around WAC-designated courses that were increasingly being taught by adjuncts and instructors rather than full-time faculty. Departments were finding that upper division WAC courses were being taught by the same faculty semester after semester, which became a source of frustration. They were burning out. WEC proposes a solution to this problem at the upper division by enabling departments to distribute efforts of teaching writing across the major rather than designating specific WAC or WEC courses. Furthermore, the pilot process enabled us to build slowly to develop the necessary processes, strategies, and revisions to improve our work with departments on an ongoing basis.

The *developing stage* began with our first department, Languages, Linguistics, and Comparative Literatures, and has continued for the past five years. Developing processes have included liaison and faculty meetings, transcription of these discussions, tracking which departments are at which points in the process, all document templates, and an online management system. Rather than simply importing the assessment processes NC State or the University of Minnesota have devised, we are working out a model with the pilot departments that better fits the context at FAU, a point made by Fodrey and Hassay in Chapter 7 of volume). We have held two meetings for WEC liaisons and chairs in Fall 2018 and Spring 2019 to develop the assessment model and will begin implementing tracking processes later this year. This process has enabled us to gain departmental input and buy-in for the assessment process, a step I would recommend any program developing a WEC initiative to take.

While the ideal time for developing SIs is in the planning stage of a program or one of its new projects, FAU's WEC pilot began a few years before the WSA and its SI methodology was formulated. Thus, we introduced SI development for FAU's overall WAC program in the fourth stage of the WSA, *leading*. As shown in Figure 8.2, this last stage reflects on the work of the other three and looks beyond implementation to communicating program accomplishments and outcomes, creating wider circles of connections beyond the specific program initiatives, improving what has already been put in place, and anticipating what changes to the program and its various projects might make it stronger still. This is the stage during which the data for SIs are collected and evaluated.

While this work will likely question the sustainability of WEC at FAU, it also provides us a roadmap for addressing these concerns and tracking sustainability into the future, and it provides other programs ways to imaging what using this system might look like at their own institutions. The remainder of this chapter lays out the process formulating and tracking the WEC program SIs and demonstrates the power of using this process.

SUSTAINABILITY INDICATORS FOR WAC PROGRAM DEVELOPMENT

SIs are critical to the WSA for WAC for several reasons. The use of SIs:

- requires the use of a participatory process that seeks to build consensus about sustainability goals
- compels this stakeholder group to articulate in concrete terms what sustainability means in relation to WAC
- helps WAC leaders notice threats to program and project sustainability and figure out steps for addressing them
- brings together data points from multiple systems (rather than relying on one data point, such as program budget) to create a more nuanced understanding of a program or project's sustainability
- creates clear data that may be communicated to stakeholders as evidence of a program's viability (or lack thereof)
(Cox & Galin, 2019, p. 42)

Unlike most other forms of WAC program assessment, SI tracking is self-reflective, focused primarily on improving and sustaining the program. It is inward-facing and formative. Typically, WAC program assessments are outward-facing, and summative, concerned primarily with proving that the program is successful. With an emphasis on improving rather than proving, SI tracking need only be concerned with the least number of indicators that are sufficient to track program viability over time. As I explain below, this data provides a clear picture of shifts in program viability, but it can also prove extremely useful to administrators who need to argue for additional resources when clear threats are revealed by the radar charts of resulting data. By emphasizing formative assessment, I am not arguing that summative assessment be neglected. Rather, SI tracking should become one facet of a full program assessment package that is tailored to each specific WAC program within its institutional context.

Because of their importance to the WSA, SIs are integrated across all four stages, as indicated in Figure 8.2. In the understanding stage, proto-SIs are developed to determine across campus the status of existing attitudes and perceptions about student writing, practices for teaching writing, student support for writing, etc. For example, if a university is developing a WAC program to address a concern that student writing needs to be improved and supported in the upper division, then it is important to determine the current state of writing in the upper division before an intervention takes place. Such information could be collected in faculty, student, and external stakeholder surveys, or existing university-wide assessment data. The aim for these proto-SIs is to inform the stakeholder group conversations so that they can work to shift the culture of writing on campus as they formulate mission, goals, and SIs to track those goals.

With mission and goals established, WAC program SIs can be identified for each primary component of the program and the program overall. As new projects are added, SIs should be included for those as well. During the developing stage, these SIs are operationalized so that data can be collected and graphed in radar charts to provide snapshots of the program each time the data is collected. During the leading stage, these radar graphs are aggregated and analyzed to determine program stability over time. It is worth noting that most new WAC initiatives will not be establishing more than a couple of primary projects for the program at the start. For instance, while FAU has five current projects (supporting faculty, maintaining WAC courses, assessing outcomes, enriching departmental curriculum, and recognizing excellence), it only began with two, WAC course management and faculty training. Had we integrated SI tracking from the start, we would have operationalized these two sets and a third small set for the program overall.

Developing SIs for a well-established WAC program will likely be more complex, requiring sets for all established and developing projects; however, this work can move at a more leisurely pace than that of a newly forming program, unless the program is facing significant challenges that warrant faster action. An established program is not typically under time constraints to implement programs, so its primary work is reflective and self-evaluative. A new WAC program that will involve shifts in the university's curricular ecology from the start, like writing in the disciplines (WID), communication across the curriculum (CAC), or revision of the undergraduate core curriculum, may have pressure to move more quickly from inception to planning, even if implementation slows down. Nonetheless, I have discovered at FAU that two or three meetings a semester of a WAC committee are not sufficient to foster the process of forming mission, goals, SI, and operationalize the SIs. It took our committee two years meeting three times a term to work through this process, when it could have been completed in one or two semesters if the mission had been established at one meeting, goals at another, and SIs developed at a full-day retreat. For programs just getting started, the process would be even shorter with fewer projects for which to develop SIs, so a half-day retreat would likely suffice.

FAU's recently revised mission and goals provide a useful context for understanding how to establish a set of program SIs. The committee reduced our original two-paragraphs mission into one, eliminated jargon, emphasized support for faculty, focused on critical thinking for students, and added emphasis on reading and writing rather than writing alone. The resulting program-wide mission is clearer, more focused, and more concise:

> The University's Writing Across the Curriculum (WAC) program supports faculty to strengthen teaching and learning writing across all levels and disciplines in undergraduate education. We collaborate with individual faculty and departments to instill in their students critical thinking and complex problem solving through the complementary processes of reading and writing (see https://www.fau.edu/wac/).

Once the mission statement was finalized, the committee turned its attention to goals, which had not previously been articulated. The committee developed five, one for each of the program's primary projects. Goal four, focusing on the WEC project, is as follows:

> (4) Enrich Departmental Curriculum: Lead departments, schools, and colleges through the processes of integrating writing systematically throughout their majors and concentrations (e.g., facilitating department-wide discussions to identify desired student outcomes, mapping departmental curricula, creating assessment plans, and designing departmental proposals for revising curricula in majors and concentrations).

Goals are concrete, lead to direct deliverables, and can be assessed directly. Each goal represents a primary function of the program. And each goal has associated SIs. Once the goals were defined, I facilitated committee discussions to develop and narrow program SIs for each the following semester using a four-step process that maximized stakeholder input. This is the work that would be best carried out during an all-day retreat.

> *List* all SIs that come to mind without censoring or critiquing but still focused on the goal of sustainability.
>
> *Qualify* and narrow the list by determining if each SI is

relevant, easy to understand, reliable, durable, and assessable, does not duplicate others, and asks whether it reveals impacts as it offers historical patterns.

Select the 5–10 most feasible SIs by considering the resources needed to track them, relative importance, and greatest insight.

Unpack each SI to identify implementation procedures by determining if it can be quantified and set the minimum and maximum thresholds (bands of equilibrium). Further revise, narrow, and eliminate SIs through the operationalization process. (Adapted from Bell & Morse, 2008, p. 174, in Cox & Galin, unpublished manuscript, pp. 7–8)

The most productive work the committee engaged in during this entire collaborative process involved SI development and narrowing conversations. As we listed all possible indicators, we began the hard work of noting indicators of distress and success across the WAC program. The obvious stressors were the lack of sufficient funding and insufficient administrative support time to scale the program. But we also identified indicators that could measure university commitment/engagement, student outcomes, and departmental follow-through for WEC proposals.[1]

We winnowed the list of necessary but sufficient SIs from 11 to six for goal four. Part of the narrowing process took into account several of the 15 strategies of the WSA, particularly understanding the interconnected web of writing goals, mandates, programs, initiatives, and resources to help locate points of leverage that can foster greater integration of the program across the university and more significant engagement and change. Once we narrowed the list, we operationalized them on a scale of 0–6, with 1 being the lower limit of sustainability and 5 being the upper limit. These ranges are called the bands of equilibrium (BOE). After introducing the six indicators below, I explain the process of setting these ranges.

1. Number of departments expressing interest in participating in the WEC process in the next 4 years
    0. 0
    1. 1–2
    2. 3–4
    3. 5–6
    4. 7–8
    5. 9–10
    6. 11 or more

---

1   Readers will find discussions of the tactics that Galin, Cox, and Melzer (2018) used to facilitate these conversations in Sustainable WAC.

2. Percentage of departments with assessment results that demonstrate student improvement in their writing abilities over time.
    0. 0–9
    1. 10–24%
    2. 25–39%
    3. 40–54%
    4. 55–69%
    5. 70–84%
    6. 85–100%

3. WEC initiative enables departments to improve teaching of writing as demonstrated by faculty perceptions and student outcomes.
    0. not at all
    1. to a minor degree
    2. to a below-acceptable degree
    3. to an acceptable degree
    4. to an above-acceptable degree
    5. to a strong degree
    6. to an extraordinary degree

4. Percentage of departments meet the goals they set in their proposals/revisions (within a semester leeway) on the schedule that they established
    0. 0–9
    1. 10–24%
    2. 25–39%
    3. 40–54%
    4. 55–69%
    5. 70–84%
    6. 85–100%

5. Estimated average number of available administrative hours needed per semester to administer the WEC program
    0. over 41 hours surplus
    1. 31–40 hours surplus
    2. 10–30 hours surplus
    3. 9 or less hours surplus or deficit
    4. 10–30 hours deficit
    5. 31–40 hours deficit
    6. over 41 hours deficit

6. Percent of funds available that are needed to support the WEC program per year.
    0. over 15% less needed

1. about 10% less needed
2. about 5% less needed
3. No additional needed
4. about 5% more needed
5. about 10% more needed
6. over 15% more needed

A good set of indicators serves as a snapshot at a moment in time of a given WEC program, or in this case, program initiative. If the number of departments interested in participating drops below the number of available slots to support new start-ups for a given year, then the program faces a challenge. Any indicator at 1 or below requires intervention. If enough indicators are at or below this minimum, then the program is not likely to succeed unless long-term changes are made. While the upper limit of SI 1 is not likely to cause the program to fail, if enough departments want to get involved and are prevented from doing so because there are not sufficient resources to support their interest, risks increase that departments will get impatient over time and may lose interest. This problem is exacerbated in a program like FAU's because we can only support one department a year. This has meant that we have chosen not to publicize the program widely to overstimulate demand, but it also means that we are always scrambling to find the next department during spring semester. This indicator may need different ranges for a university that can manage multiple departments a year.

Indicator 5 represents the number of available hours that my assistant director and I can reasonably provide support in a given term, and indicator 6 represents the costs of cycling programs through the 7-year process. Indicator 6 is a simple percentage of amounts needed to support the slate of departments participating in a semester or year. If the amount of time exceeds available administrative time, then cost projections go up. If the program is able to scale to more than one department per year, then costs go up considerably.

The scales for each SI should not be set arbitrarily but grounded in university and program practices. Once drafted by the WAC administrator, who has best access to necessary data to determine ranges, they should be discussed with the stakeholder group. Once the lower and upper bands of equilibrium are set at 1 and 5 for each indicator, the rest of the ranges are easy to determine, with three being the midpoint. The typical target for each indicator is in the range of 2–4. As long as all indicators are in these ranges, the program is deemed soundly sustainable. Even an indicator like the third one above, which tests the level of improved teaching of writing, marks unsustainable levels in the 5 range because there is only so much improvement that can be accomplished over time before outcomes level out as judged in improvements of student writing over time. For example, if the abilities and characteristics of successful student writing in a department are being evaluated on an analytical scale that departments have devised, there is only so much room within a 4-point scale that improvement can occur over time.

Each institution will work at a slightly different pace to establish SIs and operationalize them. FAU will start tracking SIs by the fall of 2019 so that we can generate our first official radar graphs with all SIs represented on a single figure. I have, however, generated provisional data for the past five years in order to demonstrate what a radar graph looks like and to discuss how that data reflects on our program's sustainability (see table 8.1).

From this data one can surmise that the initiative has not yet reached a relatively balanced state. When we were first gathering data to prove that such an initiative was warranted, we had a high number of departments interested in getting involved. I visited each college to explain the program at the Dean Council of each college. Over time, we drew from that initial list, tapping the most interested departments. By the fourth year, several had remained non-committal while others had changed their minds, leadership, or both. Since the assessment process is just going to get underway for the first time this coming academic year, we have no data for indicator 2. Indicators 3 and 4 show that the departments that started working early to create changes in their curricula have begun to see impacts on teaching. One department got a slow start, so the results are not quite aligned to start-up rate expectations. Indicators 5 and 6 both represent the pilot status of the program, that we have maxed out our current capacity to grow above 1 program a year.

Table 8.1. Preliminary data for FAU WEC initiative

	Fall 2014	Fall 2015	Fall 2016	Fall 2017	Fall 2018
Number of departments not yet involved expressing interest in WEC	6	5	3	1	1
Percentage of departments demonstrating student writing improvement	0	0	0	0	0
WEC initiative enables departments to improve teaching of writing	0	1	1	2	2
Percentage of departments meeting proposals/revisions targets	0	1	1	2	3
Average available administrative hours needed per semester to administer WEC	3	3	5	5	5
Percentage of available funds necessary to support the WEC program per year	1	1	4	4	5

In fact, this last point is quite important when considering the sustainability of any type of WAC program, but particularly WEC initiatives. Most WAC programs are not sustainable in their first three to five years because it takes a significant amount of time to establish a critical mass of support and interest university-wide and shift the curricular ecology of academic institutions. Cox, Melzer, and I did not realize this implication of program start-up in our previous work together. Nor had we considered what implications this realization might have for the program stages that Condon and Rutz (2012) proposed in their WAC program taxonomy. They identified four program types—foundational, established, integrated, and institutional change agent (Condon & Rutz, 2012, pp. 362–363). While we note in our book that this taxonomy does not explain why the latter two types tend to outlast the former two types (Cox et al., 2018, p. 14), we do not note the point that opens this paragraph. Even in their description of the "established" type of program, Condon and Rutz note that funding is often tentative. I suggest further that a large proportion of WAC programs that remain at the first or second levels are more susceptible to failure because they have not become "integrated" into the university's curricular and administrative ecologies and reward systems. The litmus test for impact within a department is demonstrable curricular change, ongoing commitment to support student writing broadly defined, and a fundamental shift in department practices; if this work remains siloed in individual departments with limited external support, recognition, and benefits for their efforts beyond the initial few years, a WEC initiative is not likely sustainable over time. The WSA uses resilience theory to highlight the importance of introducing change, adapting over time, and maintaining a desirable steady state for university-wide for complex systems like universities and their curricular ecologies. This theory also explains the importance of change across multiple scales, from individual faculty and students, to departments, colleges, divisions, and other administrative units and programs. In essence, without a university commitment to institutional change, a WEC program that focuses on work in just a few departments will remain siloed and thereby trapped in smaller scale reforms. The money, energy, and visibility of the program will revert over time as departmental support dries up. WEC programs should be long term university-wide commitments, not just departmental decisions to make some changes, no matter how productive those departmental changes become.

This is not to say, however, that programs in the upper two levels of Condon and Rutz's taxonomy are always sustainable. In fact, we note in *Sustainable WAC* that Washington State's own WAC program went through a challenging stretch in the late 2000s when it became leaderless for a period of time as a result of some political changes at the university ("Improving Rather than Proving"). Every WAC program is susceptible to failure, which is likely why sustainability rates across the country are no better than chance. Perhaps the most important takeaway of this realization is that we should not be alarmed that programs we are developing have not yet crossed the sustainability threshold early in the start-up process. After all, a pilot program, by definition, is not sustainable until it is no longer a pilot and has permanent funding, stable leadership, and established policies, procedures, and practices. This realization means that evaluating SIs once a year is likely to be sufficient to track program viability and longevity because several years of data are necessary to be able to see trends, recognize problems, and implement solutions. Figures 8.3 and 8.4 offer snapshots of FAU's program after years one and five and demonstrate visually the data in Table 8.1.

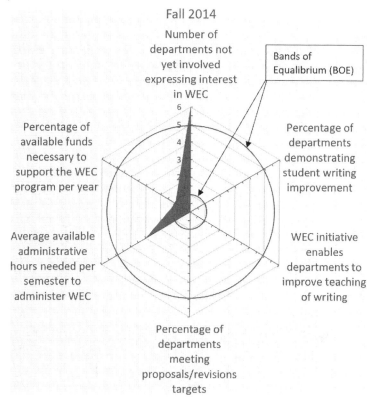

Figure 8.3. First year of FAU WEC pilot before most data could be collected

In the first year of implementation with one department, there were only three measurable indicators, which is why there is no data for three categories. We had an oversized interest and high demands on administrative time with a manageable budget. We started this first year with $5k less support than we needed but had ample surplus to cover the extra cost.

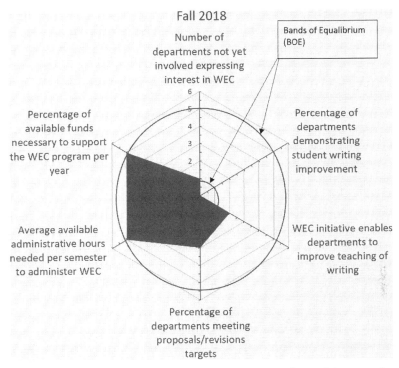

Figure 8.4. Most recent fall semester data demonstrating three of the six indicators verging on unsustainability and one for which data has not yet been collected.

By fall of 2018, with five departments involved, we were able to measure five of the six indicators, all of which were within sustainable range, but three on an inner or outer BOE. We were asked to take a one-year hiatus from starting a sixth department this coming year because the Center for Teaching and Learning lost a previously stable funding source. While we anticipate regaining this money in the future, a recent conversation with the provost made clear to me that future requests for additional funding will be predicated a demonstration of impact on currently participating departments. We hope by Spring 2020 to have assessment data from each participating department on the student abilities that they identified in their initial proposals. It is clear that this data is likely the single most important indicator within our set of SIs to justify expansion. Once we can provide reliable demonstration of curricular impact, we are likely to be able to move the needle on other indicators after the current budget crisis has been addressed. This point cannot be understated. While most of the SIs are geared to provide formative assessment measures, student improvement in writing is essential to both formative and summative measure to assess sustainability and prove the program is working to the upper administration.

Bell and Morse (2008) extol the value of using these radar charts for SIs. The power of such figures arises from their ability to tell the story of the program in a single visual snapshot. A mostly symmetric shaded area within the BOE (not on its boundaries) would represent a stable and sustainable initiative. While the trend in these SI has been improving over time for FAU, we have a great deal of work still to do to stabilize the program. The initial process of setting up these charts is greatly facilitated with the use of a template, which Cox, Melzer, and I will soon make available on our WAC Consortium website, along with a step-by-step process for chart creation. Once the data is added to the table, it is as easy as selecting the correct data for the new year and pasting the chart onto a new sheet in Excel to add additional iterations.

NOT ALL WAC PROJECTS WARRANT SIS

Not all program elements for WAC are worth the effort to track program sustainability. For instance, an annual faculty recognition ceremony may not be necessary to track. But the complexity of WEC programs makes them particularly good candidates for this type of assessment. It is easy to see the value of systematic departmental change that such programs can bring to a university when one is working with departments over a seven-year timeframe. But it is equally easy to ignore important indicators of unsustainability in such a program as we highlight the remarkable curricular changes that individual departments are making. In a recent conversation with Stacey Sheriff (personal communication, December 8, 2018) about her work at Colby College, I asked her how her program was proceeding. Like me, she is sold on the process and the clear impact it has on the departments that participate. Yet when I asked her about funding, staffing, and numbers of departments participating year over year, it was immediately clear that her program is not yet sustainable either. A soon-to-expire grant has been underwriting Colby's program, and even though she has a part-time assistant to help with the program, they have had to scale back how many departments they can accommodate in a given year. She has, at least, been able to establish an assessment process that can provide data to the university. I expect that we are not alone as new WEC initiatives trying to maintain traction at our respective universities. Clearly, tracking sustainability is a high priority.

FINAL THOUGHTS

Every institution that starts a WEC initiative will need to work during the understanding phase of building a program to determine what is possible and realistic. By undertaking a collaborative self-assessment process of instituting SIs for the five major program initiatives and the program overall, the WAC committee has enabled us to uncover program-wide issues we anticipated and others we did not. Had we known to identify these SIs from the outset of the program, we would likely have done a few things differently, which is perhaps the most important takeaway for others considering building WEC programs. Few of us start curricular reform initiatives that we expect to fail, yet we often convince ourselves that we know better than others how to avoid pitfalls or that we just need to get things started before building in more sustainable practices. Most WAC programs begin with energy, commitment, and a loose mandate. Directors jump in head-first with the best intensions. Without a systematic process in place to initiate WEC with stakeholder input, the odds are against program sustainability. For FAU, the most important tools in our arsenal are the upcoming departmental assessment, the recent faculty recognition ceremony that publicized the impressive work of WEC departments, development of a WEC website, and the radar charts of our program to help us prioritize which facets of the program need the most attention.

Programs with existing WAC initiatives have an advantage because of existing infrastructure and staff, established relationships, and a developed understanding of campus support networks, mood, and ideologies concerning writing across the university. At the same time, existing programs that take on WEC initiatives also have existing practices and time commitments that will likely need to be rebalanced and changed, a whole new level of complexity and scale that likely dwarfs what had previously existed, and a potential problem with university buy-in because the upper administration needs to be convinced that such a significant increase of resources for an existing program is warranted.

The obvious solution to many of these problems is to start with a pilot process with one or two departments and to scale over time so that the administrators managing the program have time to develop procedures and strategies for each phase of program development. But scaling from a pilot process to a full-scale WEC program that might work with three to four departments a year requires a more systematic approach that is more than a matter of following a model that has worked at another university. During a pilot phase, a stakeholder group can be formed, practices for public acknowledgement of the program need to be formalized, and use of the WSA, including SIs, can dramatically improve formative assessment of program progress. Since over 50% of WAC programs continue to fail over time (Thaiss & Porter, 2010), it stands to reason that the same will be true for WEC initiatives. Having seen the value of this kind of intensive work first-hand, I can't imagine anyone wanting to launch such an initiative without wanting to ensure its longevity.

REFERENCES

Bell, S. & Morse, S. (2008). *Sustainability indicators: Measuring the immeasurable?* (2nd ed.) [Adobe Digital Editions version]. https://www.u-cursos.cl/ciencias/2015/2/CS06067/1/material_docente/bajar?id_material=1210909.

Condon, W. & Rutz, C. (2012). A taxonomy of writing across the curriculum programs: Evolving to serve broader agendas. *College Composition and Communication, 64*(2), 357-382.

Cox, M. & Galin, J. R. (2018). Building sustainable WAC programs: A whole systems approach. *The WAC Journal, 29,* 64-87. https://doi.org/10.37514/WAC-J.2018.29.1.03.

Cox, M. & Galin, J. R. (2019). Tracking the sustainable development of WAC programs using sustainability indicators. *Across the Disciplines, 16*(4), 38-60. https://doi.org/10.37514/ATD-J.2019.16.4.20.

Cox, M., Galin, J. R. & Melzer, D. (2018). *Sustainable WAC: A Whole Systems Approach to Launching and Developing Writing Across the Curriculum Programs.* National Council of Teachers of English.

Hardi, P. & Zdan, T. (1997). *Assessing sustainable development: Principles in practice.* International Institute for Sustainable Development. https://www.iisd.org/system/files/publications/bellagio.pdf.

Thaiss, C. & Porter, T. (2010). The state of WAC/WID in 2010: Methods and results of the U.S. survey of the international WAC/WID mapping project. *College Composition and Communication, 61*(3), 534-570.

United Nations World Commission on Environment and Development. (1987). *Report of the world commission on environment and development: Our common future.* http://www.un-documents.net/our-common-future.pdf.

PART THREE. EXTENSIONS AND CONTEXTUAL VARIATION

CHAPTER 9.

GOING WILD: ADDING INFORMATION LITERACY TO WEC

Susanmarie Harrington, Dan DeSanto, Graham Sherriff, Wade Carson, and Julia Perdrial

University of Vermont

The University of Vermont adapted the writing enriched curriculum model in a collaboration between the writing in the disciplines program and the university libraries. Our writing and information literacy in the disciplines (WILD) program invites departments to reflect on the ways writing and information literacy are intertwined and disciplinarily situated. Collaborative attention to the intersections of writing and information literacy helps departments refine their disciplinary goals. Our work is grounded in an emerging set of four principles, which we explore in three programmatic contexts: biomedical & health sciences, engineering, and geology. WILD's productive boundary blurring of writing and information literacy encourages deeper dives into both fields.

The WEC model offers many benefits to participating institutions, not least among them a way out of the perpetual literacy crisis mode that plagues American higher education. As a project that tackles rigorous reflection on and definition of disciplinary priorities, as Anson's introduction in this volume describes, it creates a rich environment for curricular and pedagogical change. The WEC model flips the crisis mode script, inviting participants to focus not on what students can't do, but on what disciplinary practitioners themselves do—and thus what disciplinary faculty want students to achieve. It changes the conversation from *what makes writing good?* to *what kinds of effective writing are done here in this discipline?*

UVM's emerging version of WEC expands focus to include both information literacy and writing. What it means to be *information literate* is as elusive as what it means to *be a good writer*, and writing scholars know that literate achievements, or "good writing," are iterative and nuanced. In her Conference on College Composition and Communication Chair's address, Adler-Kassner noted, "writing is never 'just writing'," for writing is learned in specific places, at specific times, and realized in particular ways in given contexts (2017, p.

DOI: https://doi.org/10.37514/PER-B.2021.1299.2.09

323). Information literacy, too, is shaped in and realized by contextual factors, and knowledge of this—among students and teachers—is uneven and tacit. (Mis)conceptions about how both writing and information literacy are learned can contribute mightily to faculty discontent about why student performance doesn't always match expectations. The project described here builds on transformations in the field of information literacy to broaden the focus of department-based WID/WAC work. Our Writing and Information Literacy in the Disciplines (WILD) model treats information literacy as an equal partner to writing and explores the intersections of our two fields in the workings of other disciplines. WILD is directly inspired by WEC: our work begins with student/faculty/community partner surveys and curriculum maps, and leads to departmental implementation plans. The survey process provides a systematic backdrop for departmental conversations about desired outcomes, and the curricular mapping process offers the opportunity to examine how those desired outcomes are currently realized—and how they might be. WILD reinforces some dimensions of current practice and creates plans for change. But WILD's intellectual challenge is unique in that it asks departmental faculty to consider how students' writing skills, abilities, and dispositions are fundamentally intertwined with students' abilities to evaluate, synthesize, and contextualize information.

Each WILD team—17 to date—brings together WID, the library, and a department faculty leader, who jointly coordinate a departmental process for reflecting on faculty, student, and community partner assumptions about writing and information literacy; creating learning goals; and exploring how those goals are—or could be—implemented via the department's curriculum. By bringing together WID, departmental faculty, and the library, WILD recognizes that writing and information literacy are intertwined and disciplinarily situated. This intertwining is a hallmark of UVM's general education reforms.

UVM has come relatively late to the work of developing curricular general education expectations. Historically, its general education has had quite a loose structure (each of seven undergraduate colleges has its own degree requirements, and university-wide requirements are few in number). Only in 2014 did all UVM undergraduates have a common first-year requirement involving writing—and that new requirement asked faculty to attend to foundational writing *and* information literacy in a foundational course. The Faculty Senate adopted this requirement with the explicit recognition that communication and information literacy outcomes are developmental and not learned in any single course. While the institution neither structured nor funded any particular implementation of disciplinary attention to writing and information literacy in the majors, the general education initiative did shape the ways in which the campus' writing in the disciplines work proceeded. UVM, despite its relatively prominent history in writing across the curriculum (WAC) thanks to Toby Fulwiler's iconic Faculty Writing Workshop, has never had a fully institutionalized approach to WAC. Rather, it has relied on a WAC—now WID, writing in the disciplines—director to cultivate and organize grassroots individual and departmental attention to writing. WEC, with its department-by-department framework, was an attractive model for organizing attention to the disciplinary evolution of the foundational outcomes the faculty senate had identified. The creation of the foundational writing and information literacy requirement was a powerful boost for WAC/WID on campus. As we sought to build on the new first-year requirement, it was only natural that WID and academic librarians collaborate to engage departments in curricular reform. WEC alone wouldn't address the priorities the Faculty Senate had identified, given the emphasis on writing *and* information literacy as a core undergraduate learning outcome. As Fodrey and Hassay argue in Chapter 7 of this volume, it is critical that WEC implementation evolve to suit the contexts and "nuanced details" of each institution. Thus WILD became a way to systematically connect with departments seeking to build on our new foundational requirement. With seed funding from the Davis Foundation, we launched a program that brought together WID, the library, and departmental faculty to investigate the way communication and information literacy outcomes are situated in departments and nurtured over time across multiple courses.

ADDING INFORMATION LITERACY TO WEC: EXPANDING THE MODEL

WEC's lever for change is its emphasis on disciplinary expertise: departments are invited to articulate how writing outcomes are an inextricable part of their discipline, rather than an add-on that requires outside expertise and intervention. When we began adapting WEC into WILD, we expected a simple extension that would broaden WEC's focus to include information literacy. In fact, our first concern was that WEC might collapse under the addition, since we wanted to equally privilege writing and information literacy and thus our first department survey drafts were quite long. As we worked through the adaption (eventually creating surveys of reasonable length as we consulted with departments about the information they hoped to capture), we found that information literacy enhanced WEC principles and changed them.

WILD's attention to threshold concepts from information literacy invites departments to use extradisciplinary concepts to create disciplinary insights. Participating departments had extensive experience with disciplinary research, of course, but very little awareness of instructional librarianship as an academic discipline. Some judicious attention to threshold concepts in academic librarianship created productive collaborations in which the department is central and is supported by WID/WAC and information literacy approaches. Faculty confidence in their own roles as disciplinary researchers often made it easier for them to imagine and articulate a picture of a successful student researcher. Articulations of disciplinary research spurred conversations about disciplinary writing, which was particularly helpful in departments where the belief that writers are born, not cultivated, was strong. Faculty felt more comfortable seeing themselves as teachers of disciplinary research than they did as teachers of disciplinary writing, and so addressing writing and information literacy together often provided a foothold for faculty to grapple with creating student outcomes.

While we initially envisioned WILD prompting departments to create distinct writing and information literacy outcomes, we quickly realized that the interplay of students seeking information, shaping insights, and communicating information made it difficult and unnecessary on our part to try to force outcomes into our own artificial "writing" and "information literacy" buckets. As an example, nurses created the outcome: "Students will be able to apply the information they find into their clinical and scientific practice." This outcome necessitates student abilities in both writing and information literacy in order to perform as pre-professionals in the lab or the clinic. We finally came to the conclusion that it simply did not matter in which field we placed this outcome if it was useful to faculty for thinking about work in their discipline.

Subject librarians were an integral part of each WILD team and helped to facilitate departmental conversations that developed disciplinary outcomes. Librarians often have an expansive view of student abilities and challenges as they work with different courses and encounter students at multiple levels of a program. Their broad perspectives across departmental curricula proved useful in tracing student expectations and outcomes throughout a department's sequence of courses. In addition, the timing was right to include academic instruction librarians in the process. The focus of the ACRL's *Framework for Information Literacy for Higher Education* (2016) on threshold concepts made an enormous impact on academic librarians in North America and helped them to better articulate the conceptual foundation students must have in place to be successful seekers, evaluators, and communicators of information. In WILD, librarians supported departmental faculty in moving beyond skills-based thinking in the discipline toward a more holistic articulation of changes in student understanding. In Human Development and Family Studies, in fact, it turned out that the *Framework's* concept of "scholarship as conversation" helped to unstick an emphasis on proper APA citation that had been read by students solely as an injunction about formatting a bibliography. The phrase "scholarship as conversation" helped faculty to better articulate a goal around APA formatting that centered on developing a sense of the field's authoritative conversations about current issues—which was, they articulated, their original goal all along and the reason they emphasized citation conventions so much. As the WILD team worked, library voices helped the department find more appropriate language for its own expectations. Academic librarians are well positioned to be valuable contributors to departmental WEC discussions. They are primed for formulating and articulating disciplinary outcomes and, in many cases, librarians can draw upon years of subject-liaison experience and relationships to help departmental faculty through the outcome-articulation process.

While librarians were an essential part of each department's WILD team, they also benefited greatly from inclusion in departmental big-picture curricular discussions. WILD was well received by subject librarians and proved particularly effective at on-boarding two newly hired subject librarians by acclimating them to the departments with which they would work. Often, librarians find themselves in the place of reacting to an instructor's or department's curricular decisions rather than helping to shape them. The WEC model, as adapted by WILD, involves librarians in deep disciplinary conversations about the students with whom they work each semester. By being part of the curricular planning process, librarians help faculty to create rich research-based instructional experiences that are meaningful to students and are reinforced throughout a department's curriculum. Subject librarians can also help scaffold a systematic curriculum that develops student facility at seeking out, considering, and integrating researched information in a disciplinary context. This benefits everyone—faculty, students, and librarians—and focuses time and effort accordingly. The WEC model is particularly attractive not only as a blueprint for shaping departmental outreach but also as a means for articulating the particular ways of thinking and doing that are valued in a department and highlighting the mutually reinforcing interests at the intersection of WID/WAC, academic librarianship, and academic departments. As Sheriff notes in Chapter 6 of this volume, the WEC model provides a heuristic that fosters "key 'realizations' in the process of unearthing their writing expectations and reckoning in with the tacit dimensions and curses of disciplinary expertise." Similarly, WILD unearths tacit expectations and knowledge regarding information literacy and research.

LEARNING IN THE WILD: PRINCIPLES FROM COLLABORATION

Each departmental collaboration began with a common survey, but our WILD process adapted to each of our participating departments (some of whom preferred to work as a committee of the whole, some of whom preferred smaller working groups). Despite the variations in process, a set of core principles emerged from these varied collaborations, and they have become the threshold concepts that guide our work (and make departmental work so productive).

- Information literacy, like writing, responds to disciplinary context
- Contextual needs dictate the ways in which one searches for, selects, and communicates information

ACRL identified a need to evolve beyond its *Information Literacy Competency Standards* largely because of the *Standards'* failure to recognize contextual complexity—which would include disciplinarity—as an influence on information literacy behaviors. A statement from the *Standards* such as "students will identify a variety of types and formats of potential sources for information" (ACRL, 2000, p. 211) quickly becomes problematic in practice because disciplines create, use, and value information types and formats differently (Anson et al., 2012). Psychologists may place a premium on current empirical studies while historians might spend a majority of their time working with primary archival material. Engineers might need to search patents to research devices' specifications and functions, while geologists might be more concerned with organizing and analyzing data sets. Even within a discipline, contextual situations may necessitate rhetorical responses for different audiences. A nurse might choose to search for a health consumer factsheet for a patient rather than present the patient with a scholarly article; a business student might need to recognize that a broad industry report will not suffice for pitching a nuanced idea to a local business; a special educator might select a summary source rather than specialized language to describe a behavioral intervention. Disciplinarity governs much about how a writer creates and communicates new information but also how they seek out, evaluate, manage, and disseminate that information.

Those working in any discipline approach their work with values and expectations about how texts are composed and circulated, and particular assumptions about the history of work in the field (Lerner, 2015). Writing both enacts and shapes the discipline—and many of the ways it does this are central to the field of information literacy. The kinds of information that are valued, the terms used to describe or analyze that information, and the ways in which information is stored and circulates are all reflective of, and influential on, the nature of the discipline.

THRESHOLD CONCEPTS IN INFORMATION LITERACY AND WRITING HELP FACULTY CREATE DISCIPLINARY OUTCOMES

Writing and information literacy have connections to every discipline, and while they are indeed part of every discipline, they are often a *tacit* part of every discipline. Faculty may not be aware of their abilities to teach research and writing in their fields and are likely to be unfamiliar with the language of information literacy or even unaware of the term itself. And yet, faculty are more likely to see "research" as a teachable endeavor, something that is naturally scaffolded over time. So pairing information literacy and writing provides opportunities for overcoming faculty resistance to change. For some faculty, the (incorrect!) belief that writers are born, not made, or that they don't have time to add writing, or responding to multiple drafts, to already quite busy courses means that directly addressing how to scaffold writing in the major can be off-putting. Conversations exploring what it means to seek, create, and use information in the discipline naturally give rise to conversations about writing in the discipline.

Considering the palimpsest of writing and information literacy promotes reflection within the discipline. Schön's (1983) notion of reflection-in- and reflection-on-action emphasizes the unity of action, reflection, and knowledge-generation: it is in the reflection on particular situations that professionals develop new, sometimes surprising knowledge and perspectives. Action, for Schön, is embodied knowledge: professionals express their expert knowledge without thinking about it, as a matter of course. But in moments of reflection (which may be structured, or may simply arise in response to troubling or complex events), new insights are generated which affect further action (Schön, 1983, p. 50). This is exactly the dynamic that WILD opens up: tacit disciplinary expertise is expressed in pedagogies that may not welcome student newcomers, and the WILD process creates repeated opportunities for faculty to reflect in action about their work with students. WILD starts conversations about what students should know, offering faculty in any one discipline the chance to situate their expertise in relationship to information literacy and writing studies. Everyone involved has a chance to learn, in an unjudgmental space. Faculty have permission to discuss past failures or obstacles, as well as aspirations and disciplinary goals. The reflection is pragmatic and generates new perspectives on tacit disciplinary expertise about how students should demonstrate their learning, how students can practice skills that support their disciplinary work, and what kinds of information students need to be able to access, understand, and use to do so.

INFORMATION LITERACY, LIKE WRITING, MUST BE SEQUENCED ACROSS A COURSE OF STUDY AND OVER TIME

For both information literacy and writing, there is always more to learn, do, and know. As students enter disciplines and eventually the professional world, they experience new contexts and advanced expectations. New contextual expectations may cause confusion about what sorts of information will serve their needs, how to process tasks, or how to shape texts for particular audiences. Repeated and scaffolded attention to the ways a discipline frames questions, cultivates data, and creates genres will nurture both writing and information literacy abilities and demonstrate that the application of critical research and writing practices must be ongoing.

Information literacy, like writing, isn't a natural activity. It's learned with other people, and it's learned in particular places and moments. Curiosity may be a natural human trait, but curiosity alone doesn't spontaneously create an information literate individual. Behaviors that work in one context may not be right for another. As students move from course to course, they experience different vocabularies, bodies of information, and expectations. A term as simple as "research" may denote poring over books and articles for one class and yet may denote taking and recording measurements in another. A tried and true archival database like JSTOR may be a good search tool for history courses but will prove almost useless when looking for current scientific information. A student may be adept at locating information typically published in western countries but all of a sudden that same student may need to develop new search strategies for a global economics class that requires local information generated in the countries he or she is studying. In each case, there is no blueprint or guidebook. Information literacy is unique and shaped by contextual experiences.

Because critical work must be ongoing, students cannot be made information literate in one class period, one course, or even one academic year. In fact, no single course can provide an inoculation that will set students up for perfect future performance. Rather, each course can present the opportunity to transfer forward knowledge and composing practices, ready to be amplified by new learning. By drawing on the WEC model in creating learning outcomes and scaffolding progress toward those outcomes across a curricular map, WILD requires that disciplinary faculty consider both writing and information literacy as learning that is best sequenced throughout their major's curriculum—and in fact, as learning that is part and parcel of the major's curriculum.

INFORMATION LITERACY AND WRITING ARE, AT POINTS, INSEPARABLE

It is impossible to teach information literacy without attending to writing, and impossible to teach writing without attending to information literacy—and impossible to teach any given discipline without also teaching some form of expression or communication that draws from both writing and information literacy. As the many contributions to *Information Literacy: Research and Collaboration across Disciplines* attest, both writing and information literacy are shared responsibilities across the university, and it benefits everyone when the two broad fields are worked together in disciplinary contexts (D'Angelo et al., 2016). The processes that support the revision of texts also support the revision of search strategies; the work that supports researchers learning to evaluate information also supports writers learning to evaluate needs within a rhetorical context. While parallels between the disciplines have cropped up as a topic at many conferences and presentations and by notable librarian/writing instructor pairs (e.g., D'Angelo & Maid, 2016), we came to understand early in the WILD project that certain threshold concepts were not just operating on parallel writing and information literacy tracks; rather, they were two sides of the same coin (DeSanto & Harrington, 2015). Without a label of "writing" or "information literacy," certain threshold concepts can be applied to either the seeking and consideration of information or its communication. These boundaryless concepts are mutually reinforced by attention from our two fields and point us to ways in which context shapes how writers seek out and articulate information.

One of the threshold concepts in *Naming What We Know* (Adler-Kassner & Wardle, 2015) is that *writing is a knowledge-making activity*. It's also an *information-seeking activity*, and information-seeking activities are overwhelmingly those involving writing and reading. Reconceiving writing and information literacy as two sides of the same coin has enormous effects on how we teach and discuss composing. When revision is viewed as a re-evaluation of what information is needed for what purpose, writing is information literacy. When a writer seeks out data on a phenomenon they're studying, that's building information literacy.

Becoming more conscious of the relationship between writing and information literacy emphasizes the act of knowledge creation embedded in writing.

DEPARTMENTAL LESSONS

To illustrate the ways these threshold concepts work in departmental contexts, we turn our attention to three collaborations. The very different ways in which WILD was adapted in each department is a testament to the power of this flexible model: it can be shaped in ways that speak to the challenges, opportunities, and constraints in particular departments and disciplines.

BIOMEDICAL AND HEALTH SCIENCES

While the WILD initiative's very nature encourages departments to view writing and information literacy as something diffused in all courses, some departments have used the WILD program to focus attention on one foundational writing-intensive course. Although a faculty focus on one particular course can lead to an "inoculation" or "one and done" approach to writing and information literacy, a foundational writing-intensive course can, if well-structured, form the basis for a sequenced approach across the curriculum. Planning for a foundational course introduces faculty to larger conversations about the touchstones on which they hope to build in other courses. Minnesota's original WEC initiative began in order to address gaps in a writing-intensive course requirement system. Thus it may seem counterintuitive that our WILD initiative has helped create some writing-intensive courses—but in the UVM context, where attention to disciplinary writing instruction has often been scarce, the creation of a writing-intensive course can be something that unites a department around shared outcomes that ripple throughout a major. The biomedical and health sciences department (BHSC) collectively designed a foundational course introducing the core writing genres expected in its major, and in so doing, has created a deep and networked understanding of how students are expected to work as professional writers, researchers, and data managers in multiple programs in a newly restructured department.

Biomedical and health sciences offers three clinical majors that each require slightly different skills in their respective professions. Through work in the WILD program, the department has developed a course broad enough to encompass writing and information literacy abilities in radiation therapy, medical laboratory science, and health science, yet specific enough to allow a sequential approach across each curriculum. In essence, BHSC has created its own foundational writing and information literacy class as a gateway to other activities within the major. This foundational experience within the program provides a rhetorical, disciplinary context for the later writing and research work that involve students in writing for different audiences and searching for and validating quality data relevant to their profession. The department's goal is to ensure students are ready for more advanced writing work and that students develop a broad understanding of how writing and information literacy are relevant to their professions.

BHSC's involvement in WILD originated when faculty noticed that students were challenged by selecting the appropriate genre for an audience. They were further challenged by performing a literature search using primary sources, and composing a paper based on that primary literature. Although each student in the BHSC department completed the university's foundational first year writing and information literacy course (FWIL), faculty determined that the general FWIL course could not, on its own, prepare students to successfully write in the discipline; faculty determined that some kind of disciplinary introduction to writing was needed, to build on FWIL. (We note that this claim wouldn't surprise those associated with the FWIL courses, which are intended to prepare students for more discipline-specific learning—but that faculty in a discipline used WILD to themselves unlearn a fundamental, yet persistent, misconception that writers should already know how to write in the major is exactly what makes WILD so valuable.) These observations were validated through the survey completed by both faculty and students as part of the WILD process. Students in the major validated the faculty's didactic sense that more disciplinary practice with writing and research is needed. The collaborative efforts to create a disciplinary foundation that can be shared across multiple majors led faculty to emphasize the rhetorical similarities faced by health professionals regardless of specialty. The new focused course was offered for the first time in 2019–2020. In the lead-up to this course's debut, faculty have identified ways to name and sequence assignments to highlight transferable skills; they have also identified the particular ways their existing writing and research assignments reinforce students' professional development.

ENGINEERING

UVM's engineering departments started with a deceptively simple goal: students needed more experience seeking out, evaluating, and communicating information. For example, local employers had reported dissatisfaction with newly graduated engineers' research skills and writing. As part of their participation in the WILD project, engineering faculty developed curricular learning outcomes for writing and information literacy. These were mapped to the current curriculum to locate courses where these outcomes were being addressed (and where they were not). Significant gaps were visible in the sophomore and junior years. For instance, students only had the opportunity to reflect on the appropriateness of different academic and technical sources for different situations at the senior level, and some outcomes concerning intellectual property were not addressed at all. These gaps seemed to be a systemic problem, and Engineering decided to approach the challenge in part by creating a new course that would bridge the gaps identified in its existing curriculum.

Like biomedical and health sciences, engineering took up a counterintuitive-in-terms-of-WEC approach by adding a writing-intensive course to their department. While we are aware of the limitations of writing-intensive courses, the department's collective determination to create a course that has analogs in other engineering or technical communication programs honors the local governance component of the WEC model: even given the WILD team's presumption that addressing writing and information literacy outcomes across a network of courses would be our product, the department chose to start by creating an elective curricular space that would highlight disciplinary writing and informa-tion literacy, structured around the new learning outcomes. A three-credit course titled "Engineering Communications" was developed and opened to all students in any engineering program. Over the course of two years, multiple engineering faculty attended a week-long course development institute, facilitated by WID and the library, in order to refine the course, which sought to address some of the gaps in departmental outcomes. In the course students practice various modes of communication used in professional and academic engineering, including technical publications and documentation. They read and evaluate engineering genres, as well as draft technical reports and give presentations. The course meets with its subject librarian at multiple points in the semester.

Students have reported that this kind of detailed and explicit research and writing development is not available to them elsewhere in their departmental curriculum.

Since the course's initial year, more engineering faculty have attended the spring course design institute in order to solidify the network of outcomes that culminate in senior design seminars. Over the course of the project, UVM restructured its organization of Engineering and diffused curricular decision-making throughout multiple departments. Yet, the WILD project has spurred more faculty engagement with and attention to scaffolding written and oral performance in the discipline. UVM Engineering continues to consider ways in which disciplinary writing and information literacy instruction might be threaded throughout its curricular sequence.

GEOLOGY

The geology department's WILD work revealed a situation exactly opposite than that faced by engineering: the department's mapping of its outcomes led to a realization that the curriculum appeared to be tightly scaffolded, with clear and shared expectations across the undergraduate degree program, and opportunities to practice and develop key skills from course to course, level to level. The only problem: faculty reported that students consistently failed to apply knowledge from prior courses in subsequent ones. The curriculum mapping process initially felt like a disappointment, as the map we produced didn't explain faculty per-ception of student experience. However, as we explored the working of the cur-riculum, faculty realized that the tight sequencing of the map could be exploited to make core disciplinary concepts more explicit, and could be used as the foun-dation of a new common assignment. Thus was born the "RoCKs Document," an assignment that is shared across courses in the department (RoCKs stands for Record of Core Knowledge and Skills). Geology faculty created a shared framework for the RoCKs Doc—identifying strands of knowledge that students need to call back to in order to make progress toward the department's learning goals. The RoCKS document is an evolving written compilation of knowledge and skills that, guided by the instructor, is compiled by the students for each course. This approach was piloted in earth materials and included exercises and reflections on knowledge and skills. The department continues to assess the effectiveness of this approach with student feedback and improve accordingly. Assessment plans moving forward include investigating the effects of the RoCKS document on student performance in higher level Geology courses. However, in its early period, the initiative has already improved scaffolding of materials within and among courses and improved consistency in the curriculum.

The WILD process also created the opportunity for a newly hired sciences librarian to begin working with foundational classes in the major. While the curriculum itself appeared to be addressing topics in a productive sequence, the department reframed its relationship with the library in order to better support students. The department's subject-area librarian thus has increased contact with courses and has been involved with a greater number of the department's students. Involvement with the department's librarian enabled yet another avenue for greater continuity between classes and better knowledge transfer as students progress through the major.

WILD LEGACIES

The WILD initiative is still nascent. Shifting financial pressures, a wave of senior leadership changes, the promise of another round of general education reform that may (or may not) institutionalize attention to writing and information literacy in the upper levels all lead to cautious optimism: yet it's unclear how these factors will affect departments. Whatever the institutional winds may bring, WILD has built powerful bonds between WID and the UVM libraries, as well as with the emerging campus assessment and program review initiatives. As of this writing, WILD remains a voluntary program, available to departments or programs seeking support. It is firmly institutionalized as a partnership, for collaboration between the libraries and writing in the disciplines addresses similar challenges and offers mutual benefit. Those of us working in either of these roles face similar challenges. With or without structured upper-level writing requirements, both programs often seek partnerships with disciplines, departments, and individual faculty, and in many cases these partnerships grow out of faculty members' sense that there is some kind of problem: an outdated curriculum needs revising, students can't complete assignments properly, or students these days simply can't work as well as they used to. Introducing faculty to intersecting writing and information literacy threshold concepts shifts the conversation from "What's wrong with students these days?" to a more helpful discussion of "What research and writing is most important our discipline? What concepts in this field are necessary and challenging? What do students absolutely need to fully engage in our major?" This reframing, as our experience demonstrates, invites a whole new conversation about the curriculum and repositions the discipline in relation to writing and research. WILD's extension of WEC, blending writing and information literacy, situates writing as a core part of disciplinary work while inviting a more thoughtful conceptualization of information literacy.

The WILD program's grassroots implementation of WEC proved a good match for our campus where departments have a large degree of autonomy and can be suspicious of programs that feel like administrative mandates. Throughout our work with each of these departments, the emerging and evolving intersections between writing and information literacy have been a generative connection that has inspired both individual and collective attention to teaching and learning. As time has passed, everyone involved in the projects have found that creating or maintaining strict boundaries between *writing* and *information literacy* was counterproductive to how disciplinary faculty understood, discussed, and taught the process of creating researched information. WILD's productive boundary blurring of writing and information literacy encouraged deeper dives into both fields and made it easier for disciplinary faculty to imagine ways that partnering with either or both of the library and writing in the disciplines programs would be productive.

The writing-information literacy palimpsest leads disciplinary faculty to a deep understanding of the fact that *my discipline is not the universe.* Adler-Kassner and Majewski (2015) point to the boundary-shaping function of this understanding: faculty who come to see that their own expectations are indeed context-specific, not universal, realize the need to make those expectations more explicit. At the same time, we have found that faculty also come to see the ways that their contextual expectations have connections to expectations nurtured in other fields. Seeing the connections among disciplines—and having the opportunity to learn from other departments' language and processes, as well as having the opportunity to learn from information literacy and writing studies scholarship—creates an academic community in which disciplinary boundaries become clearer, and in which the roles of adjacent or complementary disciplines become clearer, too.

As we reflect on the WILD initiative's progress to date, we realize that, as with any good assignment, the value of the product is secondary to the learning. Our participating departments have created outcomes and assessment plans, but the real value of this work lies in the conversations along the way. Many of the benefits we can identify from the program (better understandings of information literacy as a concept, a commitment to scaffolding writing, more nuanced and sequenced research expectations, a greater willingness to collaborate with departmental colleagues on curriculum, more focused department assessment plans) do not really depend upon the particular tasks the departments set out for themselves. Rather, the success comes from discussions of departmental priorities in the structured environment of the WILD project and the threshold concepts departments articulate and commonly recognize as needed to effectively teach writing and research. The rethinking and learning that faculty accomplished in WILD, the process of thinking through the work, was as important as the products and curricular revision WILD sponsored.

REFERENCES

Adler-Kassner, L. (2017). Chair's address: Because writing is never just writing. *College Composition and Communication, 69*(2), 317–340. https://library.ncte.org/journals /CCC/issues/v69-2/29421.

Adler-Kassner, L. & Majewski, J. (2015). Extending the invitation: Threshold concepts, professional development, and outreach. In L. Adler-Kassner & E. Wardle (Eds.), *Naming what we know: Threshold concepts of writing studies* (pp. 186–202). Utah State University Press.

Adler-Kassner, L. & Wardle, E. (Eds.). (2015). *Naming what we know: Threshold concepts of writing studies.* Utah State University Press.

Anson, C. M., Dannels, D. P., Flash, P. & Gaffney, A. L. H. (2012). Big rubrics and weird genres: The futility of using generic assessment tools across diverse instructional contexts. *Journal of Writing Assessment, 5*(1). http://journalofwritingassess ment.org/article.php?article=57.

Association of College and Research Libraries (2000, January). *Information literacy competency standards for higher education.* https://alair.ala.org/handle/11213/7668.

Association of College and Research Libraries (2016, January 11). *Framework for information literacy for higher education.* http://www.ala.org/acrl/standards/ilframework.

D'Angelo, B. J., Jamieson, S., Maid, B. & Walker, J. R. (Eds.). (2016). *Information Literacy: Research and Collaboration across Disciplines.* The WAC Clearinghouse; University Press of Colorado. https://doi.org/10.37514/PER-B.2016.0834.

D'Angelo, B. & Maid, B. (2016). Creating collaborations through connecting national writing guidelines to the framework for information literacy: Writing program administrators' outcomes statement for first year composition. ACRL e-Learning Webcast Series: Framing the Framework Series. http://learningtimesevents.org/acrl /creating-collaborations/.

DeSanto, D. & Harrington, S. (2015, March 22–25). *Harnessing the intersections of writing and information literacy* [Paper presentation]. *ACRL Proceedings.* Conference Proceedings of ACRL 2017, At The Helm: Leading Transformation, Baltimore, Maryland, USA. http://www.ala.org/acrl/sites/ala.org.acrl/files/content/conferences

/confsandpreconfs/2017/HarnessingtheIntersectionsofWritingandInformation Literacy%20.pdf.

Lerner, N. (2015). Writing is a way of enacting disciplinarity. In L. Adler-Kassner & E. Wardle (Eds.), *Naming what we know: Threshold concepts of writing studies* (pp. 40–41). Utah State University Press.

Schön, D. (1983). *The reflective practitioner: How professionals think in action.* Basic Books.

CHAPTER 10.

SUSTAINING WEC THROUGH PEER TUTORS

Heather Bastian

University of North Carolina at Charlotte

This chapter explores how the WEC model may be integrated with embedded peer tutors (EPTs), a staple initiative of many WAC programs. It begins by outlining the tensions between WAC and WEC and the resulting challenges. It then considers how the WEC model and EPTs might function together productively within the underlying tensions to support student learning and development and to reinforce curricular and instructional change.

Many institutions of higher education support WAC programs. As the National Census on Writing found, 53% of four-year institutions (n=642) reported that they have a WAC program and/or writing requirement beyond first-year writing (Gladstein, 2013). WAC programs take many forms and undertake a variety of initiatives, including writing-intensive courses, faculty development institutes or academies, learning communities, workshops, consultations, etc. Another common WAC initiative is embedded peer tutors (also referred to as curriculum-based or classroom-based peer tutors and writing associates, consultants, fellows, or mentors); in fact, scholars have long pointed to embedded peer tutors (EPTs) as a way to enrich and reinvigorate WAC programs (Hall & Hughes, 2011; Mulin, 2001; Mulin & Schorn, 2007; Soven, 1993). It is not surprising, then, that 151 four-year institutions reported having EPTs (Gladstein, 2013).

The WEC model also may be appealing to WAC programs as they look to enrich existing initiatives or launch new initiatives (see Anson's Introduction and Scafe & Eodice, Chapter 11 of this volume). Those who do seek to integrate WEC and WAC, however, may be met with underlying tensions: WAC initiatives tend to focus on individual faculty and student engagement at the course-level while the WEC model tends to focus on collective faculty engagement at the department-level. This does not mean that the WEC model precludes individual engagement or that WAC initiatives preclude collective engagement. Instead each has a distinct focus and emphasis that when combined has the potential to compete with rather than complement each other, especially when either is applied or approached reductively.

Given the underlying tensions between WAC and WEC, this chapter explores how the WEC model may be integrated with EPTs, a staple initiative of many WAC programs. While this chapter focuses on EPTs, I believe it will be of use and interest both to WAC programs pursuing other initiatives and to those adopting the WEC model outside of WAC programs. I undertake my exploration in two parts. In the first part, I outline the tensions between WAC and WEC and the resulting challenges. I do so by placing the theoretical framework for EPTs in relation to the WEC model and by briefly describing the history of WEC efforts and EPTs at UNC Charlotte. In the second part, I consider how the WEC model and EPTs may productively function together and conclude by outlining concrete steps for integrating WEC and EPTs that attempt to work within the underlying tensions.

UNDERSTANDING THE TENSIONS BETWEEN EPTS AND WEC

The embedded peer tutoring model, inspired by Harriet Sheridan's work at Carleton College and Tori Haring-Smith's work with Sheridan at Brown University, is situated within WAC and WID principles with an emphasis on the shared responsibility of all faculty for writing instruction and the connection between writing and learning (Haring-Smith, 1992). In this model, EPTs are understood as potential agents of change who work to shape student writing practices and attitudes while also influencing faculty teaching practices and beliefs about writing and learning (Haring-Smith, 1992). EPTs are able to do so by working directly with students, faculty, and WAC programs. Specifically, undergraduate (and, at times, graduate) students working as EPTs are assigned to a specific course or section of a course (often a discipline-based one), they collaborate with their peers in that course or section to provide writing support and assistance, and they work in partnership with the course faculty without taking on any grading or evaluation responsibilities.

While embedded peer tutoring programs share these three key characteristics, implementation varies significantly between programs. For example, some programs assign students as generalist/WAC tutors to a course outside of their programs of study, while others ask faculty to identify students in their major or minors to work as specialist/WAC and WID tutors in their courses (see Gladstein, 2008; Haring-Smith, 1992; Macauley, 2014; Soven, 2001; Zawacki, 2008). In another example, some EPTs primarily support students outside of class by providing feedback on written assignments and meeting with students to discuss it; others provide this kind of support but also attend class to support writing-to-learn and writing-related activities during class (see Spigelman & Grobman, 2005). In one final example, the partnerships between EPTs and faculty can range from a few meetings throughout the semester and some conversation regarding writing assignments to several meetings throughout the semester, frequent conversation regarding writing assignments and students' experiences, and even co-facilitation of activities during class.

Regardless of this variation between programs, the embedded peer tutoring model seeks to support both students as writers and faculty as writing instructors with EPTs directly interacting with students and faculty. In doing so, they serve as connections between faculty and students and also between faculty and the WAC program. It is in the in-between spaces that EPTs occupy where scholars locate EPTs' potential to act as agents of change. By operating in what scholars refer to as intersections, interstitial positions, gray spaces, and middle spaces, EPTs resist, disrupt, and, at times, transform common binary relationships—e.g., teacher/student, teaching/learning, expert/novice, generalist/specialist, and content/writing—that structure how the university and those within it operate (Carpenter et al., 2014; Gladstein, 2008; Hughes & Hall, 2008; Mulin et al., 2008). Scholars have suggested that working in and from these in-between spaces provides EPTs and, by extension, those with whom they work insight into disciplinary and pedagogical practices. As Mullin et al. (2008) demonstrated, EPTs can "help raise the visibility of assumptions and practices for all, making evident the hidden complexity of the community practices necessary to master written knowledge in a discipline" (para. 3) by prompting faculty to recognize their "expert blind spots" (see Sheriff, Chapter 6 of this volume). By resisting binary relationships, EPTs, especially those who work with students and faculty during class, also can decenter the power relations and hierarchy typical to a classroom by encouraging tutors, students, and faculty to work together as active participants in knowledge construction and composing practices (Spigelman & Grobman, 2005). Whether EPTs are working to make the implicit explicit or to decenter power relations, they ideally engage in what Gladstein (2008) has called a "cycle of inquiry and dialogue" to create "symbiotic relationships" (p. 3) between faculty, students, and WAC programs and act as agents of change.

Like EPTs, the WEC model seeks to affect instructional and curricular change by adopting foundational principles of WAC and WID; however, there are four key differences between the WEC and EPT models that result in the underlying tensions I noted above. The first difference between the models is the primary driver of change. In the WEC model, faculty drive change by articulating and interrogating their understanding and conceptions of writing and writing instruction throughout a series of structured conversations facilitated by a WAC/WEC consultant (see Flash, Chapter 1 and Luskey & Emery, Chapter

4 of this volume). In the EPT model, students acting as EPTs drive change by operating in the in-between spaces to provide formative feedback to their peers on their writing and to faculty on their instructional practices and student experiences. A second difference is the primary location of change. The WEC model seeks to affect change at the department level with faculty participating in structured conversations during departmental meetings. The EPT model seeks to affect change at the course level with faculty, EPTs, and students participating in conversations outside of class and, at times, during class. The third difference between the two models is the source of change. While the WEC model is data-driven with locally collected data serving as the driving source of change (see Flash, Chapter 1 of this volume), the embedded peer tutoring model is experience-driven with student and EPT experience serving as the driving source of change. These three differences taken together result in the fourth difference, the kind of change each model seeks to initiate. Both models seek to achieve curricular and instructional change, but each takes one as its primary focus and starting point. The WEC model with its focus on faculty engagement with local data at the department-level works to achieve curricular change by integrating writing across the curriculum of a program of study (see Flash, Chapter 1 of this volume). The EPT model with its focus on student engagement and experience at the course level works to achieve instructional change by integrating writing into the pedagogy of a class and a faculty's teaching practices. Neither model advocates stopping at curricular or instructional change; rather, the WEC model sees curricular change as a way to instructional change and the EPT model sees instructional change as a way to curricular change. These four differences pose potential challenges when the two models are integrated, as the EPT model's focus on individual engagement at the course-level has the potential to work against collective engagement at the department-level.

To further complicate the integration of WEC and EPTs, recent scholarship has called into question the extent to which and with whom EPTs can act as change agents. Scholars consistently find that students generally benefit from and experience positive change as a result of working with and as EPTs (see, for example, Hughes et al., 2010; Ragaignon & Bromley, 2011; and Spigelman & Grobman, 2005). What is less consistent among scholars, however, is the extent to which they find that EPTs can and do influence faculty beliefs and attitudes, instructional practices, and curriculum (Cairns & Anderson, 2008; Hall & Hughes, 2012; Webster & Hansen, 2014; Zawacki, 2008). Some scholars find that EPTs lead to transformative changes in faculty attitudes and practices while others find little to no change and, in some cases, outright resistance to change. This range of experience makes sense given Zawacki's (2008) finding in her exploration of three case studies that it is difficult for EPTs to affect change when "a teacher is not fully invested in the WI aspects of the course and/or has deeply ingrained beliefs about 'good' writing and appropriate goals for student writers" (p. 4). When faced with situations like these, EPTs may be able to affect small, surface level changes to assignments, as Zawacki (2008) discovered, but they often lack the experience and level of understanding "to engage the teacher in more complex discussions of his assignment expectations and desired writing outcomes for his students" (p. 6).

In my own work to integrate EPTs and the WEC model in the Communication Across the Curriculum Program (CxC) at UNC Charlotte, I have witnessed the tensions and challenges that arise when combining the two models, but I also have identified some benefits. Before I joined CxC in 2016, Chris Anson coordinated with the then director from 2009–2010 to lead four volunteer departments through structured discussions to develop WEC plans. This pilot effort continued as other departments elected to undergo the WEC process, and in 2014–2015, CxC adopted the embedded peer tutoring model to complement—not replace— existing WEC efforts. The intention was that EPTs were to be closely linked to WEC plans as curricular support and financial incentive (CxC funded the EPTs). Departments identified key courses in their WEC plans where students would benefit from additional peer support. EPTs were assigned to those courses and embedded into the course curriculum and classroom. Departments selected and hired upper-level students, typically from their majors, to serve as EPTs. The intended outcomes were that EPTs would provide their peers with discipline-specific writing support and would provide the faculty and departments with feedback on how students were experiencing the changes initiated by WEC plans.

By the time I joined CxC as associate director (a year after a new executive director joined the program), twelve departments had participated in the WEC process and six of those departments were working with EPTs. All of this work was and continues to be elective. WEC plans and efforts in several of the departments were waning. The six departments working with EPTs were still engaged with their WEC plans to some extent, but the intended connections between the departments' WEC plans and EPTs had either weakened or failed to take hold. EPTs were providing their peers with feedback on writing assignments but only some were attending classes and providing faculty and departments with feedback regarding their WEC plans. Instead of working together, the WEC plans and EPTs diverged with some departments continuing curricular conversations with little to no connection to their use of EPTs and with other departments focusing on their use of EPTs and particular courses with little forward movement on their overall curriculum and WEC plans.

As the executive director and I entered this milieu, we witnessed some challenges that arise when integrating EPTs and WEC. The biggest challenge for us was maintaining a focus on curricular change at the departmental level while EPTs support particular courses in a department. Curricular conversations in some (but not all) departments became focused and stuck on EPT supported courses, which made shifting the department's attention to change across the curriculum and into other courses a challenge. When attention remained focused on a few courses and not all faculty within a department taught those courses, department-wide efforts in which most if not all faculty participated were difficult to maintain. Issues of ownership and dependency also presented challenges, but we witnessed them to a much smaller degree. While the embedded peer tutoring model advocates that EPTs complement, never replace, faculty writing instruction and feedback, in a few cases, faculty were relying on EPTs as the primary means of writing instruction and feedback. In these cases, faculty were not necessarily altering their own instructional and feedback practices or the course curriculum in response to WEC plans but, instead, were relying on EPTs to provide writing instruction and feedback outside of class. These challenges, most likely, are not surprising given the underlying tensions between WAC and WEC, and they certainly resonate with concerns raised in EPT scholarship. Moving between individual engagement at the course-level and collective engagement at the department-level proved difficult with departments gravitating toward one end of the spectrum.

While we saw that integrating EPTs and WEC presented challenges, we also identified positive aspects of integration at our institution. Most notably, EPTs allowed CxC to maintain a physical connection to the classroom and presence in the department. EPTs presence in the classrooms allowed us to gain insights into how WEC plans were and were not moving forward; EPTs, in this sense, have served for us as a sustainability indicator (see Galin, Chapter 8 of this volume) of a department's progress and investment in WEC plans. For example, when a department's use of EPTs has radically changed or has departed from standard practices, this indicated to us that the department's WEC plan had either changed, or more likely, waned. This has been especially helpful for CxC because we are an elective program and do not have a formal standing body through which WEC plans are reviewed and approved, and, as a result, our WEC process is less structured and has less oversight than at other institutions. We also found that EPTs' physical presence in the department often allowed us as CxC directors to keep department and faculty focus on or, more often, return focus to writing, curriculum, and pedagogy by creating some consistency and stability in CxC's work with departments. For example, we can request meetings with chairs and faculty to discuss their consultant use but also use these meetings to inquire about the status of WEC plans or about other relevant curricular developments. As another example, we can offer departments professional development opportunities that relate to working with EPTs but focus on pedagogical and curricular changes that support EPT integration and WEC rather than on EPT practices.

Given the history of CxC at UNC Charlotte and our observations regarding EPT and WEC integration within this context, we are at a point of reflection as a program. EPTs are the primary way in which CxC can financially support and incentivize elective WEC and WAC efforts; our administration has a strong interest in funding student employment on campus since many UNC Charlotte students need to work to support themselves and, at times, their families. As a result, EPTs continue to be an important element of WEC planning with existing and new departments and a thriving element of the CxC program at large. We need to decide how to move forward as a program taking into consideration our historical context and current institutional reality. Rather than abandon WEC efforts or EPTs or allow them to develop and function as separate branches of our program, we have elected to try to navigate the tensions and challenges integration present because we also see potential and opportunities for student learning and curricular change that integration may bring.

NAVIGATING THE TENSIONS BETWEEN EPTS AND WEC

In this exploratory section, I consider how the WEC model and EPTs might function together productively to support student learning and development and to reinforce curricular and instructional change. This exploration, admittedly, imagines ideal circumstances and best-case scenarios but doing so has allowed me to develop some concrete steps that CxC plans to take to realize the potential and address the challenges of EPT and WEC integration.

Integrating WEC and EPTs introduces a student dynamic to the WEC process that could work to further support student learning and development. Students serve as EPTs and EPTs serve as peer educators for students by providing one-on-one writing and learning support. The WEC model focuses on providing direct support for faculty development, which makes sense—more informed beliefs about teaching and writing and more effective curriculum and instructional practices support student writing development and learning. Certainly faculty play a crucial role in student learning and development; however, peer teaching and feedback can play an equally important and different role in student development and learning. It is important to note here that I am not advocating nor does any EPT scholarship advocate that EPTs replace faculty teaching and feedback or that faculty outsource their work to EPTs; rather, EPTs should complement faculty teaching and feedback by providing a different kind of learning experience for students. Ideally faculty teaching and feedback and

EPT peer support mutually reinforce each other, allowing students to engage more deeply with a writing-enriched curriculum.

EPTs provide direct support for students by engaging their peers in conversation about their writing and development as they meet with them either one-on-one or in small groups. EPTs' peer status and non-authoritative position provides for a different kind of social context and learning experience for students, one that tends to be more collaborative and active in nature than traditional, teacher-led learning contexts (Bruffee, 1995; Spigelman & Grobman, 2005). Additionally, EPTs' in-between status as neither an expert nor a novice provides them with a language and perspective that may be more accessible to their peers (Mulin et al., 2008). This kind of peer support has been found to have a positive impact on student learning and development. Regaignon and Bromley (2011) found that students who work with EPTs demonstrated measurable and statistically significant improvement in their writing over the course of the semester while students who did not work with one did not. Students who work with EPTs also report gaining insight into disciplinary academic genres and language as well as confidence in their own abilities (Buyske, 1995; Mulin et al., 2008; Spigelman & Grobman, 2005).

In addition to supporting student learning and development, integrating EPTs and WEC could help to reinforce curricular and instructional change at the department level by providing faculty support at the course level. One way EPTs could do so is by prompting faculty to engage in reflective practice at the course level that complements the reflective practice occurring at the department level. Throughout the WEC process, departmental faculty, facilitated by a WEC consultant, engage in structured, locally situated discussions in which they articulate and interrogate their conceptions of writing and writing instruction. The WEC consultant provides essential support for engaging faculty in this reflective activity at the department level. EPTs could provide another, complementary source of support for engaging faculty in reflective activity at the course level. While the WEC consultant works "behind the scenes to enable and mediate productive reflection" focused on conceptions of writing and writing instruction (Flash, 2016, p. 247), the EPT could work "on the scene" as a facilitative partner to enable productive reflection focused on instructional practices and student learning. For example, EPTs can provide faculty with immediate feedback on their instructional practices that are informed by their changing conceptions of writing and writing instruction so that they can continue to reflect on and refine both their instructional practices and conceptions of writing instruction.

Given that, as Zawacki (2008) has found, EPTs have limited success when faculty already have deeply ingrained beliefs about writing and writing instruction, faculty may be more receptive to EPTs' feedback on instructional practices and student experiences if that feedback aligns with their new understandings of writing and writing instruction and their overall WEC plan. Faculty may even be more inclined to actively seek out and act on EPT feedback if they understand how EPTs fit into their WEC plans and overall departmental curriculum and if both EPTs and faculty are working from similar understandings of writing and writing instruction and developing them with each other.

Another way EPTs could provide support for curricular and instructional change at the course level is by serving as teaching (not grading or evaluative) partners with faculty during class. When working with faculty and students during class, EPTs, as Spigelman and Grobman (2005) have noted, provide both instructional support and development because "they may introduce teachers to composing theory, writing center theory, and peer group theory; they may guide instructors to clarify their expectations, offer more consistent instruction, or develop more coherent writing assignments" (p. 9). Serving as instructional support and development allows EPTs to help facilitate instructional practices that may be new or unfamiliar to a faculty member, such as small-group work or discussions, peer reviews, or workshops. For example, an EPT could co-facilitate with a faculty member a peer review or a workshop focused on a particular aspect of disciplinary writing. When serving as a teaching partner, EPTs, again, would not replace faculty. Instead they would help support students and faculty during class as they undertake new instructional practices and curricular changes that are informed by their changing conceptions of writing and writing instruction and WEC plans.

EPTs' presence in classrooms and in departments also could serve as physical reminders of WEC plans to further reinforce curricular and instructional changes. By attending the classes in which they serve as EPTs, their physical presence alone could prompt faculty to make connections to writing that they might overlook otherwise. Not only can EPTs attend the classes that they support but they also attend other classes in the department as students. Since faculty tend to select students from their own departments to serve as EPTs, other faculty often have students in their classes who serve as EPTs in other classes. Faculty need reminders of the WEC work they have done and plan to do, especially when other institutional initiatives and departmental demands compete for their attention. EPTs with their physical presence in the classroom and department could serve as daily reminders of a department's commitments to writing, writing instruction, and their WEC plan.

These are the ways in which I have imagined EPTs and the WEC model could work together productively to support student learning and development and to reinforce curricular and instructional change. In brief, EPTs introduce student-to-student learning to the WEC process so that both students and faculty receive support for WEC plans. EPTs provide students and faculty with feedback to support their development as writers and teachers. Faculty reflective activity could benefit from both the WEC program support and the EPT perspective, much like faculty benefit from the academic librarian perspective (see Chapter 10, this collection). When EPTs encourage reflective activity at the course level through feedback on assignments and student experiences, they would build on the reflective activity facilitated by the WEC consultants occurring at the department level. Employing students from departments as EPTs also could serve to reinforce curricular and instructional change by providing faculty with physical reminders of their writing and curricular commitments and WEC plans.

I acknowledge that this ideal portrait of integration is complicated by the underlying WAC and WEC tensions and challenges that result when faculty move between individual engagement at the course level and collective engagement at the department level. These tensions and challenges most likely cannot be eliminated. I anticipate that maintaining a department's focus on curricular change at the departmental level when EPTs support particular courses in a department will continue to be challenging. I also anticipate that some faculty may rely on EPTs for writing instruction and feedback instead of altering their own instructional and feedback practices. However, I do not believe EPTs and the WEC model must be a zero-sum game. While course-level engagement may compete with faculty's department-level engagement, it need not negate or undercut it, and I have developed a few concrete steps that CxC has begun to take or intends to take to navigate the underlying tensions between WAC and WEC and address challenges that integrating EPTs and WEC pose.

First, CxC intends to work with departments more closely in terms of their EPT use so that EPTs are clearly integrated into WEC plans as a complementary form of support for curricular and instructional change. In other words, whether EPTs are introduced as a support during the first iteration of a WEC plan or later ones, EPTs must be clearly connected to departmental WEC efforts. What this means in practice is that the rationale for EPT use in certain courses should be articulated, connected to larger curricular revisions, and incorporated into the assessment plan. During later iterations of the WEC plan, EPT use should be evaluated and revised along with other WEC efforts. This might mean that EPTs move to other courses in the curriculum or that their use is paused for a period of time while curricular changes are occurring. EPTs need not be a permanent form of support but rather one that develops along with the WEC plan. When working with EPTs, departments also should have a plan for their use of EPTs in their WEC plans that includes (1) the departmental selection process for EPTs, (2) departmental expectations for faculty working with EPTs, and (3) accountability measures for faculty working with EPTs. This is especially important when EPTs are assigned to a course and faculty are expected to work with EPTs without explicitly opting-in.

Second, I have developed detailed policies regarding EPTs' responsibilities, explicitly outlined expectations for faculty and EPT partnerships, and developed a brief online faculty training to help guide EPT integration into WEC plans. Without clear policies and expectations, as CxC has found, departments and faculty "may be prone to seeing [EPTs] through the lenses they know, such as lab assistant, intern, TA, or adjunct" (Macauley, 2014, p. 47). While EPT responsibilities and faculty partnerships will vary across institutional contexts and should incorporate flexibility (Cairns & Anderson, 2008), I have observed that students, EPTs, and faculty have stronger partnerships when EPT responsibilities include meeting with students outside of class in one-to-one or small group consultations to provide feedback on written assignments and attending class to support faculty and students during writing-to-learn and writing-related activities. I also have observed that faculty and EPT partnerships benefit when faculty and EPTs meet at the beginning of the semester and then establish regular check-ins to share observations and feedback and when they collaborate as teaching partners to develop and co-facilitate writing-related activities during class.

Third, CxC intends to retain primary control of EPT training but also plans to work more closely with departments to communicate the importance of a shared training among all EPTs and to support supplemental training by departments if needed as part of their WEC plans. EPTs benefit when interacting with others from across the disciplines during shared training since it highlights disciplinary differences and connects them with a larger community of peer educators. Hall and Hughes (2011) have concluded that EPTs need at a minimum "practical, applied knowledge about reading and responding to student writing and about holding effective conferences with students" (p. 27). They further recommended that EPTs have some knowledge about how writing abilities develop so that they can provide both students and faculty with feedback (2011, p. 27). CxC is best positioned to provide this kind of training. We also have added to our EPT training explicit attention to partnerships with faculty by providing EPTs with clear guidelines for those partnerships and by role playing common situations and ways in which to provide faculty with feedback. What this training looks like will vary across institutions and be highly dependent on the students employed as EPTs. Some programs have credit-bearing courses that EPTs take (Hall & Hughes, 2011). Others, like CxC, offer intensive training at the beginning of the semester (to which we invite faculty to join us for lunch on one day) and follow it up with professional development and other activities throughout the semester.

I propose these steps here to help reduce the challenges that arise when integrating EPTs into WEC because, as I hope to have demonstrated, the embedded peer tutoring and WEC models have the potential to work together in ways that are productive. Given the underlying tensions between the two models, I doubt that all risk and challenges can be eliminated. These steps attempt to work within the tensions between WEC and WAC so that they work together rather than compete with each other. As CxC adopts these steps, develops new ones, and assesses our efforts, we will discover the extent to which integration of EPTs and the WEC model is successful, but in the meantime, I am hopeful that this exploration and concrete steps will be of use to other WAC programs that are considering adopting the WEC model and imagining how the WEC model may be integrated and interact with existing elements of their programs. I also am hopeful that this exploration will be of use to those adopting the WEC model who are considering the kinds of incentives that they can offer to departments for undertaking this work.

I wish to close by acknowledging Soven's (1993) survey of embedded peer tutoring initiatives in which she found that administrators "must be tolerant of the 'less than perfect'" because these initiatives entail several different and ultimately uncontrollable moving parts (p. 67). When combining the uncontrollable moving parts of the embedded peer tutoring model with the uncontrollable moving parts of the WEC model, one must be even more tolerant of the "less than perfect." However, I side with Zawacki's optimism when it comes to the "less than perfect." Zawacki (2008) has argued that even though not all EPT and faculty partnerships are successful in reaching the WAC goals of transforming faculty teaching practices and influencing curricular change:

> negotiations around assignment and response practices that occur between teachers and their [EPTs] ultimately lead to a better understanding of overall learning and writing goals for student writers. In that way, every [EPT] placement, even those that are less than successful, becomes part of a network for change, thereby helping us to build and sustain the rich culture of writing at our institution. (p. 13)

Integrating EPTs and the WEC model has the potential to support student learning and development and to reinforce curricular and instructional change. Ideally and in the best-case scenarios, EPTs and WEC plans would work harmoniously and mutually reinforce each other, but even when in reality the integration is "less than perfect," I believe that it still can contribute to a network for change at an institution that helps to build and sustain a culture of writing.

REFERENCES

Bruffee, K. (1995). Peer tutoring and the "conversation of mankind." In C. Murphy & J. Law (Eds.), *Landmark essays on writing centers* (pp. 87–98). Hermagoras Press.

Buyske, S. G. (1995). Student communication in the advanced mathematics classroom. *Primus, 5*(1), 23–32.

Cairns, R. & Anderson, P. V. (2008). The protean shape of the writing associate's role: An empirical study and conceptual model. *Across the Disciplines, 5*. https://doi.org /10.37514/ATD-J.2008.5.2.07.

Carpenter, R., Whiddon, S. & Dvorak, K. (2014). Guest editor introduction: Revisiting and revising course-embedded tutoring facilitated by writing centers. *Praxis: A Writing Center Journal, 12*(1). http://www.praxisuwc.com/from-the-guest-editors/.

Flash, P. (2016). From apprised to revised: Faculty in the disciplines change what they never knew they knew. In K. Yancey (Ed.) *A rhetoric of reflection* (pp. 227–249). Utah State University Press.

Gladstein, J. (2008). Conducting research in the gray space: How writing associates negotiate between WAC and WID in an introductory biology course. *Across the Disciplines, 5*. https://doi.org/10.37514/ATD-J.2008.5.2.02.

Gladstein, J. (2013). The national census of writing. https://writingcensus.swarthmore .edu/.

Hall, E. & Hughes, B. (2011). Preparing faculty, professionalizing fellows: Keys to success with undergraduate writing fellows in WAC. *The WAC Journal, 22*, 21–40. https://doi.org/10.37514/WAC-J.2011.22.1.03.

Haring-Smith, T. (1992). Changing students' attitudes: Writing fellows programs. In S. H. McLeod & M. Soven (Eds.), *Writing across the curriculum: A guide to developing programs* (pp. 123–131). Sage.

Hughes, B., Gillespie, P. & Kail, H. (2010). What they take with them: Findings from the peer writing tutor alumni research project. *Writing Center Journal, 30*(2), 12–46.

Hughes, B. & Hall, E. B. (2008). Guest editors' introduction. *Across the Disciplines, 5*. https://doi.org/10.37514/ATD-J.2008.5.2.01.

Macauley, W. J., Jr. (2014). Insiders, outsiders, and straddlers: A new writing fellows program in theory, context, and practice. *Praxis: A Writing Center Journal, 12*(1), 45–50.

Mulin, J. (2001). Writing centers and WAC. In S. H. McLeod, E. Miraglia, M. Soven & C. Thaiss (Eds.), *WAC for the new millennium: Strategies for continuing writing-across-the-curriculum programs* (pp. 179–199). National Council of Teachers of English.

Mulin, J. & Schorn, S. (2007). Enlivening WAC programs old and new. *WAC Journal, 18*, 5–18. https://doi.org/10.37514/WAC-J.2007.18.1.01.

Mulin, J., Schorn, S., Turner, T., Hertz, R., Davidson, D. & Baca, A. (2008). Challenging our practices, supporting our theories: Writing mentors as change agents across discourse communities. *Across the Disciplines, 5https://wac.colostate.edu/atd/ special/fellows/*. https://wac.colostate.edu/atd/special/fellows/.

Regaignon, D. R. & Bromley, P. (2011). What difference do writing fellows programs make? *WAC Journal, 22,* 41–63. https://doi.org/10.37514/WAC-J.2011.22.1.04.

Soven, M. (1993). Curriculum-based peer tutoring programs: A survey. *WPA: Writing Program Administration, 17*(1–2), 58–74.

Soven, M. (2001). Curriculum-based peer tutors and WAC. In S. H. McLeod, E. Miraglia, M. Soven & C. Thaiss (Eds.), *WAC for the new millennium: Strategies for continuing writing-across-the-curriculum programs* (pp. 200–223). National Council of Teachers of English.

Spigelman, C. & Grobman, L. (2005). Introduction: On location in classroom-based writing tutoring. In C. Spigleman & L. Grobman (Eds.), *On location: Theory and practice in classroom-based writing tutoring* (pp. 1–13). Utah State University Press.

Webster, K. & Hensen, J. (2014). Vast potential, uneven results: Unraveling the factors that influence course-embedded tutoring success. *Praxis: A Writing Center Journal, 12*(1), 51–56.

Zawacki, T. M. (2008). Writing fellows as WAC change agents: Changing what? Changing whom? Changing how?" *Across the Disciplines, 5.* https://doi.org/10.37514/ATD-J.2008.5.2.05.

CHAPTER 11

FINDING WRITING WHERE IT LIVES: DEPARTMENTAL RELATIONSHIPS AND RELATIONSHIPS WITH DEPARTMENTS

Robert Scafe and Michele Eodice

University of Oklahoma

This chapter offers tactics for moving toward a sustainable, faculty-driven WEC process when the very conditions of working with a department seem to preclude faculty involvement. In the WEC initiative at the University of Oklahoma, our approach has been like that of a social activist doing grassroots work behind the scenes before they have achieved the critical mass to effect institutional change. The chapter first aims to update the general WAC conversation about social movement tactics with recent literature about relational dynamics (Tarabochia, 2017), including the rhetoric of respect (Rousculp, 2014) practiced in community-oriented writing centers. These relational dimensions are especially important for new or small WEC programs that must flexibly build coalitions and one-with-one ties to foster a campus culture of writing. We present evidence from WEC's work with the OU Department of Chemistry and Biochemistry. Drawing on faculty focus group responses and curriculum development materials, we demonstrate how one curriculum specialist, guided by WEC, gradually initiated a departmental conversation through one-with-one conversations, coalitions with other teaching initiatives, and strategically chosen curricular interventions.

BRINGING WEC TO THE UNIVERSITY OF OKLAHOMA

"Organizing 101!" proclaimed historian Anne Hyde, punctuating a WEC focus group conversation in which the Department of Chemistry's instructional lab

DOI: https://doi.org/10.37514/PER-B.2021.1299.2.11

designer Tami Martyn had described her "grassroots" efforts, similar to those of Blank in Chapter 5 of this volume, to engage individual faculty members in discussions about student writing. Here's the context: In 2016, Dr. Martyn approached our WEC coordinator for assistance integrating writing instruction across the four-year undergraduate curriculum in chemistry. With the approval of the chair, we slightly revised and distributed a WEC-style survey that collects instructors' perceptions about student writing. But while the department appreciated the data and blessed Tami's work on a WEC-inspired curriculum map, they believed it impossible for the faculty of over 32 to be involved in a concerted two-year project of curricular and pedagogical change related to writing. Thus, while WEC fell short of one of its fundamental principles—open and extensive faculty involvement in developing a plan for curricular development—we continued to consult with Dr. Martyn as she worked, both overtly and "behind the scenes," to create a departmental buzz about student writing.

Our story, then, reveals a kind of outsourcing of expertise that could be one of the challenges of implementing WEC at many universities. Yet while our focus group revealed the trying conditions under which faculty labor, Dr. Hyde's "Organizing 101" remark also suggested that WAC's history of borrowing tactics and strategies from social movements might offer solutions. As Anson and Dannels (2018) put it in their case study in *Sustainable WAC*, "the departmental model [e.g., WEC] requires a kind of community activism that at once respects the autonomy and values of departmental cultures while also providing them with new perspectives, knowledge, and strategies" (p. 6). To be sure, WEC can be seen as part of an effort to overcome the limitations of the "social movement" model's reliance on micro-level, decentralized pedagogical work (Cox et al., 2018, p. 17). But as Anson and Dannels' allusion to "community activism" suggests, this concern with strategic issues such as program administration in no way implies abandoning the "movement" tactics of earlier WAC approaches. Consistent with the strategies recommended in Cox, et al., WEC builds on the relational wisdom gleaned from grassroots WAC to create a *flexible* system—one that thoughtfully respects disciplinary prerogatives, faculty autonomy, and a bottom-up ethic of inductive work. When this "work with other movements" takes the form of collaborations and partnerships, we argue, relational work that employs tactics is required. Drawing on recent theory about the link between social relations and larger WAC conversations (Geller, 2009; Rousculp, 2014; Tarabochia, 2017), we show how WEC facilitates collaborative labor and mutual respect in ways that move toward a systemic writing plan, even when labor and administrative constraints incline departments to "doubt" (Geller, 2009) this goal from the start.

This chapter illustrates our experience adapting the WEC model to our situation in three stages. First, we will provide an overview of WEC at our university, the origins and connections to the writing center's existing WAC efforts and collaborative ethos. Then we will describe three interrelated approaches that have the explanatory power to help us better understand our WEC efforts: a *rhetoric of respect*, or attention to the dynamics of reciprocity and to the relational dynamics that go into forging sustained collaborations; *co-inquiry*, which emerges from valuing both techne and episteme during collaborative work; and the *coalition-building* strategies that enable WAC movements to be legible to all stakeholders. After showing how collaborative work and attention to relationships work together, we'll present a case study—chemistry—that illustrates the potential of collaborative micro-work in environments that turn to outsourcing expertise. Overall, this chapter offers tactics for moving toward WEC's staged, faculty-driven process when the very conditions of working with a department seem to preclude faculty involvement. Our approach is like that of a social activist doing grassroots work behind the scenes before they have achieved the critical mass to effect institutional change. At OU we have often been pleasantly surprised by how the material practices of the WEC model—the faculty survey, the insider/outsider assessment, the curriculum map—scaffold faculty to conferring about disciplinary writing, the value of collaborative work, and curricular goals in ways that administrative mandates fail to inspire. We believe that this universally desired outcome would be welcome in almost any higher education context.

INCUBATING WEC IN A WRITING CENTER CULTURE

What we did for many years at OU would hardly be classified as systemic or sustainable (Cox et al., 2018). Our approach was basically a neighborly one, with a peripatetic writing center director interested in talking with faculty about teaching writing in their discipline as well as about the writing they were doing in their discipline. For example, over the past ten years we have made a space for informal faculty discussions of writing across disciplines through brown bags, guest lectures, year-long symposia, writing groups, and Write Track Workshops. At times we had embedded graduate student writing fellows with departments to help facilitate a makeover—one that might have been required to meet program review standards to improve capstone writing, for example.

Because we intentionally developed a relational ethos for our writing center, we wished to extend that intentionality into thinking about WEC (Tarabochia, 2017). We wanted to find models that aligned with our values and offered some explanatory power. Our most useful affordance was the relationships we had already built, the trust that the writing center (through the director) had engendered. We were also pretty set on not adopting an overdetermined model. So at the start we were thinking about how to retain the good will and informality we had cultivated with faculty while transitioning to an actual programmatic model.[1]

In our context, a public R1 flagship with about 25,000 undergraduate students, adopting the WEC approach as described in the introduction to this collection was less like creating a WAC program from scratch and more like building on the OU Writing Center's existing grass-roots effort to reach faculty across campus and engage them in conversations about writing—student writing and their own writing. Yet the WEC approach included elements we had not employed, most particularly making our efforts more transparent and deliberate with plans and goals.[2]

The Rhetoric of Respect

As the OU Writing Center and WEC staff collaborated to achieve this more systematic engagement with departments, we took advantage of the affinities between the "rhetoric of respect" which Rousculp (2014) has articulated in the context of community writing centers and the practices of listening and cultivating faculty expertise which are so essential in WEC's work with departments. The OU Writing Center, as a site for developing WEC, already demonstrated the organizational wisdom of social movements because of its existing social justice partnerships across campus. We saw WEC's "community activism" idea as helping us transplant WEC to an environment where, in the absence of funding incentives and an administrative mandate, building relationships and alliances would be at a premium.

There are strong homologies between WEC's approach to working with departments and the main tenets of the "rhetoric of respect" that Rousculp (2014) has outlined for an activist community writing center. For Rousculp, the rhetoric of respect is meant as an alternative to rhetorics of "tolerance" and "acceptance," which may imply a patronizing and unequal stance toward writing center visitors and partners. The cultivation of mutual esteem demands agility in balancing listening and expertise in adaptation to local partnerships. Rousculp

---

1   When Michele arrived at OU (2006), she invoked a book that she had been thinking about for several years when she was asked about developing big programs. OU did not want/ still does not want, a campus-wide writing intensive initiative or a systemic WAC initiative, which fit well with her intentions and set the tone for WEC at OU. See *Small is beautiful: a study of economics as if people mattered* (Schumacher, E. F., 1973).

2   Late in 2012, we invited Pamela Flash to visit OU and provide some overview of the University of Minnesota writing enriched curriculum program to selected faculty and the provost. Soon after, because we sensed a positive reaction to the model by the provost, we submitted a proposal to fund a WEC initiative.

learned, on the one hand, those doing this work need to "believe the organization (in our case, departments) are capable of knowing what they want and what is best for them and their clients (in our case, students)" and attend planning meetings in a "blank" listening state. On the other hand, genuine reciprocity requires the "perception of worth, in esteem for another—*as well as* for the self," a kind of situational self-awareness that will sometimes withhold advice, but at other times offer expertise (2014, p. 25, italics ours). Crucially, for all its intentional "fuzziness," Rousculp's approach is guided less by general feeling or theory than it is by discursive practice: "how we collaborate [and] problem-solve" in the field. In other words, we build strong relationships by foregrounding practical work, trusting that collaborative, problem-solving activity will reveal the proper balance of listening and expertise better than standardized guidelines.

CO-INQUIRY AND LABOR

WEC work reveals the extent to which the virtues of "co-inquiry" depend on understanding the process of inquiry as empirical *work*—the almost magical ability of work to lead people to insights that no amount of abstract discussion or lecturing could induce. Geller (2009) has argued that WAC workers who participate in egalitarian dialogue with faculty will be able to play with disciplinary differences and reveal the underlying principles of teaching writing. Beyond egalitarianism, however, what's essential to Geller's concept of co-inquiry is the work process of empirical inquiry. Here she provides a method: "we can think our differences, rather than just thinking about our differences . . . and thinking our differences together is slow work," she explains, "the stuff of retreats, intensive weeklong workshops, and the very best collaborative assessment research" (2009, p. 33). Tarabochia (2017), too, has theorized the value of such "slow work" to generate meaningful relationships with (and among) faculty in her discussion of "establishing expert techne" in WAC work. Tarabochia's conversations with WAC developers reveal that many can establish expertise in a dialogic way when they "[make] visible the methodological dimension of their expertise—the craft-ful practice of teaching writing" (2017, p. 36). We think she's saying that techne leads to episteme better than the other way around.

These concepts of expert techne and co-inquiry reveal the hidden value of early WEC tools such as the faculty survey and initial assessments and curriculum maps—tools that may provide occasions of co-inquiry even before departments have assented to the idea of a writing plan. We might see these empirical tools as gestures of "productive humility" that Luskey and Emery have described in Chapter 4 of this volume—as places where the WAC worker can perform their disciplinary naiveté, and where the faculty members can work in the liminal space between "good writing" and thinking and expression in their specific discipline. The faculty survey might seem like just setting a quantitative benchmark for future assessment—but its true value lies in the preparatory process of calibrating disciplinary writing outcomes by comparing them with several samples of student writing: practical work that does more to help faculty to understand the concept of teaching "writing in the disciplines" than venting about student writing quality. The same can be said of initial assessments of student writing: initial assessment is not so much a pretense to scientific comparison; there's an ulterior motive—namely, involving faculty in the process of developing disciplinary-specific criteria themselves (Flash et al., 2018). Small scale, initial assessment can be used to generate dialogue with early adopters about disciplinary writing and to create a sense of agency and investment by mixing their labor with the process. In short, for WEC initiatives, we think "co-inquiry" means the first priority may not be getting a slot at the department's next faculty meeting to pitch a two-year writing plan to the assembled professors; instead, it should be creating occasions of co-work on student writing with faculty, and consciously leveraging any activity that makes visible the epistemological thresholds of disciplinary writing and curricular design.

But the concept of co-inquiry also suggests some ways we had to modify our initial understanding of the WEC approach. We thought WEC meant, much as Rousculp (2014) counsels, an ethos of minimal response—going into meetings "blank," withholding expertise, even when faculty say things that would rankle our comp/rhet comrades. In practice, however, the relational dynamics of working with faculty have led us to revisit the "co" in "co-inquiry." Tarabochia (2017) counsels flexibly offering and withholding expertise, depending on labor needs of a particular person/department. Geller advances the value of equity between WAC worker and patron—not a "division of labor" or a patron-client relationship, or between a generic pedagogy coach and a disciplinary expert, but a reciprocal exchange between two disciplinary experts "working their differences together." Patton (in Geller, 2009) describes the scene:

> The dialogue I've had with him and others isn't just one-way—we share lots of reading, lots of philosophical inquiry about our assumptions, as well as questions about my teaching and assignments. But my point here is that to embrace egalitarianism is not to deny expertise, much of which is *practiced* even if not *preached*. (p. 30)

Here Patton nicely connects both sides of the co-inquiry equation: "practiced" techne can become more explicit episteme when it's approached with the playful, cross-disciplinary dialogue between WAC worker and faculty member.

Coalition-Building

Respectful dialogue and collaborative work acquire greater legitimacy when they are perceived as part of a grassroots movement rather than primarily as part of a top-down initiative. Even back in the 1990s, as early WAC leaders began to construct a vision for the future, Walvoord (1996) characterized WAC as a *movement*, one based on strategic collaboration that maintains an anti-state, pro-faculty stance. For Walvoord, WAC programs could emulate the social movements' "dissemination of tactics and personnel" in intentional alliances with other campus stakeholders such as teaching centers, offices of assessment, and gen-ed initiatives, while carefully avoiding losing WAC's "pro-faculty" stance (1996, p. 70). To Walvoord, seeing WAC within the paradigm of social movements is a more positive way to frame the challenges, each of which then suggests a possible solution: work with other movement organizations" (p. 68–74). Susanmarie Harrington et al. (this volume) describe a contemporary example of this type of coalition building: "By bringing together WID, departmental faculty, and the library," WEC at the University of Vermont was able to demonstrate "that writing and information literacy are intertwined and disciplinarily situated." We believe our version of WAC/WID, developed from the WEC model, depends vitally on such coalition-building relationships. And coalitions remain focused on members, people who, however named, have joined a group and are moving along together.

As the ensuing case study will show, this dynamic of collaborative work has played out in Robert's work in chemistry, too. On the one hand, Robert and Tami both identify as "in-sourced" labor, similar to Gary Blank's early role in forestry (this volume). Just as Dr. Martyn's role as the "Instructional Lab Designer" for the chemistry department delegates the work of curriculum development and TA management to an internal specialist, Robert's first WAC project was as the "Writing Coordinator" for the U.S. History Survey. At that time, he was charged with injecting writing into a curriculum that was not going to give up the "Sage on the Stage" style of teaching. Thus, he was given the work of TA training and writing curriculum development, labor that would not be taken up by senior faculty at the time. In addition to bonding over the similarities of their institutional status, Robert and Tami's working relationship thrived on the sort of cross-disciplinary co-inquiry that Geller (2009) and Tarabochia (2017) have discussed.

Now we want to show how these three elements—rhetoric of respect, of relational work/co-inquiry, and coalition-building—influenced our work with one department—chemistry.

CASE STUDY: DEPARTMENT OF
CHEMISTRY & BIOCHEMISTRY

Prior to WEC we were quite familiar with trying to make change happen within small groups—a coalition of the willing, so to speak.[3] We were also aware that some departments were fractured—and fractious. We intuited deep historical political divides within departments that could have prevented any interaction from being positive. We also saw, in some cases, how bringing in outside expertise was perceived as the best solution; some departments wanted us to do all this work or to work on an individual basis with instructional designers to deal with matters of curriculum and pedagogy. To better theorize the relations between these campus-wide, departmental, and individual aspects of WAC/WID work, we developed an IRB-approved study to facilitate focus group discussions with faculty members we have worked with over in a WEC capacity over the last five years. We will use our work with chemistry to illustrate how we've flexibly applied WEC instruments to departmental cultures resistant to WEC's collective approach. The case study also illustrates how relational dynamics condition adaptations of WEC's long-term staged process.

The WEC team's work with chemistry began three years ago when the department's full-time instructional lab designer, Tami, contacted us about incorporating writing instruction into their general education offerings. This unusual institutional situation—working with an embedded instructional designer—quickly presented advantages and obstacles. One the one hand, we had a built-in liaison, a chemist with knowledge of disciplinary writing, and one who was "thoroughly convinced—I convinced myself before working with WEC—that you don't know if a student understands until they can put it into words." But Tami's insider expertise also posed a problem for WEC's participatory, inductive approach to curriculum development. Although a WEC-style faculty survey pinpointed critical writing abilities and suggested the need to map them over the curriculum, the department said "No" to our proposal to discuss these results with the faculty. Instead, the department delegated responsibility for developing a curriculum map and instructional materials to Tami, alone, in consultation with WEC. How were we to move toward a sustainable curriculum when the engine

---

3   Our earliest efforts under the WEC banner were with construction science, computer science, and music. George Cusack [now at Carleton College] is credited with bridging our informal approach to a more structured process and, especially with music, was appreciated for "giving us just what we needed to work on this" in terms of direction and guidance. George acknowledged the tensions in the department, made the participatory, inductive, and labor-intensive process transparent, and focused the attention and energy on the task at hand—"fixing the Capstone."

of WEC work—faculty dialogue about actual student writing—was off the table from the get-go? In this case study we want to show how such circumstances may require tactically flipping your original WEC script now and again, focusing early on curriculum development activities that allow WEC personnel to build working relationships both with and within departments. While we found it necessary to depart from an optimal WEC sequence at certain moments, we were ultimately convinced of the importance of maintaining the overarching narrative at every step of the way in a "grassroots" process of gradually inducing faculty participation.

Robert responded to chemistry's unwillingness to collectively discuss their writing goals by offering to help develop a few "low-stakes" writing assignments for students integrating data tables and figures in their general chemistry lab reports. He initially thought he was throwing away the WEC playbook by getting into the weeds of assignment creation without the involvement of teaching faculty; it was Tami who had the tactical sense to foresee how focusing on tables and figures would move us toward the long-term goal of faculty participation. Her approach was to use the success of an assignment focused on a skill that faculty would not initially see as "writing"—constructing data tables and graphs—to induce individual faculty members to adopt language and approaches others had had success with. As she explained to the focus group:

> Yeah, [you have] to have an example to say, "This is what it
> will look like if you do this." And then they can say, "Yeah,
> that makes sense." Instead of just abstractly "We want you to
> write" or "we want your students to do better" or "What do
> you think writing is?" at which point they just shut down and
> say, "We don't write in my class."

Tami explained that the demonstrable impact of the tables and figures curriculum in first-year chemistry encouraged *Chem 2* instructors to integrate a similar language—"Titles, Tables, and Text"—on their own syllabi or learning management systems. Most importantly, Tami foresaw how flipping the WEC script—far from throwing away the playbook—could initiate a "grassroots" approach to gradually creating a departmental conversation one professor at a time:

> We're hoping to incorporate more faculty as we go. As I said,
> we really haven't incorporated all across our curriculum yet.
> And to do that, we have a conversation with that next instruc-
> tor: how are we going to frame this, and how is it going to
> show up in your class? Can we make a statement on your
> syllabus? Can we put together this one page that you can just
> put onto your Canvas site? So that it makes it obvious that it's

part of a system. But it's one faculty member at a time, and saying "Okay, we have an overall plan, we want to incorporate your course into it. How can we work together on this?"

In lieu of the best-case scenario—inductively generating learning outcomes in faculty meetings and committees—Tami is creating a de facto "system" by using the tables and figures curriculum to have conversations about chemistry writing with individual professors, and to persuade them to adopt consistent language across the curriculum. Tami and Robert agree gradually luring faculty into participating in a shared curriculum (similar to the activities preceding WEC implementation in some departments described in Chris Anson's chapter in this volume) is not as good as having open faculty discussions from the start—but we believe we can move toward that goal one professor at a time.

Developing working relationships to carry forward such "grassroots" strategies may require WEC workers to temporarily shelve their preferred method of coaching and to claim some writing expertise. Tarabochia (2017) shows that WAC workers often establish "expert *techne*" by sharing their own practices of teaching and writing and comparing them with the methods of faculty they're working with. For example, a WAC worker might leverage the practical suggestion about grade norming to arrive at the epistemological principle of the "rhetorical nature of writing and the complex reality of multiple audiences" (Roozen, 2015, pp. 38-39) through conversations about their common experiences with the scholarly peer review process. In a similar vein, Geller has argued that creating practical occasions of "co-inquiry" with departmental faculty requires not only "believing" in the faculty member's writing expertise, but also "owning up to" our own writing—"admit[ting] what we know—and don't know" about writing in our discipline and as WAC experts (2009, p. 31). Like Tarabochia, Geller (2009) believes that such practices of "thinking our differences together" (p. 33) requires exposing deeper epistemic assumptions, "learning how to make explicit the thinking that leads you to say what you say" (p. 29). The practical work of comparing differences as teachers and practitioners of writing can lead tacitly to the deeper realizations—that writing is disciplinary, that it's rhetorical—that enable faculty participation in WAC/WID work.

Robert's work with Tami to create the "Tables and Figures" curriculum for Chemistry suggests how such practical work done in the spirit of mutual humility can lead departments toward these epistemological thresholds. Tami and Robert developed their thinking about this in a co-presentation at the OU Writing Center's Year of the Scientific Writer Symposium—a fact worth underscoring because it shows how WEC's work with individuals and departments builds on Michele's "coalition-building" approach to developing a campus culture of writing. In their presentation Tami and Robert used the subtitle "Just a Chemist . . . Just a Writing

Teacher" to convey the productive messiness of co-discovering the writing in student data tables and figures. Tami, persuaded that writing about data makes it *meaningful*, sought out Robert's expertise as "writer"; she didn't want so much to be prompted neutrally to develop her own consciousness of chemistry writing as to engage in playful dialogue with someone who approaches "writing" from a different disciplinary angle—as a historian, as a "writer" (Robert's Ph.D. is in history, and he teaches composition in the Expository Writing Program). As she explained in the YSW presentation:

> At this point I wanted an "expert's opinion"! Though I had put together what I thought was the most important parts of writing a good paper and had gotten feedback within the department to support the curriculum, I really wanted to know how a writer would view it. I also know that we are educating a wide variety of students and I wanted to know what assumptions I was making of students' understanding that non-chemists would not understand. I NEEDED an outside perspective.

What is interesting about Tami's characterization of Robert's role here is how it alludes simultaneously to his "expertise" as a practitioner and teacher of writing and his (useful) ignorance of what counts as meaningful in a chemistry context. The same experience that made Robert an "expert" in creating curriculum materials like this also rendered him useful as an uninformed "outsider."

As Tarabochia (2017) and Geller (2009) have emphasized, developing such working relationships of mutual respect both requires and reveals deeper reflection on pedagogical process—in our case, on *how* we found a common language about meaningful writing across our disciplinary divides. At first, Robert struggled to grasp what Tami was presenting as "meaningful" in tables and graphs—choices about where to start the x-axis, the ordering of columns of data, and so on—and to relate to his own stock of ideas about interpreting evidence (the Toulmin model from composition, primary source criticism from history). The breakthrough happened when Robert and Tami read together the following passage from Heard's *The Scientist's Guide to Scientific Writing*: "Do not expect readers to interpret a graphic unassisted. The text should indicate what pattern they should look for, how that pattern relates to the point being made, and how to see the pattern in a complex graphic" (2016, p. 117). Tami and Robert dubbed this passage their "magic quote," because, after Tami exclaimed "that's what I want!" upon hearing it, this invocation to audience awareness greatly helped both of them focus on a few of the most important "meaning-making" aspects of putting together tables, labeling them, and explaining them in the text. Reflecting on the totemic status of this single quotation throughout their collaboration,

Robert and Tami explained that they had stumbled upon the value of the deep learning goal—audience awareness—as the guiding principle that would help them focus the curriculum on just a the most "meaning-generating" aspects of table or a graph. Tami summarized the payoff of this collaboration in a way that pinpoints the value of thinking across disciplines: "Again, we really wanted to focus on what is *meaningful*, not necessarily the rhetoric. In my mind I was considering (1) What our science-minded TAs would be able to grade comfortably and consistently, and (2) What first-year student scientists could grasp and master at this point." Having created this relationship of meaningful disciplinary practice and "rhetorical" writing in a working dialog about a single feature of chemistry writing, Tami and Robert made their approach more "shareable" by identifying the deeper pedagogical principle that made their work possible.

By learning how to talk to one another about chemistry writing, Tami and Robert also learned how to revisit the idea of a WEC-style faculty conversation about writing with the department administration. Tami created a buzz about the tables and figures curriculum by conducting a formal assessment of its impact on General Chemistry lab reports and co-presenting these results at OU's Assessment Forum. Tami and Robert also hatched a plan to propose a WEC-style "insider/outsider" assessment of capstone writing to initiate a conversation about the learning outcomes in a course that represents the culmination of students' four-year curriculum. The department chair responded to Tami's proposal with enthusiasm. Noting that he already had somebody in mind for the outside assessor, he also embraced the underlying logic of this approach by approving of Tami's suggestion to re-orient the capstone writing assignment to a more "real-world" scenario modeled on examples from John Bean's *Engaging Ideas*. In her proposed curriculum, students choose to be a research scientist for a public agency like the EPA or NASA and write a research-based proposal to maintain funding for one of these agencies' chemistry-related projects. The initial success of this capstone initiative illustrates the relational, performativity aspect of WEC work.

Recalling the chair's remark that he "already had someone in mind" as the outside assessor affirms how concrete, personal relations can authenticate abstractions such as the assertion that writing is what chemists do in their professional work. The fact that the same department head who initially said "No" to a faculty meeting on writing outcomes then approved of similar conversation as part of the assessment process illustrates the relational wisdom baked into WEC instruments. The faculty who may say "we don't teach writing" are more likely to perceive that they have something to discuss when presented with the practical work of assessing student writing with working chemists outside of academia. But we also need to emphasize how Robert and Tami's co-inquiry with tables and figures cleared the way for this breakthrough on capstone assessment. Particularly with some aspects of data, the use of "real-world" examples of bad tables from chemistry journals created the narrative about writing as meaningful to students when a real audience is introduced.[4]

At the one-with-one level, focusing on a particular (and particularly) disciplinary form of writing—tables and graphs—allowed Tami and Robert to build a working relationship and develop "shareable" epistemic knowledge about curriculum development. At the departmental level, they were able to leverage that small success to win broader acceptance for faculty discussion of chemistry writing by using WEC's "insider/outsider" assessment method to appeal to the department's strong relations with professional chemists outside of academia. But all of it was further enabled by WEC's tactical cooperation with multiple campus pedagogy initiatives—the office of assessment, science librarians, and temporary coalitions such as the science faculty who supported the "Year of the Scientific Writer" symposium. As Tami explained to the focus group, the opportunity to present and revisit her curriculum development work in multiple forums legitimized her efforts in the eyes of her faculty in ways that only working with WEC would not have.

In the process of developing a WEC-inspired curriculum map (Figure 9.1), Tami was able to engage individual faculty in discussions about what writing abilities are taught in their courses, and then to re-present her findings in a graphic that was both descriptive and prescriptive.

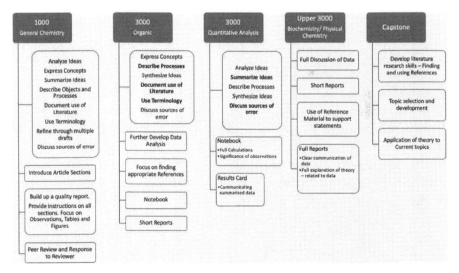

Figure 9.1. Martyn & Scafe, "Strategies for Assessing a Writing Enriched Curriculum in Natural Sciences," OU Assessment Forum, 2018.

---

4   Although student responses in this case were not part of The Meaningful Writing Project data, the way the term is used here points to two interconnected reasons students named a writing task meaningful—authenticity and relevance. See Eodice et al. (2017) and meaningfulwritingproject.net/.

In our focus group, which was held shortly after the 2018 OU Assessment Forum, Tami explained how documents such as this helped her coordinate faculty conversations about writing even outside of the departmental meeting forum:

> I think it's been really good that the university has had
> the [Year of the Scientific Writer] forum in spring and the
> Assessment Forum this fall. And having [all this work] come
> almost like a grassroots type of thing: maybe the idea came
> from WEC to our department, but then our department
> starts spreading, "Hey this is what we're doing and this is
> working well for us." So even if it didn't come as a top down
> "everybody is going to do this" getting to us and starting that
> conversation, then it was also valued when we go present that
> somewhere. Other people agreed with it, and they said, "Oh
> and I like the way you're doing that. We should do something
> like that." And that's the type of feedback I got from last week
> [at the assessment forum]. So, yeah, I think that makes a big
> difference to our faculty when they hear other departments
> like what you're doing.

Tami's remarks corroborate Russell's argument that a discourse on writing in the disciplines can be more effectively dispersed throughout a community instead of only "through the determination of individual faculty or at the insistence of maverick administrator" (Russell, 1990). When new WEC programs find themselves occupying just one niche in a larger ecosystem of campus pedagogy initiatives, they may find, as Tami and Robert did, that work presented in multiple forums outside of the WEC-department relationship lends an interdisciplinary vitality that can further legitimize those departmental efforts.

The WEC approach contains a great deal of relational wisdom, which is why we wanted to adopt the model. Our work with chemistry shows that a WEC worker can operate within a "coalition of the willing" reaping the benefits of a campus culture of writing, of distinctive departmental cultures, and of one-with-one relationships by adopting a kind of informed opportunism. At first, we wondered if we had made the right decision to bring WEC. Would it be a nimble enough platform to allow us to preserve some of the artisan ways we had been working with faculty and departments? Would it signal a regulatory programmatic shift? Would it be perceived as the "fix" (as some hoped) for faculty and departments? Overall, we believe integrating the WEC model was possible because of, not despite, the highly relational "small" WAC effort we had developed.

CODA

We have come to realize the social justice potential of WEC has been latent in our work with departments, and we are right now (early 2021)—in part spurred by events on our campus and nationally—making inclusive writing pedagogy intentional and embedded in the WEC process of developing curricular writing plans. As we integrate inclusive writing instruction into the process, we have come to see WEC's *relational* ethos as a healthy alternative to the potentially missionary and colonizing elements of some WAC programs, elements that have been critiqued as assimilationist or accommodationist (see Guerra, 2015; Kareem, 2020; Kells, 2013; LeCourt, 1996; Mahala, 1991; Russell, 1990; Villanueva, 2001). What if WEC's collaborative, grassroots methods offer a better way to work toward social justice? And what if our through-line of the relational extended from our work with groups of faculty to inclusive and collaborative pedagogies within disciplinary writing contexts? For example, a capstone revision in chemistry echoed WEC's relational ethos by offering opportunities for meaningful writing, where personal connection to self and future happens within an authentic writing assignment (Eodice, et. al, 2017). We can learn from research projects that look at the student writing experience through Writing Across Communities models and studies of students' writing experiences outside and beyond school, such as the Wayfinding Project, as well as learn from the findings of the research group *(Re)Examining Conditions for Meaningful Learning Experiences* at Elon University.

We believe WEC can better live up to the social justice potential of its relational ethos if it serves not only the curriculum but also the student learning imperative. With Kells (2019) we see all writing as an "ecology of relationships" (p. 20) that must include relationships with the student writing experience, yet the students are often absent from the process and imagined as a monolithic problem in the abstract when we cook up our assignments.

In Chapter 4 of this volume, Luskey and Emery reach a similar conclusion: "our own liminality with disciplinary concepts and discourses enables us to approximate students who are themselves apprenticing in their disciplinary fields . . . [yet] throughout the WEC process, students, themselves, are rarely present in the conversation." Certainly, as we write this in early 2021 there is some exigence to trade the deficit model for a developmental approach and the disciplinary for the democratic. As Kells (2019) advises us, "WAC programs must become more culturally responsive and structurally de-centered. Otherwise, we risk reproducing the dominant narratives of oppressive educational systems which replicate themselves hierarchically to benefit those already in power and to serve the most elite (rather than the most vulnerable) constituencies in our communities" (p. 27). This would mean not only including students in the WEC conversations as partners (Cook-Sather et al., 2014), but also shifting our focus from building programs to building communities. We are slow learners, but twenty years ago Villanueva (2001) pointed the way: "We should enter into a dialogue across the disciplines so as to better to understand the social processes that could relegate such a large number to the troubleheap" (p. 170). This critique of the social underpinnings of the deficit model requires, as Poe (2020) notes, that the "discussions about adequate standards for writing that fueled WAC long ago now become discussions about negotiation, perspective, and change" (p. xiii). Ultimately, for us, after all the work with faculty across a table, the goal is really to keep building the core capacity for collaborative change, the type of change made possible in our context through crafting relationships within institutional, disciplinary, and personal contexts.

REFERENCES

Alexander, J., Lunsford, K. & Whithaus, C. (2020). Affect and wayfinding in writing after college. *College English, 82*(6), 563–590.

Anson, C. M. & Dannels, D. P. (2018). Handing over the reins: Ownership, support, and the departmentally-focused model of communication across the curriculum. In M. Cox, J. Galin & D. Melzer (Eds.), *Sustainable WAC: A whole systems approach to launching and developing WAC programs* (pp. 5–7). National Council of Teachers of English.

Bean, J. C. (2011). *Engaging ideas: The professor's guide to integrating writing, critical thinking, and active learning in the classroom.* John Wiley & Sons Inc.

Cook-Sather, A., Bovill, C. & Felten, P. (2014). *Engaging students as partners in learning and teaching: A guide for faculty.* John Wiley & Sons.

Cox, M., Galin, J. & Melzer, D. (2018). *Sustainable WAC: A whole systems approach to launching and developing writing across the curriculum programs.* National Council of Teachers of English.

Eodice, M., Geller, A. E. & Lerner, N. (2017). *The meaningful writing project: Learning, teaching and writing in higher education.* Utah State University Press.

Flash, P., Huesman, R. & Bendzick, M. (2018). Rating student writing and working with rating data. 2018 WEC Institute. Unpublished. 2018 WEC Institute, University of Minnesota.

Geller, A. E. (2009). The difficulty of believing in writing across the curriculum. *Journal of the Assembly for Expanded Perspectives on Learning, 15*(1), 6.

Guerra, J. C. (2015). *Language, culture, identity and citizenship in college classrooms and communities.* Routledge.

Heard, S. (2016). *The scientist's guide to scientific writing.* Princeton University Press.

Kareem, J. M. (2020). Sustained communities for sustained learning: Connecting culturally sustaining pedagogy to WAC learning outcomes. In L. E. Bartlett, S. L.

Tarabochia, A. R. Olinger & M. J. Marshall (Eds.), *Diverse approaches to teaching, learning, and writing across the curriculum: IWAC at 25* (pp. 293–308). The WAC Clearinghouse; University Press of Colorado. https://doi.org/10.37514/PER-B.2020.0360.2.16.

Kells, M. H. (2013). Out of WAC: Democratizing higher education and questions of scarcity and social justice. In C. Wilkey & N. Mauriello (Eds.), *Texts of consequence: Composing social activism for the classroom and community* (pp. 117–156). Hampton.

Kells, M. H. (2019). Doing democracy: The salt of the earth recovery project–citizen scholars and activist writing across communities. *Open Words: Access and English Studies, 12*(1) https://doi.org/10.37514/OPW-J.2019.12.1.02.

LeCourt, D. (1996). WAC as critical pedagogy: The third stage? *JAC, 16*(3), 389–405.

Mahala, D. (1991). Writing utopias: Writing across the curriculum and the promise of reform. *College English, 53*(7), 773–789.

Poe, M. (2020). WAC today: Diversity and resilience. In L. E. Bartlett, S. L. Tarabochia, A. R. Olinger & M. J. Marshall (Eds.), *Diverse approaches to teaching, learning, and writing across the curriculum: IWAC at 25* (pp. xi-xiv). The WAC Clearinghouse; University Press of Colorado. https://doi.org/10.37514/PER-B.2020.0360.1.2.

Roozen, K. (2015). Writing is a social and rhetorical activity. In L. Addler-Kassner & E. Wardle (Eds.), *Naming what we know: Threshold concepts of writing studies* (pp. 17–18). Utah State University Press.

Rousculp, T. (2014). *Rhetoric of respect: Recognizing change at a community writing center*. National Council of Teachers of English.

Russell, D. R. (1990). Writing across the curriculum in historical perspective: Toward a social interpretation. *College English, 52*(1), 52-73.

Schumacher, E. F. (1973). *Small is beautiful: a study of economics as if people mattered*. Vintage.

Tarabochia, S. L. (2017). *Reframing the relational: A pedagogical ethic for cross curricular literacy work*. National Council of Teachers of English.

Villanueva, V. (2001). The politics of literacy across the curriculum. In S. H. McLeod, E. Miraglia, M. Soven & C. Thaiss (Eds.), *WAC for the new millennium: Strategies for continuing writing across the curriculum programs* (pp. 165–178). The WAC Clearinghouse. (Originally published in 2001 by National Council of Teachers of English). https://wac.colostate.edu/books/landmarks/millennium/.

Walvoord, B. E. (1996). The future of WAC. *College English, 58*(1), 58–79.

AFTERWORD

Pamela Flash

University of Minnesota

In the preceding chapters, colleagues lend perspective and insight to WEC's evolving history, its design and component practices, its impacts, and its challenges. Taken together, this multifaceted investigation will likely prove useful not only to those directly involved with WAC/WID programming but also to institutional administrators who recognize the limitations inherent in many top-down, cross-curricular writing initiatives and who seek a road-tested alternative. Beyond these two groups of colleagues, I hope this collection appeals to a broader audience of educational researchers and advocates who investigate ways of inspiring and sustaining progressive systemic change.

FACILITATING, FLEXING, AND SUSTAINING

The chapters composing this collection affirm the list of WEC's essential features I describe in in Chapter 1, but they also underscore three themes central to the WEC approach. The first theme relates to the important and artful facilitation WAC consultants practice in their interactions with departments. The second relates to the model's perpetually negotiated balance of structure and flexibility, a balance that enables WEC's cross-departmental and cross-institutional portability. A final theme underscored by chapters in this collection relates to ways in which the WEC model's decentralized and iterative processes manage to circumvent factors that can threaten the longevity of WAC and WID programs.

In his forward to this volume, Michael Carter introduces the first theme when he remembers that his initial forays into departmental faculty meetings were met with a "sturdy and implacable resistance." Understanding this resistance as both politically inspired (the meetings were mandatory) and conceptually inspired (he'd been reminded that writing instruction was the dedicated responsibility of *other* departments) Carter opened the floor to complaints. "I learned that faculty needed to establish their opposition," he writes; "they wanted to be heard, to feel that they had been understood." This surprising decision productively disarmed the resistors, paving the way to constructive and productive discussion. Throughout this collection, contributors affirm Carter's approach to eliciting and working with (rather than despite) faculty resistance. They borrow strategies from rhetorical researchers, ethnographers, and community organizers. They describe

DOI: https://doi.org/10.37514/PER-B.2021.1299.3.2

listening instead of presenting, expressing an open curiosity in the face of jaded suspicion, handing control to "the room" even when the room may not want it, and partnering rather than leading. The generative results rendered by this deliberate ceding of control suggest a significant shift in the writing-missionary and change-agent roles routinely adopted in WAC work. Facilitation, as the term implies, requires facing raised challenges and considering possible means of addressing them rather than eliding concerns or presenting solutions.

The second theme, WEC's negotiated balance of structure and flexibility, highlights an attribute that lies at the heart of WEC's appeal and of its day-to-day operations. In many of the preceding chapters, colleagues describe their attraction to both the model's structural framework and to its built-in adaptability. This unusual combination inspires the participation of departments as different from one another as mechanical engineering is to theatre arts and of institutions ranging from large-enrollment research universities to small-enrollment liberal arts colleges. In each of these contexts, WEC's goal of increasing a faculty's capacity for change remains constant. The model provides objects, maps, and methods for achieving the goal of integrating relevant writing and writing instruction, it affords time and space for discursive exploration, and it establishes relationships of trust and community.

Finally, contributors to this collection draw our attention to ways in which WEC's decentralized and collaborative activity, its distributed leadership, and its ongoing rounds of implementation and assessment can enable it to withstand dangers posed by personnel changes and constrained budgets. Jeffrey Galin (in Chapter 8 of this volume) uses a whole system approach to analyze ways that a WEC model can address the sorts of structural and leadership-oriented issues that have long threatened WAC programs' sustainability. Because WEC intentionally distributes and decentralizes leadership responsibilities, it can accommodate inevitable changes in personnel, whether those changes occur on the WAC team, in participating departments, or within senior administrative offices. Although, as Galin points out, administrators may be initially surprised by the model's slow-to-scale design, we've seen its iterative cycles and gradual expansion build credibility and attract increased participation among the empirically minded and the wary. Also, as at least one of the case studies contained in this volume illustrates, the model has been successful at offering senior administrators (and external accreditors) a contextually relevant and locally assessed alternative to uniform, cross-curricular writing initiatives.

Again and again throughout this collection we're reminded that the most important glue holding WEC initiatives together over the long haul is found in the relationships the model engenders. In Chapter 4 of this volume, Matthew Luskey and Daniel Emery ask the question, "What sustains WEC once enacted?"

In answering, they point to the durable partnerships and collaborations between WAC consultants and faculty members within WEC departments, characterizing these as, "partnerships that develop through frank and open discussion . . . bolstered by the use of data and assessments." Data grounds the discussions; trust enables them to fly.

ADAPTING TO CURRENT CIRCUMSTANCES

These three themes have revealed their importance in the chapters collected here, but also in the ways that WEC programming has responded to the current set of challenging societal circumstances. Since this collection's initiation back in 2018, much in the world has changed. The onset of a global pandemic triggered a shift to online instruction and a logistical reconsideration of ways that academic writing is taught and learned across all disciplines and textual forms. Almost simultaneously, discussion of the ways that academic writing instruction and assessment have contributed to systems of structural inequity was intensified by our exposure to violent crimes perpetrated by police officers against Black, indigenous, and people of color.

Nationally and locally, the sudden and universal move to online instruction in March 2020 sparked an immediate, at times haphazard, outpouring of instructional support from technologists, librarians, and WAC consultants. In late fall, 2020, I convened a virtual meeting, "WEC in the Time of Covid," to provide WEC practitioners from across the country with an opportunity to think together about ways in which the pandemic and move to virtual instruction were impacting WEC initiatives on their campuses. Although the pandemic was (and is still) proving challenging and exhausting on all sites, colleagues also reported some affordances to moving WEC operations into virtual venues. While some described a slowdown and a de-prioritizing of activity, others reported an increased sense of urgency and motivation. In some departments, all faculty meetings had been suspended which made contact difficult and progress uneven. In others, WEC programs were quickly tapped to provide much needed guidance related to online writing instruction. Colleagues reported that the method's sequenced activity can provide a measure of forward propulsion when many other less-defined activities have become backburnered or optional. "We are practicing the technique of 'friendly persistence,'" one colleague noted. "WEC offers an island in the sea of chaos!" exulted another.

On my campus, working remotely has inspired adjustments to the ways we organize and co-facilitate departmental WEC meetings. To make the most of precious synchronous time, we've abbreviated meetings (M1-M4) but added between-meeting tasks (in-advance preview of agendas, summaries, and data, for a few examples). This works better in some departments than others, but across the board I can say that during synchronous meetings, individual participation has increased exponentially as small groups of colleagues collaborate on generating writing plan content in shared online documents and virtual breakout rooms. Also, after suspending our direct assessment of student writing for one year, we are now moving the next round of panel ratings online in a process that combines synchronous norming and debriefing meetings with asynchronous rating activity. When in-person meetings become possible once again, we'll determine which of the online meeting and assessment practices merit incorporation into what we hope will remain a primarily onsite operation.

The move to remote instruction also inspired my team to launch two versions of a virtual short course called "Teaching with Writing Online," one for interdisciplinary populations of instructors and one for instructors within any of the 60+ departments engaged in WEC. Contrasting the two versions has been instructive. When we bring the course into a WEC-participating department, we find that we don't need to spend much dedicated time in the first module surfacing participants' fundamental understanding of writing and writing instruction or introducing the importance of course-relevant writing goals as drivers of instruction. Our interpersonal history with the department and our knowledge of its curricular structure and writing expectations allow us to quickly zero-in on specific logistical or pedagogical issues triggered by the forced move to remote instruction. This background work has also allowed us to think *innovatively* with departmental instructors who recognize ways in which current circumstances are offering them unprecedented opportunities to collectively change assignment genres and modes of writing instruction that may have been previously considered immovable. As a colleague in the history department commented, "Virtual teaching just throws so many cards up in the air! Assignments that used to be considered standard—mandatory—are now up for question and trial."

After the death of George Floyd, interest in looking at ways that academic writing instruction and evaluation perpetuate systems of structural inequity was accelerated and prioritized on campuses all over the world. On my campus, WEC liaisons began to request in-house discussions of equitable approaches to evaluating student writing. Members of my team are invited into these discussions, because, as one liaison expressed it, "you *get* us." In discussions like these, we have opportunities to partner with faculty members and other instructors in a reconsideration of grading criteria they've already identified and of the ways they use them in evaluating student work. As always, our approach is inductive and responsive; we convene meetings at the faculty's request and we listen carefully to concerns and questions. We tie ideas to artifacts, drawing attention to specifics found in writing criteria, grading practices, and archived samples of student writing. We ask framing questions: Are you concerned about grading practices, about specific items on your criteria list, or both? In response to questions about alternate teaching methods, we describe possibilities and, when asked about precedent and evidence, we quote research. We sit alongside our faculty colleagues as they consider ways of working concerns into incremental or radical changes in practice.

Advocates of more direct and activistic approaches may wince at the slowness of this pace of change or challenge it as overly indirect or accommodating. As Robert Scafe and Michele Eodice in Chapter 11 of this volume remind us, however, our goal in WEC is "to keep building the core capacity for collaborative change, the type of change made possible in our context through crafting relationships within institutional, disciplinary, and personal contexts." By serving as a thinking partners in candid discussions, by supporting faculty groups as they unpack intentional and unintentional effects of writing expectations and systems used to grade writing, we walk toward change, but as importantly, we build change capacity.

In "Black Holes: Writing Across the Curriculum, Assessment, and the Gravitational Invisibility of Race" (2014), Chris Anson asks how, as a field, "WAC ha[s] neglected issues of race and racial identity in its literature and its practices, particularly in the crucial area of assessment" (p. 15). By means of address, Anson suggests that we provide faculty members with opportunities to "dig deeper into issues that until now have remained hidden or are dealt with too perfunctorily to have much meaning" (p. 28). In "Reframing Race in Teaching Writing Across the Curriculum" (2016), Mya Poe suggests that moving beyond the perfunctory can be best accomplished when our activity is guided by three interrelated principles: (1) making race local, (2) identifying expectations, and (3) acknowledging the racial aspects of linguistic diversity and its meanings in the disciplines. In this collection, we demonstrate WEC's commitment to working locally—within departmental faculty meetings—in order to identify and question writing expectations. In the role of trusted partner, WAC consultants are in an excellent position to move the discussion beyond identification and to increase attention to linguistic equity and to partner with faculty members as they find ways of addressing inequities in their teaching.

FUTURE RESEARCH AND INQUIRY

WEC is young. Throughout this collection, our colleagues have made important observations, taken up intriguing questions, and supplied us with illuminating case studies. As more institutions implement WEC initiatives, and as more colleagues engage the methods we've described in this collection, we'll be in a position to collectively ask and answer even more intriguing questions. Here is a small sampling of questions we can think about as we move forward together:

WEC's Impact on Teaching and Learning

- In what ways does WEC's emphasis on the curricular integration of writing and writing instruction increase students' ability to transfer learning within departmental curricula and between instructional contexts?
- In what ways does participation in WEC change the ways that instructors teach and evaluate critical conceptual learning?
- What specific impacts has WEC activity had on writing assessment practices in participating departments and programs? What impacts can WEC methods have on enabling departments to devise, implement, and assess equitable assessment systems?

WEC's Facilitative Methodology

- How and where are the facilitative stances and practices used in WEC methods being learned? What literature and research helps us understand this approach?
- How might WEC further involve undergraduate students in the processes of identifying writing goals, drafting departmental writing plans, and assessing writing? How would their inclusion affect results?
- Under what circumstances might WEC methods have the inadvertent effect of reinforcing and calcifying traditional disciplinary values?

WEC's Writing Plans

- What does cross-departmental and cross-contextual analysis of departmental writing plans tell us about commonly held and diverging values in academic writing? How might the local-generation and intended dynamism of writing plans enhance or curtail their use as static objects of study and/or instructional tools?

WEC's Portability, Sustainability, and Rates of Adoption.

- How might WEC methods be adapted to address graduate departments? What about international settings where majors and curricula are differently conceived?
- What has the move to online venues revealed to us about the WEC model and the interpersonal nature of WEC work?

- What level of adoption is necessary for WEC programming to sustain in institutional contexts? In terms of scope, how small is too small? In terms of scale, how slow is too slow?
- What forms of valid assessment might help institutions answer the question "What impact is WEC having on student writing across departments?"?

Although buffeted and tested by the tumult of the past year, WEC programs have held. The adaptations described in this volume demonstrate the model's inherent flexibility, an attribute that has enabled programming to continue moving forward amid circumstantial disarray. Although moving our departmental interactions into online venues affirmed my own preference for onsite interaction, the move enabled us to develop some excellent online workarounds, practices that we'll take with us post-pandemic. And although accompanying colleagues as they investigate their linguistic values and assumptions is a messy and excited business, the fact that we're being invited to participate in these local and candid discussions reveals the power of sustained and trusting partnerships. If the past twelve months have taught us anything, they've taught us that the future is uncertain. In the face of this uncertainty, I'm hopeful for the changes WEC practitioners can help effect.

REFERENCES

Anson, C. M. (2014). Black holes: Writing across the curriculum, assessment, and the gravitational invisibility of race. In A. B. Inoue & M. Poe, M. (Eds.), *Race and writing assessment* (pp. 15–28). Peter Lang.

Anson, C. M. (2021). Introduction: WEC and the strength of the commons. In C. M. Anson & P. Flash (Eds.), *Writing-enriched curricula: Models of faculty-driven and departmental transformation.* The WAC Clearinghouse; University Press of Colorado. https://doi.org/10.27514/PER-B.2021.1299.1.3.

Carter, M. (2021). Foreword. In C. M. Anson & P. Flash (Eds.), *Writing-enriched curricula: Models of faculty-driven and departmental transformation.* The WAC Clearinghouse; University Press of Colorado. https://doi.org/10.27514/PER-B.2021.1299.1.2.

Flash, P. (2021). Writing-enriched curriculum: A model for making and sustaining change. In C. M. Anson & P. Flash (Eds.), *Writing-enriched curricula: Models of faculty-driven and departmental transformation.* The WAC Clearinghouse; University Press of Colorado. https://doi.org/10.27514/PER-B.2021.1299.2.01.

Galin, J. R. (2021). Theorizing the WEC model with the whole systems approach to WAC program sustainability. In C. M. Anson & P. Flash (Eds.), *Writing-enriched curricula: Models of faculty-driven and departmental transformation.* The WAC Clearinghouse; University Press of Colorado. https://doi.org/10.27514/PER-B.2021.1299.2.08.

Luskey, M. & Emery, D. L. (2021). Beyond conventions: Liminality as a feature of the WEC faculty development. In C. M. Anson & P. Flash (Eds.), *Writing-enriched curricula: Models of faculty-driven and departmental transformation.* The WAC Clearinghouse; University Press of Colorado. https://doi.org/10.27514/PER-B.2021.1299 .2.04.

Poe, M. (2016). Reframing in teaching writing across the curriculum. In F. Condon & V. A. Young (Eds.), *Performing antiracist pedagogy in rhetoric, writing, and communication* (pp. 87–105). The WAC Clearinghouse; University Press of Colorado. https://doi.org/10.37514/ATD-B.2016.0933.2.04.

Scafe, R. & Eodice, M. (2021). Finding writing where it lives: Departmental relationships and relationships with departments. In C. M. Anson & P. Flash (Eds.), *Writing-enriched curricula: Models of faculty-driven and departmental transformation.* The WAC Clearinghouse; University Press of Colorado. https://doi.org/10.27514 /PER-B.2021.1299.2.11.

CONTRIBUTORS

Chris M. Anson is Distinguished University Professor, Alumni Association Distinguished Graduate Professor, and Director since 1999 of the Campus Writing and Speaking Program at North Carolina State University, the first university-wide WEC program in the United States. There, he teaches graduate and undergraduate courses in language, composition, and literacy and works with faculty across the disciplines to enhance writing and speaking instruction. He has published 19 books and over 140 articles and book chapters relating to writing and has spoken widely across the US and in 33 other countries. He is Past Chair of the Conference on College Composition and Communication and Past President of the Council of Writing Program Administrators, and currently serves as Vice-Chair of the International Society for the Advancement of Writing Research.

Heather Bastian is the Associate Director of Communication Across the Curriculum (CxC) at the University of North Carolina–Charlotte. Her research interests include composition pedagogy, writing program administration, WAC/WID, and genre studies. Her work has appeared in the *CCC, WPA: Writing Program Administration, Composition Studies, Composition Forum, Across the Disciplines*, and *Reader*.

Gary B. Blank is Associate Professor and Alumni Distinguished Undergraduate Professor of Forestry and Director of Undergraduate Programs in the Department of Forestry and Environmental Resources at North Carolina State University. He teaches courses concerning environmental impact assessment, historical ecology, and sustainable use of natural resources. He began his appointment at NC State in 1976 and initiated WEC work in forestry in 1979. His publications include papers in wide ranging scientific and technical journals, book chapters, essays, book reviews, and poems.

Wade Carson is clinical assistant professor of medical radiation sciences and director of the University of Vermont's radiation therapy program. His interests include clinical research in radiologic sciences and also health care administration.

Michael Carter is Emeritus Professor of English and Associate Dean of the Graduate School at NC State. His research and teaching have focused on rhetoric and writing in the disciplines, with publications in a variety of journals, including *Written Communication, College Composition and Communication*, and *Research in the Teaching of English*. He is the author of *Where Writing Begins* and was honored with the Braddock Award for the Best CCC Article of the Year in 2008. His NSF grants have concentrated on writing and learning in the sciences, including the LabWrite project.

Dan DeSanto is Libraries Associate Professor in the Information and Instruction Services Department of the University of Vermont's David W. Howe Memorial Library. His scholarship with Susanmarie Harrington investigates the intersections of writing and information literacy. His other interests include measures of scholarly impact, and open access.

Daniel L. Emery (Dan) serves as an assistant director of writing across the curriculum at the University of Minnesota. He earned his Ph.D. in communication studies and Graduate Certificate in Rhetorics of Inquiry from the University of Iowa. Previously, he served as Term Associate Professor of Business Communication at the University of Minnesota and Assistant Professor of Communication and Writing at the University of Utah.

Michele Eodice is the Senior Writing Fellow in the Center for Faculty Excellence at the University of Oklahoma. Previously she directed the OU Writing Center and was an editor of the Writing Center Journal. She is a co-editor of *Learning from the Lived Experiences of Graduate Student Writers* and a co-director of the Meaningful Writing Project.

Pamela Flash serves as director of writing across the curriculum programs, co-director of the Center for Writing, and affiliate graduate faculty for the Literacy and Rhetorical Studies Minor at the University of Minnesota where she has taught and administered teaching-oriented programming since 1991. She is founding director of both the University of Minnesota's Writing-Enriched Curriculum (WEC) Program and of its interdisciplinary Teaching with Writing Program. She chaired the 2014 International Writing Across the Curriculum Conference, serves on the Association of Writing Across the Curriculum's executive and mentoring committees, and consults both nationally and internationally on WEC and WAC programming. Her consulting work, research, publications, consultations, and presentations focus on the WEC model, writing pedagogy, and the use of qualitative research methods (particularly inductive consultation, collaborative action research, and ethnographic methodologies) to enable sustainable pedagogic change on individual, departmental, and institutional levels.

Crystal N. Fodrey, director of the Writing at Moravian Program, is Associate Professor of English at Moravian College in Bethlehem, PA., where she teaches courses in rhetorical theory, writing studies, digital writing, professional writing, first-year writing, and creative nonfiction. Her scholarship has appeared in *Across the Disciplines, Composition Forum, Kairos: A Journal of Rhetoric, Technology,* and *Pedagogy, Assay: A Journal of Nonfiction Studies,* and elsewhere. In addition to leading first-year writing and WEC efforts at Moravian, she is currently working with colleagues to develop a conceptual framework for promoting digital multimodal teaching praxes across the disciplines.

Jeffrey R. Galin is Professor of English at Florida Atlantic University and founding director of FAU's writing center, WAC program, and community writing center. He teaches academic and multimedia writing. His most recent co-authored book is *Sustainable WAC: A Whole Systems Approach to Launching and Developing Writing Across the Curriculum Programs.* He has published edited collections on technology and teaching, teaching writing in college, and has published articles on literacy theory, teaching writing, managing writing programs, copyright, and online publishing. He is currently outgoing chair of the CCCC WAC Standing Group, outgoing chair of the Association for WAC, and past co-chair of the WAC Summer Institute.

Susanmarie Harrington is Professor of English and Director of the Writing in the Disciplines Program at the University of Vermont. With Dan DeSanto, her recent scholarship explores the relationship of threshold concepts in writing and information literacy.

Chris Hassay is a co-researcher with the writing-enriched curriculum at Moravian College, where he also teaches first-year writing and worldbuilding courses. His scholarship has appeared in *Composition Forum,* and he has presented on WEC research and FYW pedagogy at the Writing-Enriched Curriculum Institute, College Composition and Communication Conference, International Writing Across the Curriculum Conference, Small Liberal Arts College Writing Program Administrators Conference, and Watson Conference. His current research centers on the connections between transfer-centric writing practices and creative writing experiences, as well as WEC research practices and methodologies.

Matthew Luskey is an assistant director of writing across the curriculum at the University of Minnesota. He holds a Ph.D. in English from the University of Oregon and has taught undergraduate and graduate courses in writing and rhetoric, literature, film, media aesthetics, Liberal Studies, and Education. He has directed National Writing Project sites at the University of Pittsburgh and the University of Washington and edited several collections of writing.

Julia Perdrial is Associate Professor of geochemistry at the University of Vermont. She studies the intersection of the geosphere, biosphere, and hydrosphere, and teaches geochemistry and earth materials.

Robert Scafe is the director of the Writing-Enriched Curriculum Initiative in the Center for Faculty Excellence at the University of Oklahoma. He earned his Ph.D. in French history from Stanford University and has taught interdisciplinary composition courses in the Expository Writing Program at OU since 2006. After a three-year project of developing and coordinating a writing curriculum for the general education U.S. History survey, he assumed leadership of WEC at OU in 2016.

Stacey Sheriff is the founding Director of the Writing Program at Colby College in Waterville, Maine. She teaches first-year writing, rhetoric, and professional writing at Colby, and she has a background teaching technical writing. Her research interests include WAC and WID, rhetorical theory and histories, and multilingual writing. She has published in *Rhetorica, Rhetoric Society Quarterly, Technical Communication Quarterly* and recently co-authored chapters in *Writing Program Architecture* (Finer & White-Farnham, 2017), *The Internationalization of U.S. Writing Programs* (Rose & Weiser, 2018), and *Diverse Approaches to Teaching, Learning, and Writing Across the Curriculum* (Bartlett et al., 2020). Stacey started Colby's writing-enriched curriculum initiative with collaborative support from Pamela Flash and a grant from the Davis Educational Foundation.

Graham Sherriff is the Instructional Design Librarian in the Information and Instruction Services Department of the University of Vermont's David W. Howe Memorial Library. He serves as the editor of *The Journal of Web Librarianship*. His scholarly interests focus on digital learning objects and online learning. He is the subject librarian for the College of Engineering and Mathematical Sciences.

Kathleen Blake Yancey, Kellogg W. Hunt Professor of English and Distinguished Research Professor at Florida State University, has served as the elected leader of several literacy organizations, including NCTE, CCCC, and CWPA. She has edited two journals, *Assessing Writing* and *College Composition and Communication*, and guest edited several others, including a special issue of *Across the Disciplines* addressing WAC and writing assessment. Currently, she is the lead PI for a series of CCCC-funded research studies on the efficacy of the "Transfer of Transfer" curriculum. Author, editor, or co-editor of 16 scholarly books, she has authored co/authored over 100 articles and book chapters, often with colleagues. She is the recipient of several awards, among them the FSU Graduate Teaching Award; the FSU Graduate Mentor Award; the CCCC Exemplar Award; and the NCTE Squire Award.